# MORAL RESPONSIBILITY

# MORAL RESPONSIBILITY

Edited by

JOHN MARTIN FISCHER

Cornell University Press

ITHACA AND LONDON

First published 1986 by Cornell University Press.

International Standard Book Number 0-8014-1828-3 (cloth)
International Standard Book Number 0-8014-9341-2 (paper)
Library of Congress Catalog Card Number 86-6282
Printed in the United States of America
*Librarians: Library of Congress cataloging information
appears on the last page of the book.*

*The paper in this book is acid-free and meets the guidelines for
permanence and durability of the Committee on Production Guidelines
for Book Longevity of the Council on Library Resources.*

# Contents

Introduction: Responsibility and Freedom
JOHN MARTIN FISCHER     9

## I. ACTING FREELY AND MORAL RESPONSIBILITY

1. Freedom of the Will and the Concept of a Person
HARRY G. FRANKFURT     65

2. Free Agency
GARY WATSON     81

3. Three Concepts of Free Action: I
DON LOCKE     97

4. Three Concepts of Free Action: II
HARRY G. FRANKFURT     113

5. Understanding Free Will
MICHAEL SLOTE     124

## II. FREEDOM TO DO OTHERWISE AND MORAL RESPONSIBILITY

6. Alternate Possibilities and Moral Responsibility
HARRY G. FRANKFURT     143

7. Ability and Responsibility
PETER VAN INWAGEN     153

8. Responsibility and Control
JOHN MARTIN FISCHER     174

9. Behavior Control and Freedom of Action
P. S. GREENSPAN    191

10. Free Will as the Ability to Will
BERNARD GERT AND TIMOTHY J. DUGGAN    205

11. Asymmetrical Freedom
SUSAN WOLF    225

12. The Incompatibility of Responsibility and Determinism
PETER VAN INWAGEN    241

Bibliography    251

Index    257

# MORAL RESPONSIBILITY

# Introduction:
# Responsibility and Freedom

JOHN MARTIN FISCHER

*Moral Responsibility*

Suppose that one day you discover something very startling about
your best friend—you discover that he is being electronically manipulated by a team of scientists at a research institute in California. The
researchers secretly implanted a sophisticated device in your friend's
brain when he was quite young. This extraordinary device allows the
scientists to monitor all the activities of your friend's brain; in particular, the researchers are able to tell exactly when your friend is deliber-
ating about courses of action, both significant and mundane. Furthermore, the device can be used to stimulate the brain electronically to
induce certain decisions in your friend. This direct manipulation is
not something that can be "felt" or detected by your friend. Whenever your friend deliberates, the scientists briefly consult one another
and agree as to which decision to induce electronically. Over time,
they attempt to achieve a certain coherence in the pattern of induced
decisions—the decisions and actions of your friend are not in any
sense "random" or unpredictable.

At first it would be hard to know how one would react to such an
unusual situation. But, I think, once you had been convinced that
direct manipulation exists, a striking thing would occur: many of your
most basic *attitudes* toward your friend would change. Your friend
would no longer seem to be an appropriate object of such attitudes as
respect, gratitude, love, indignation, and resentment. Furthermore, it
would seem somehow out of place to praise or blame your friend on
the basis of his behavior. Imagine, for instance, that your friend fails

to pick you up at the airport (although he had previously agreed to do so); surely, it would be inappropriate to resent the failure, for after all, his decision not to pick you up was a product of direct electronic stimulation by the scientists in California. If it is fitting to be indignant or resentful on anyone's account, it would seem that the *scientists* would be the appropriate objects of the attitude. Furthermore, suppose that, instead of coming to pick you up at the airport, your friend devoted his afternoon to collecting money for the United Way. It would not be in any way fitting to commend him for his efforts. If anyone is to be praised for the charitable activity, it would seem to be the group of scientists and *not* your friend.

It would appear impossible to maintain any sort of friendship with a person whom you knew to be under the sort of direct manipulation described above. The whole range of attitudes characteristic of friendship would have to be abandoned. But we needn't imagine such wholesale and systematic manipulation in order to see how our attitudes toward others might change. Imagine that the scientists very infrequently manipulated your friend, but on the occasion of his failure to pick you up at the airport, the manipulation occurred. Now, although one might still have toward him the fabric of attitudes constitutive of friendship, it would nevertheless be inappropriate to be indignant at him for his failure to pick you up. Similarly, if the charitable work was the result of manipulation, it would not be fitting to praise your friend for this activity. Our attitudes and responses to particular bits of behavior, as well as whole ranges of activity, are sensitive to the kinds of discoveries described above.

Other kinds of discoveries about individuals—similarly unusual and alarming—would result in parallel changes in attitude. Imagine that you discover that, on the morning of your birthday, a hypnotist secretely hypnotized an acquaintance of yours, inducing her to call you. Unhappily, your feelings of gratitude and affection after the telephone conversation now seem wholly inappropriate. Or suppose that you discover that someone secretly slipped a pill into the drink of a friend of yours who, you believe, smokes too much. The pill induces an aversion to the thought of smoking. When your friend abstains from smoking, you might feel happy and relieved, but it would seem out of place to give any credit to your friend for refraining from smoking—he does not deserve your *respect* for his decision.

There are two separate points I wish to make about these cases. First, the new information acquired convinces us that certain actions are not, in some important sense, *free* actions. For example, when you discover that your friend is being directly manipulated by the scientists, you realize that, in an important sense, he is not in *control* of what he does—he has "no choice" about what happens, and he is not free to do other than what he does. If anyone has a choice about what your friend does, it is the scientists. The locus of control is *external* to your friend. Second, *because* of your friend's lack of freedom, it seems inappropriate to have certain important attitudes toward him. When you discover that the telephone call was hypnotically induced, you realize that your acquaintance did not *freely* make the call, and because of this, it is not fitting to be grateful to her for the phone call. I wish to discuss both of these points, starting with the latter.

When we discover that a form of behavior or a range of actions is outside an agent's control—that the agent lacks freedom with respect to it—certain kinds of responses seem inappropriate. These responses, it is quite clear, are of central importance to our lives. Imagine a life without gratitude, respect, love, indignation, resentment, and so on. Such a life would be very thin and radically different from the lives we now lead. We care very deeply about these attitudes and about the activities of praising and blaming that are bound up with them. Insofar as we consider these attitudes and activities to be of critical importance to our lives, and we believe that lack of freedom threatens them, we have reason to worry about whether human beings have freedom. That is, the question of whether human beings have freedom is of interest to us—we care so deeply about it—because certain attitudes and forms of behavior that are extremely important to us seem to presuppose some sort of freedom. This point is made and elegantly elaborated in Peter Strawson's insightful and influential essay "Freedom and Resentment."[1]

Some attitudes—frustration and relief, sadness and happiness—can be appropriate, even if the object of the attitudes lacks "control" or freedom. One might be frustrated that one's friend has failed to meet one at the airport and glad that charitable work has been done. But these attitudes seem crucially different from attitudes such as gratitude, respect, indignation, resentment, and so forth. It is inappropriate to *resent* your friend or to feel any sort of gratitude toward the acquaintance who telephones you. Strawson calls these latter attitudes "reactive attitudes," and they seem appropriate only as reactions to free actions performed by free agents.

To understand the nature of reactive attitudes further, imagine

---

1. P. F. Strawson, 1962 (works cited throughout this chapter are listed in the Bibliography). For interesting discussions of the issues raised by Strawson, see Stern, 1974; Bennett, 1980; and Wolf, 1981.

that you are a psychologist performing an experiment on rats. There is a "Y-shaped maze," and you are attempting to induce the rats always to take the left fork in the maze rather than the right. To this end, you employ a pattern of positive and negative reinforcements on the rats. Today you are hoping that the rats will always go to the left. When you place a rat in the maze, you note that, unfortunately, it takes the right fork. There is certainly nothing inappropriate about your feeling of frustration and even perhaps sadness and disappointment in the result, but it seems wholly out of place to feel *indignant* at the rat or to *resent* the rat for its behavior. Imagine that you give the rat an electric shock on the basis of its behavior. In applying a "negative reinforcement" to the rat, you are certainly "conditioning" the rat—stimulating it in such a way as to induce a certain pattern of behavior. But it seems wrong to say that you are *punishing* the rat, because punishment involves an element of condemnation that is inappropriate to the rat. A rat's behavior is presumably dictated by instinct and impulses not under its control; a rat's behavior is not free. Thus while certain responses to the rat are not out of place, the *reactive* responses are inappropriate.

I have claimed, following Strawson, that there is a cluster of attitudes and also activities (praise and blame, punishment and reward) that are appropriate only to agents who are, in a suitable sense, "free"—in control of their activity. I shall say that an agent is "morally responsible" insofar as he is accessible to such attitudes and activities. That is, of course, a rather broad and vague account of moral responsibility, but I think that it captures an important intuitive notion (even if it is not the only idea that people have in mind when they speak of moral responsibility). On this sort of account, a person is a morally responsible agent when he is an *appropriate candidate* for the reactive attitudes and for such activities as praise and blame and punishment and reward. It is not irrational to blame or punish a responsible agent in the same way that it is irrational to blame an individual whose movements are being electronically (or hypnotically or instinctually) induced. Furthermore, an agent is morally responsible *for a particular action* to the extent that he is accessible to the reactive attitudes *based on the action in question.* That is, a person is morally responsible for (say) pulling the trigger insofar as he is a candidate for being blamed *for pulling the trigger.*

Of course, a morally responsible agent—an agent morally responsible for at least some action—may not be morally responsible for *all* his behavior. Also, an agent may be morally responsible for an action on the basis of which *no* reactive attitude ought to be taken. That is, an agent who is morally responsible for an act must be *accessible* to (say) praise or blame—must not be an inappropriate object of praise or blame. But it does not follow that he ought actually to be praised or blamed for his act. An act for which an agent is morally responsible must be an act about which the question of punishment (or reward) can coherently be raised, but, of course, it needn't follow that the punishment must be (or ought to be) carried out. On this approach, then, there is a conceptual connection between moral responsibility and *accessibility* to activities such as reward and punishment, but an agent can be morally responsible for an action for which he ought not be either praised or blamed. (This sort of theory of responsibility is particularly attractive when one considers that there are certainly cases of morally neutral actions for which an agent is nevertheless responsible.)

One of the most striking and important of the connections between moral responsibility and freedom is in the criminal law. Our system of criminal law demands that an agent be free—be in control of his actions in some sense—in order for him to be criminally responsible. (On the account of moral responsibility presented here, criminal responsibility is a type of moral responsibility—accessibility to criminal sanctions.) An individual might lack control if he were insane. This possibility gives rise to the "insanity defense."[2] In the American history of the insanity defense, the most celebrated case—until John Hinckley's—was that of Charles Guiteau, who shot President James Garfield. Despite testimony about Guiteau's "insane delusion" that God had instructed him "to remove the president for the good of the American people," he was convicted under the McNaughten Rule. The McNaughten Rule essentially defined insanity as a mental impairment that produces an inability to distinguish right from wrong (or to understand the nature of one's act). Guiteau was convicted despite his claim: "My free agency was destroyed. . . . I had to do it. That's all there is about it."

Since the time of Guiteau's trial, the insanity defense has changed considerably. Now one can be judged insane if one can't distinguish right from wrong *or* one can't conform one's conduct to the law. So the test for insanity is now not simply a "cognitive" test; if through some defect in one's capacity for self-control one literally can't make one's behavior conform to one's judgment about right and wrong, one can be considered legally insane and can thus not be held respon-

2. For an interesting discussion of the insanity defense with particular emphasis on the Hinckley trial, see Caplan, 1984 a & b.

sible. Hence, criminal responsibility—accessibility to criminal sanctions—requires both a cognitive and an "affective" or "executive" ability, without which it is natural to think that an individual would lack self-control.

Moral responsibility, then, involves accessibility to reactive attitudes, and we care deeply about reactive attitudes. In other words, we care deeply about whether the other individuals in our lives (and we ourselves) are morally responsible. And since lack of freedom appears to threaten the appropriateness of reactive attitudes, we have reason to wonder about—and to care about—whether or not we are free.[3]

I said that the surprising sorts of discoveries discussed above would result in two separate judgments: that the individual in question lacks freedom of some important kind and that, because of this lack of freedom, the reactive attitudes are inappropriate. But there are various different kinds of freedom, and it will be useful to distinguish these kinds of freedom and to discuss their relationships to moral responsibility separately. We say that agents are free to do something (or to refrain from doing something), and that they "have a choice" about doing something, and that they are "in control of what they are doing." Also, we say that they "act freely" and perform "free actions." A very natural approach to these notions—the "traditional approach"—assumes that, in order for an agent to be morally responsible for an action, he must act freely (in performing it), *and* that in order for an agent to perform an act freely, he must have been *free to do otherwise.*

The idea behind the traditional approach is very attractive. The idea is that, in order to be held responsible for an action, I must have a genuine choice about what happens—I must be able to do other than what I actually do. There is at least one sense of "control" according to which I lack control over what happens insofar as I don't have freedom both to perform the pertinent action *and* to refrain from performing it. It is very tempting to think that, when I lack this sort of control (and I can't do otherwise), I *have* to do what I do, and thus I am *compelled* to act as I do, and I don't act freely. The directly manipulated agent (or the hypnotized agent and so forth) has no choice about what he does, and he thus doesn't act freely; hence, we can't legitimately hold him morally responsible for what he does.

Later I shall discuss various strategies that *reject* the traditional ap-

---

3. For skepticism about the claim that we care about whether or not we are free (in the sense of "free to do otherwise"), see Dennett 1984a & b.

proach to moral responsibility. But since the traditional approach is quite appealing, and it claims that moral responsibility requires that an agent be free to do otherwise, it is important first to focus on this sort of freedom.

### Freedom to Do Otherwise

There are various kinds of freedom, but traditionally it has been supposed that moral responsibility requires freedom to do otherwise. In the cases described above, it might seem plausible to think that the lack of freedom to do otherwise renders the agents inappropriate candidates for the reactive attitudes. I shall discuss this claim below. Here I wish first to understand a bit better our feeling that, in the cases described, the agents lack freedom to do otherwise. To do so, I shall begin by considering a very popular strategy for explaining freedom to do otherwise.

Intuitively, the cases that have been sketched above—cases of direct electronic stimulation of a thoroughgoing kind, hypnosis, potent drugs—are examples in which the agent clearly lacks freedom to do otherwise. But I have simply relied on intuitive judgments about the occasions when an agent has such freedom; it would be desirable to give an analysis of freedom to do otherwise that could be applied generally (and even to intuitively less clear cases).

We often think that we have more than one genuine option. When the rat is caused by an instinctual urge to go on the right fork of the maze, perhaps it couldn't have done otherwise. But under ordinary conditions, when I take the Merritt Parkway rather than I-95 to New York, it seems as though I could have done otherwise. Given that my car is operating well, that the roads are open, and so on, I genuinely could have taken I-95 rather than the Merritt Parkway. In such a situation, we agree with Borges that "the future is a garden of forking paths": I am free to take the Merritt Parkway (which I do), and I am also free to take I-95 (that is, to do otherwise).

In this case, there are no special *obstacles* or impediments to my taking either road; nothing prevents me from taking I-95 (or *compels* me to take the Merritt). We normally distinguish between factors that simply make us disinclined to do something (for example, the ugly scenery along I-95) and factors that actually *prevent* us from doing something (for example, a flood that has caused the road to be closed). When one refrains from doing something simply because one doesn't want to do it, it needn't follow (we think) that one *couldn't* have done it. Underlying this view is the natural and plausible supposition that, when a person controls what happens, his actions *depend on* his motivational states (states such as choosing, deciding, trying, willing, and so forth). Since there are no special circumstances that would prevent my taking I-95, it is true that if I had chosen to take I-95, I would have taken I-95. (Of course, had the road been flooded, then I would not have taken I-95 even if I had chosen to do so.) When I am free either to do or to refrain from doing something, my act depends on my choice in the appropriate way: I choose to take the Merritt and do so, and had I chosen to take I-95, I would have done so. So the mere fact that I don't want to go on I-95 and that I thus choose not to take I-95 does not show that I am not *free* (in the pertinent sense) to do so.

On this account of freedom, when I am free, my action depends on my choice; this dependence is captured by certain "conditional" statements—"if-then" statements. The conditional analysis of freedom is as follows: an agent is free to perform an action just in case, if he were to choose to perform it, he would do so.[4] Thus, the mere fact that I don't choose to take I-95 doesn't imply that I can't take I-95. When an agent does one thing X, and the conditional analysis of freedom tells us that he could have done another thing Y instead, then it tells us that he was free to do otherwise.

The conditional analysis of freedom claims that freedom is a kind of "disposition," a disposition to act in accordance with choice. In this respect, freedom can be compared with other dispositional concepts, such as solubility, malleability, fragility, and so forth. It might be suggested, for example, that a piece of salt is soluble in water insofar as it would dissolve if it were placed in water. There are interesting parallels between the analyses of such "passive" dispositions as solubility and the "active" disposition freedom.[5]

The conditional analysis of freedom yields intuitively plausible results in a number of cases. It seems to be sensitive to certain external and internal obstacles in just the right sort of way. If I-95 is flooded, then the conditional statement "If I were to choose to take I-95, I would do so" will be *false* (as it should be). And there can be internal impediments parallel to external impediments such as the flood. For

4. Various conditional analysts pick different "motivational states" (trying, willing, deciding, etc.) for the analysis. For a classic presentation of the conditional analysis, see Moore, 1912. Some important discussions of the conditional analysis are Austin, 1961; Chisholm, 1964 and 1966; Lehrer, 1966a, 1968, and 1980; Aune, 1967 and 1970; Pears, 1975b; Davidson, 1973; Anscombe, 1976; Ginet, 1980; Walton, 1981; and van Inwagen, 1983, pp. 114–26.
5. See Goldman, 1970, pp. 199–200; McCann, 1975; and Anscombe, 1976.

instance, if I am an addict and I have an irresistible urge to take a certain drug, then I *can't* refrain from taking it. In this case, the conditional analysis yields the correct answer: if I were to choose to refrain from taking the drug, the urge would overwhelm me and I would still take it.

But whereas the conditional analysis of freedom seems quite plausible and appealing, I believe that it is inadequate, because freedom of action can be undermined by lack of freedom of choice, and the conditional analysis fails to be sensitive to this fact.[6] Consider someone who was bitten by a snake as a child and who, because of this traumatic incident, has an extreme psychological aversion to snakes. Let us suppose that this aversion renders him unable to choose to pick up a snake. In virtue of the fact that this person can't choose to pick up a snake, it seems that he *can't* pick up a snake. And yet it might be true that, if he were to choose to pick up a snake, he would do so. The aversion renders him unable to choose and thus unable to act, but the conditional analysis tells us that he *can* so act. Thus the conditional analysis seems to be inadequate. The truth of the conditional is not *sufficient* for freedom.

The basic problem for the conditional analysis posed by this case (of the aversion to the snake) arises from the fact that the agent can't choose otherwise. Remember also the case of your best friend who is directly manipulated electronically to produce all of his choices and so forth. Now, when he chooses, let us say, to play softball this afternoon, the scientists produce his choice and action in such a way that it seems plausible to say that he is *not* free to do otherwise. And yet it might be true that, had he chosen to do otherwise, he would have done otherwise. (Of course, had he chosen to do otherwise, the scientists would have been manipulating him in a different way.) Again, the truth of the conditional specified by the conditional analysis of freedom is *not* a sufficient condition for freedom.

I have supposed here that it is coherent to say that an agent can't choose to do something. Some philosophers have defended the conditional analysis by denying that it is coherent to apply the notion of "can" to choice. And some have developed conditional analyses that employ not choice but rather some other notion to which "can" apparently does not coherently apply.[7] So, for instance, one might suggest that an agent can do something just in case, if he were to have

---

6. See Lehrer, 1966, 1968, and 1976; for the example of the pathological aversion to the snake, see Lehrer, 1976.
7. For such an approach, see Davidson, 1973. Cf. Locke, 1976.

(sufficient) reason to do it, he would do it. And it is not so clear that it is coherent to say that an agent can't have sufficient reason to do something—after all, having (or even recognizing) a reason is not an action or something one *does*.

Even if this claim about the relationship between "can" and having reasons is correct (and it is controversial), such a defense of the conditional analysis is deficient. Consider the proposal that an agent can perform an action just in case, if he were to have sufficient reason to perform it, he would perform it. This is clearly inadequate, since individuals (even intuitively free individuals) do not always act on good (and sufficient) reasons (even those reasons that are recognized to be good and sufficient). Suppose I know that I have good and sufficient reason to abstain from drinking a carafe of wine tonight. (It is late, I need to get up early, and so forth.) Nevertheless, I might be "weak-willed" and go ahead and drink the wine despite my reasons not to do so. And insofar as my desire to drink is not irresistible, it is reasonable to say that I was free to abstain from drinking. But on the conditional analysis proposed here, we cannot say that I was free to abstain, since it is not true that, if I were to have sufficient reason to abstain, I would abstain. After all, I *did* have sufficient reason to abstain, but I went ahead and drank anyway. I think, then, that the conditional analysis cannot be defended in the way proposed here. If the conditional analysis employs an "actlike" mental event such as "choice," then the question as to whether one can choose arises; if the analysis eschews such mental events, then it will be implausible.

Let's return to the case of the individual with a pathological aversion to snakes. He cannot choose to pick up the snake, and thus we said that he cannot pick up the snake. An assumption of this inference is that he cannot pick up the snake without choosing to do so; if he could pick up the snake without choosing to do so, then his inability to choose wouldn't necessarily translate into an inability to pick up the snake. So the point is that, from the facts that the person can't choose to pick up the snake and that so choosing is a necessary condition of picking up the snake, it follows that he cannot pick up the snake.

This inference is very plausible, and I wish to formulate a general principle that seems to underlie it as well as other inferences we are disposed to accept. Let us say that when a person has no choice about whether a proposition (or statement) obtains—he cannot prevent that proposition from obtaining and so it is unavoidable (relative to him) that it obtains—it is "power necessary" for him that it obtains. Power necessity is that kind of necessity which holds when an individual lacks control over whether a proposition obtains, that is, he is not free to prevent it from obtaining. The abbreviation "$N_t^S p$" will be used to stand for: it is power necessary for $S$ at $t$ that $p$, that is, $S$ is not free at $t$ to do anything that would prevent $p$ from obtaining.

Suppose that $S$ is the person who cannot choose to pick up the snake, let $p$ be the proposition that $S$ doesn't choose to pick up the snake, and let $q$ be the proposition that $S$ doesn't pick up the snake. Now it is clear that, in the example,

(1) $N_t^S p$

is true at the pertinent time $t$ (in virtue of the pathological aversion). And since $S$ cannot pick up the snake without choosing to do so,

(2) $N_t^S$ (If $p$, then $q$)

is also true. But then we can, it seems, infer:

(3) $N_t^S$ ($q$).

Let us call the principle that allows us to go from (1) and (2) to (3) the "principle of transfer of powerlessness." It says that, if you cannot prevent one thing, and you cannot prevent that thing's leading to another, you cannot prevent the other. The principle explains why the individual cannot pick up the snake, and it seems to underlie our judgments about various other agents who lack freedom.[8]

Remember the first case, in which you discover that your best friend is subject to systematic surveillance and electronic stimulation by the scientists. It is clear that your friend does not control what happens; rather, the scientists do. There is an obvious sense in which your friend does not possess the freedom to alter the course of his behavior from the path chosen by the scientists.[9] Exactly why is your

8. Ginet and van Inwagen use this principle to argue against the conditional analysis: Ginet, 1980; and van Inwagen, 1983, pp. 122–26.

9. One might describe the case in two different ways. First, one might say that (because of its genesis) your friend's behavior is not *action* but mere bodily movement. Your friend does not and cannot act (in the appropriate sense) at all and therefore is not capable of free action. He is not free to *do* otherwise. Another description of the case has it that your friend acts but that he does not control his actions in the sense that he is not free to do other than what he does. He lacks the kind of freedom required by the traditional approach to moral responsibility. I shall, for simplicity's sake, adopt the second method of description. I shall talk about what manipulated agents "do," but nothing crucial philosophically will depend on this method of description—one could, if one preferred, simply switch to the first method, according to which certain manipulated agents merely "behave" but do not act. What is important is that all such agents obviously lack the pertinent type of freedom: freedom to do otherwise.

friend, who is subject to the electronic manipulation by the scientists, *unable* to do other than what he does? Well, the answer seems quite obvious: he lacks control over the scientists' activity, and he lacks control over the fact that, given their activity, he does certain things; thus, he lacks control over what he does—he is not free to do otherwise. This pattern of explanation of unfreedom is the same as that which explained the unfreedom of the person who is afraid of snakes.

Consider also the case of your acquaintance who is hypnotically induced to telephone you on your birthday. Suppose (as above) that she is completely *unaware* of the hypnotist's activity (and thus has not consented to it); furthermore, suppose that the hypnotist is firmly committed to hypnotizing her—nothing she could do would in any way deter him from hypnotizing her. Imagine, here, that, even if she had discovered the hypnotist's intention and had tried to resist, he would overpower her and would submit her to the hypnosis. Now, since she had no choice about the hypnosis, and she had no choice about the fact that, given the hypnosis, she telephoned you, she clearly had no choice about telephoning you—it was not in her power to refrain.

We could contrast this case with one in which she *consents* to the hypnosis. Perhaps she contracts with a hypnotist who would not have intervened at all but for her request. In this case, at least at the time just prior to the contract, your friend *is* free not to telephone you on your birthday. After the hypnosis she is not free, but *before* it there doesn't seem to be any reason to deny that she is free to refrain from telephoning you on your birthday. What makes it true (in the original case) that she lacks at any relevant time the freedom to refrain from telephoning you on your birthday is therefore not simply that she's hypnotized but also that she lacks control over the fact that she's hypnotized.

Similarly, recall the case of the friend who swallowed with his drink a pill that induced an aversion to smoking. If he had freely contracted with the person who slipped the pill into his drink, then (at least just prior to the contract) he was free to continue smoking. One can certainly enter *freely* into contracts that (subsequently) limit one's options, like Odysseus binding himself to the mast. But insofar as we imagine that he had no choice about the drug's being in his drink, and he had no control over his not smoking, given the effects of the pill, then he genuinely had no choice about refraining from smoking.

From these cases, a kind of pattern seems to emerge that supports the principle of transfer of powerlessness. The principle will need to be specified with greater care and precision, but it suffices for now to note that some such principle seems intuitively quite plausible; it evidently explains and justifies judgments that we are inclined to make in several "clear-cut" cases of powerlessness, and it has been used to show that the conditional analysis of freedom is inadequate.

We started this section with the intuitive feeling that we are sometimes genuinely free to pursue any of several alternative paths into the future. One kind of analysis of this sort of freedom—the conditional analysis of freedom—has been shown to be inadequate. But of course, it doesn't follow that we cannot explain such freedom or that we are never free to do otherwise; for all that has been said, *other* accounts of this sort of freedom may be adequate. Along the way, a principle has been articulated that both explains our rejection of the conditional analysis and also seems to underlie various judgments of powerlessness in *clear* cases: the principle of transfer of powerlessness. A problem, however, emerges here, because this principle can be used to generate a rather distressing sort of argument. This argument would show (if it were sound) that we very well might *never* have freedom to do otherwise (contrary to our commonsense view). That is, the argument purports to show that our intuitive distinction between cases in which we have freedom to do otherwise and cases in which we don't have such freedom might be *illusory*. The argument—using the very plausible principle of transfer of powerlessness—threatens an *epidemic* of powerlessness.

### Foreknowledge and Fatalism

An extremely natural, plausible principle has been sketched and can be appealed to in justifying our uncontroversial judgments about some admittedly rather unusual cases—cases in which there are direct manipulations, hypnosis, pathological aversions, and so forth. But what is perhaps surprising and worrisome is that the same sort of principle apparently shows that we are *never* free, that, even under what we take to be "normal" circumstances, we have no choice about what we do. The attractive explanation of our lack of freedom in the obvious cases might also show that certain conditions such as the existence of God or the truth of causal determinism *similarly* undermine our freedom. Thus the intuitive difference between (say) action induced by hypnosis and action that is produced by the "normal" human deliberative mechanism is in danger of being obliterated, if (say) God existed or if causal determinism were true. We would have proceeded from fairly uncontroversial claims of unfreedom to rather more controversial claims.

Most people presumably are not certain that God does not exist or that the doctrine of causal determinism is false. Most of us believe that there is at least a nonnegligible chance that God exists or that causal determinism is true. But we maintain nevertheless that there is some sort of distinction (even if we can't fully explain it) between cases where we have freedom to do otherwise and cases where we don't. But if we can employ the principle of transfer of powerlessness to generate an argument that, if God exists (or causal determinism is true), then no human being is ever free to do otherwise, there would be a collapse of the intuitive distinctions. Worse yet, in light of the apparent connection between moral responsibility and freedom to do otherwise, it would seem to follow that, if God exists or causal determinism turns out to be true, then we cannot legitimately hold agents to be morally responsible. But then, for all we know, our very most basic attitudes toward ourselves and others—the "reactive attitudes"—might be inappropriate and rationally indefensible. The threat that looms on the horizon is that we are all relevantly similar to your friend who is directly electronically stimulated or your acquaintance who is hypnotized and so forth.

I shall consider the argument for the incompatibility of God's existence and human freedom to do otherwise in this section. In the next section, I shall consider the parallel argument concerning causal determinism.

How exactly would the existence of God threaten our freedom in a way that is parallel to the way in which hypnosis or aversive conditioning or phobia does? Take a very ordinary action of yours, like going to the movies tonight. If you do go, and God exists, then God knew (and thus believed) in the year 1000 that you would go to the movies tonight. But you now have no control over the past, so you now have no control over which beliefs God had in the year 1000—after all, if a person held a certain belief in the remote past, there is nothing you can now do about it. And since God is essentially omniscient, you can't control whether or not his beliefs turn out to be true; necessarily, if God believes a certain proposition, the proposition is true. A familiar pattern seems to emerge again: you now have no control over whether God held the belief (in 1000) that you would go to the movies on July 24, 1985, and given that God held this belief, you have no control over whether it turns out to be true. Thus, by the transfer principle, it would seem that you have no choice about going to the movies tonight; you are not free to do otherwise, any more than a person who is hypnotically induced to go to the movies or goes as a result of some kind of brainwashing or compulsive desire. The seemingly innocuous transfer principle appears to extend the range of unfreedom in what might be a surprising way.

The argument can be set forth a bit more carefully. Suppose you go to the movies tonight (Thursday). Then if God exists and is omniscient, He believed in the year 1000 that you would go to the movies tonight. But since the past is "fixed" and out of our control, it follows that

(4) $N_{\text{Thursday}}^{\text{you}}$ (God believed in 1000 that you would go to the movies on Thursday.)

But since God's beliefs must be true,

(5) $N_{\text{Thursday}}^{\text{you}}$ (If God believed in 1000 that you would go to the movies on Thursday, then you go to the movies on Thursday.)

And then, by the principle of transfer of powerlessness,

(6) $N_{\text{Thursday}}^{\text{you}}$ (You go to the movies Thursday.)

From the assumption of God's existence, we have apparently proved that you cannot avoid performing an ordinary act such as going to the movies. And the argument can clearly be generalized to apply to *any* action.[10]

Of course, the argument sketched above presupposes a number of things. It assumes that God is temporal and that His eternality consists in "sempiternality"—existence at all times. It assumes that God is essentially omniscient in the sense that it is necessarily true that God believes a proposition at a time $T$ if and only if the proposition is true at $T$. Also, it assumes that, if you go to the movies tonight (Thursday, July 24, 1985), then it was true in the year 1000 that you would go to the movies on July 24, 1985. (This is the assumption that "future contingents" have a determinate truth value.) These assumptions are certainly not uncontroversial, but they are also not radically implausible. Relative to this set of rather attractive and widely held assumptions, one's freedom seems to be threatened. This argument shifts our attention from cases in which it seems clear that one has no control over (say) the application of hypnosis or aversive conditioning to cases in which, it is claimed, one has no control over the *past*.

10. For a different development of essentially the same sort of argument, see Pike, 1965 and 1970.

Whereas the argument for the incompatibility of God's existence and human freedom to do otherwise is plausible, it can be rejected in various ways, and it will be illuminating to consider at some length one of the strategies of response. First, one can deny one (or more) of the argument's assumptions. Some philosophers would deny that God's existence is temporal; they claim that God's eternality is "atemporal" eternality and that God's omniscience thus doesn't constitute *foreknowledge*.[11] Also, some philosophers would deny that "future contingents" are determinately true or false; that is, they would deny that it follows from your going to the movies on Thursday that it was *true in the year 1000* that you would go to the movies on Thursday, July 24, 1985.[12]

Another strategy of response to the argument denies that one of the premises, (4), is true. That is, this sort of response denies that it is out of your control on Thursday whether or not God believed in 1000 that you would go to the movies on Thursday. This strategy is associated with the medieval philosopher William of Ockham. The "Ockhamist" claims (very roughly) that there are two kinds of facts about the past—genuine, "hard" facts and spurious, or "soft" facts. Whereas we have no control over the hard facts about the past, we might, according to the Ockhamist, have some sort of control over the soft facts about the past. Furthermore, the Ockhamist claims that the fact that God held a certain belief in the past is, in the relevant sense, a soft fact about the past.[13]

In what sense can a "fact" about the past be a soft fact—in what sense can we be said to have "control" over the past? There are some facts over which we certainly have no control now. We cannot now act in such a way that the Japanese bombing of Pearl Harbor would never have occurred or in such a way that John F. Kennedy wouldn't have been assassinated. These facts are genuine, nonrelational features of the past and are thus fixed now. What's done is done! But just as there may be facts involving "nongenuine," "relational" *spatial* properties, there seem to be facts involving spurious or relational *temporal* properties. Consider the "spatial" fact about a house that it is ten miles south of a pizza parlor. This sort of fact has seemed to many to be a

11. I believe that this strategy was adopted by such philosophers as Boethius and Aquinas. For a contemporary atemporal conception of God's eternality, see Stump and Kretzmann, 1981.

12. Some believe that Aristotle denies this assumption, although this interpretation is controversial. For a related strategy, see Prior, 1962.

13. Contemporary versions of Ockhamist approaches can be found in M. Adams, 1967; and Hoffman and Rosenkrantz, 1984.

merely relational, "extrinsic" fact about the house. In contrast, the fact that it has three bedrooms seems to be an intrinsic fact about the house. And there are temporal analogues to these merely relational spatial facts.

Suppose, for example, that your alarm goes off at 7:30 and that you get out of bed at 8:00. Then it is a fact about 7:30 that it preceded your getting out of bed by a half hour; yet this seems clearly to be a nongenuine, relational fact about 7:30. Furthermore, whereas you do in fact get out of bed at 8:00 (perhaps grumbling a bit), you might be free to stay in bed instead. There may be no factors inclining us to say that you are not free to do otherwise at 8:00. If you are free to stay in bed, then you are free at 8:00 so to act that 7:30 *wouldn't* have preceded your getting out of bed by a half hour. That is, you are free so to act that some fact that *did* obtain in the past *wouldn't* have obtained. Being quite explicit about the nature of the claim here might be useful. The claim is that you are at 8:00 free to stay in bed and that, if you were to stay in bed, then 7:30 *wouldn't* have had the property (which it *actually* had) of preceding your getting out of bed by a half hour. This claim, if true, shows that one might have a certain sort of control over the past—a control over soft facts about the past. It is precisely because the fact that 7:30 preceded your getting up by a half hour is a nongenuine fact about 7:30 that you may be free at 8:00 so to act that it wouldn't have been a fact. One might have a kind of control over soft facts about the past that one doesn't obviously have over hard facts about the past.

I think that it is uncontroversial that there is some kind of distinction between hard and soft facts about times. But the Ockhamist's contention is that God's having a certain belief in the past is a soft fact about the past; that is, God's beliefs are assimilated to facts such as the fact about 7:30 that it preceded your getting out of bed by a half hour. Both facts are alleged to be relational and nongenuine, and just as you might be free at 8:00 so to act that 7:30 wouldn't have preceded your getting up by a half hour, so you might be free today so to act that God would have held a different belief in 1000 from the one He actually held. In the case discussed above, you actually go to the movies tonight, and thus God believed in 1000 that you would do so; yet you are free (according to the Ockhamist) to refrain from going, and if you were to refrain, then God would have (correctly) believed in 1000 that you would refrain. Thus the Ockhamist accepts the principle of transfer of powerlessness but contends that it is *inapplicable* in the context of God's foreknowledge, since one might have control, in the pertinent sense, over God's prior beliefs.

Of course, the tenability of Ockhamism will depend on the plausibility of the assimilation of the fact about God's belief in 1000 to soft facts such as the fact about 7:30 that it preceded your getting up by a half hour. But the Ockhamist's distinction between genuine facts and spurious facts about times is an important one, and it will help us to analyze a kind of argument for "fatalism." I shall now discuss the argument for fatalism and compare it with the argument we have been considering for the incompatibility of God's existence with freedom to do otherwise. I shall then return to the Ockhamist's claim that God's belief at a time is properly construed as a soft fact about the time.

The fatalist claims that we are never free to do otherwise, and he does not purport to derive this conclusion from "substantive" assumptions, such as God's existence or causal determinism. Rather, the fatalist claims to prove the conclusion from more "minimal," basic facts. One such fatalist argument proceeds as follows.[14] Suppose you go to the movies on Thursday. It follows that it was true on Wednesday that you would go to the movies on Thursday. But since the past is fixed, you have no control on Thursday over the fact that on Wednesday it was true that you would go to the movies on Thursday. And since you have no control over the fact that "It was true on Wednesday that you will go to the movies on Thursday" entails that you will go to the movies on Thursday, it follows that you have no control on Thursday over your going to the movies. You cannot (ever) do otherwise.

The structure of the fatalist's argument is the same as that of the incompatibilist about God's existence and freedom to do otherwise. One way to block the argument (as above) would be to deny that "You go to the movies on Thursday" implies that *it was true on Wednesday* that you would go to the movies on Thursday. But the Ockhamist move seems particularly appealing here. A fact about a time such as "On Wednesday it was true that on Thursday you would go to the movies" appears to be a relational fact about Wednesday and thus not *fixed* on Thursday. If the fact about Wednesday is not fixed on Thursday, then the fatalist's argument is not sound.

Remember that the basic form of the arguments discussed so far is this: From the premises

(1) $N_i^s p$

14. This sort of fatalist argument is associated with Diodorus Chronus. For a discussion of this type of argument, see Hintikka, 1964.

and

(2) $N_i^S$ (If $p$, then $q$),

it follows that

(3) $N_i^S q$.

Now, the Ockhamist type of response to both the arguments from God's existence and the fatalist argument is to deny the "fixity-of-the-past" premise, (1). Thus, all one has is:

(1*) $p$.

And there is no reason to suppose that the following argument form is valid: From the premises,

(1*) $p$

and

(2) $N_i^S$ (If $p$, then $q$),

it follows that

(3) $N_i^S q$.

Intuitively, the principle of transfer of powerlessness transfers powerlessness from one thing to another, but if there is no powerlessness to begin with, there is none to transfer. Of course, if the inference form just presented were valid, we would be able very simply to prove that we never could have done otherwise. We would *not* need to employ any fixity-of-the-past principle. Let both $p$ and $q$ stand for the same proposition, "I am wearing a blue shirt today," and suppose that I am in fact wearing a blue shirt today, so

(1*) I am wearing a blue shirt today.

And since I have no control over logical truths,

(2) $NI_{\text{Today}}$ (If I am wearing a blue shirt today, then I am wearing a blue shirt today.)

So if the argument form is valid, it follows that

(3) $N$I$_{Today}$ (I am wearing a blue shirt today.)

But there is no reason to think that this inference form is valid. Indeed, there is no more reason to think it valid than to think that the corresponding inference for *logical* necessity is valid. If the inference form were valid for logical necessity, we could go from

(1*) I am wearing a blue shirt today.

And

(2*) $N$ (If I am wearning a blue shirt today, then I am wearing a blue shirt today.)

to

(3*) $N$ (I am wearing a blue shirt today.)

Thus if the inference form were valid for logical necessity, we could prove that *all* true statements are logically necessary. But there is no reason to think that the inference form is valid for logical necessity, and similarly, there is no reason to think that it is valid for power necessity.[15]

Insofar as the fatalist's argument does not rest on implausibly supposing that (3) follows from (1*) and (2), the Ockhamist response thus seems to be extremely plausible: the fatalist has not shown us that his fixity-of-the-past claim involves a *genuine* fact about the past. And exactly the same sort of problem appears to plague the incompatibilist about mere *human* foreknowledge and human freedom to do otherwise. Suppose again that you go to the movies on Thursday. Also imagine that Smith knew on Wednesday that you would go to the movies on Thursday. Now, it might be argued that Smith's knowledge on Wednesday is *fixed* on Thursday, and thus (by an argument parallel to those presented above) that you couldn't have refrained from going to the movies Thursday.

The problem for this argument is precisely parallel to the problem for the fatalist's argument. Since "Smith knows on Wednesday that

---

15. For a fatalist argument that seems to make the mistake of supposing this sort of inference form to be valid, see Taylor, 1963, pp. 54–59; cf. van Inwagen, 1983, pp. 43–50.

you will go to the movies on Thursday" requires for its truth that you actually go to the movies on Thursday, it seems to *depend* on Thursday's events in a way that is similar to the way in which "It is true on Wednesday that you will go to the movies on Thursday" depends on Thursday's events. Both the fact about Smith's knowledge and the fact about the truth of a certain statement seem to be relational facts—soft facts—and thus not fixed facts.

Look at the matter this way. Suppose Smith knew on Wednesday that you would go to the movies on Thursday. If you were to refrain from going to the movies on Thursday, you would be so acting on Thursday that Smith would have had a *false belief* on Wednesday. Smith (as opposed to God) is not *essentially omniscient,* so it appears that one could so act that Smith would have held the *same* belief but it would have been false. The *truth* of Smith's belief doesn't seem to be a temporally genuine feature of his state on Wednesday, and so the fact about Smith's knowledge doesn't seem to be a hard fact about Wednesday.

So far I have pointed out that the arguments from God's foreknowledge, determinate truth values, and human foreknowledge have a similar structure. I have pointed out that the Ockhamist will deny the various fixity-of-the-past premises. Also, I have claimed that, if the fixity-of-the-past premise is not established, and there is only a proposition saying that a past event occurred, then the arguments are *not* valid. But let's consider the argument from human foreknowledge a bit more closely. A person might *agree* that Smith's knowledge on Wednesday isn't a hard fact about Wednesday but might nevertheless argue as follows. If Smith knows on Wednesday that you will go to the movies on Thursday, then you *have* to go to the movies on Wednesday. After all, what is known must be true—knowledge implies truth.

In evaluating this sort of argument, it is important to distinguish two different claims:

(7) Necessarily (If a person knows that $p$, then $p$ is true),

and

(8) If a person knows that $p$ is true, then $p$ is necessarily true.[16]

Whereas (7) is true, (8) is not. What is true in the example is the analogue of (7), namely

16. Traditionally, philosophers have pointed out that one cannot go from the "necessity of the consequence," (7), to the "necessity of the consequent," (8).

(7*) $N_{\text{Thursday}}^{\text{you}}$ (If Smith knows on Wednesday that you will go to the movies on Thursday, then you will go to the movies on Thursday.)

But (7*), together with

(1**) Smith knows on Wednesday that you will go to the movies on Thursday,

does *not* entail

(6) $N_{\text{Thursday}}^{\text{you}}$ (You go to the movies on Thursday.),

just as (1*) and (2) do not entail (3) above. The fallacy of going from (1**) and (7*) to (6) is the same as that of going from (1*) and (2) to (3). We must be careful to distinguish the unacceptable (8) from the acceptable (7). But we cannot employ (7), together with other non-controversial truths, to derive the incompatibility of human fore-knowledge with human freedom.

Let me summarize the course of the discussion in this section so far. I have set out an argument from the fixity of the past to the claim that God's existence would rule out human freedom to do otherwise. I have pointed out that the Ockhamist will deny the conclusion of the argument by claiming that God's belief in the past is not a genuine feature of the past. Thus the Ockhamist claims that the incom-patibilist about God's foreknowledge and human freedom makes the same sort of mistake as that made by the *fatalist* and the incom-patibilist about *human* foreknowledge and freedom. Just as the truth of a statement about Thursday is not a hard fact about Wednesday and Smith's knowledge about Thursday is not a hard fact about Wednesday, so, too, the Ockhamist claims, God's belief is not a hard fact about Wednesday. And if it is not a hard fact about Wednesday and thus not fixed on Thursday, the incompatibilist's argument would be unsound.

It is useful to see the similarity between the arguments for fatalism, incompatibilism about human foreknowledge and freedom, and in-compatibilism about divine foreknowledge and human freedom. All seem to rest on the principle of transfer of powerlessness. The Ockhamist's response to the fatalist's argument and the argument from human foreknowledge seems convincing. But the Ockhamist's claim that God's belief at a time is not a temporally genuine feature of that time is more controversial. Why should it be thought that "God believes in 1000 that you would go to the movies on Thursday" is like such facts as "It is true in 1000 that you would go to the movies on Thursday" and "7:30 preceded your getting out of bed by a half hour"? One reason that they might all be thought to be soft facts (about the pertinent times) is that they entail that some contingent facts (of a certain sort) obtain at *later* times. That is, just as "7:30 preceded your getting out of bed by a half hour" entails that you get out of bed at 8:00, so "God believes in 1000 that you will go to the movies on Thursday" entails that you go to the movies on Thursday. So, on the one hand, the fact about God's belief is similar to the clearly soft facts in virtue of entailing a certain sort of fact about a later time.[17] On the other hand, it seems that having a belief is a temporally genuine, nonrelational property (unlike the property "preceding your getting out of bed by a half hour"). So a fact such as "God believes that *p* at *t*" involves an individual's having what appears to be a *genuine property* at *t*, and thus the fact about God's belief is in this respect different from the clearly soft facts. It is controversial, then, whether God's belief in 1000 is a soft fact about 1000.

Note that, if God's belief in 1000 were (as the Ockhamist claims) a soft fact about 1000, then it would be *different* from hard facts, but it wouldn't follow that it is not fixed after 1000. The reason is that *some* soft facts about the past are not within one's control. Consider the fact that on Monday I awakened prior to the Earth's rotating on Tuesday. Whereas this fact is a soft fact about Monday, it is not within my power to alter it on Tuesday. So even if God's belief in the past is a soft fact about the past, it wouldn't follow that it is not a fixed fact. Nevertheless, it is the Ockhamist's position that, whereas hard facts about the past *are* fixed now, soft facts about the past *needn't* be fixed now, and thus, since God's belief in 1000 is a soft fact about 1000, it needn't be taken to be fixed now. Thus, the Ockhamist denies the soundness of the incompatibilist's argument by rejecting the fixity-of-the-past premise; he claims that God's belief in the past is not now out of one's control in the way in which, say, the electronic manipulation of his brain is out of your friend's control.

It is difficult conclusively to resolve this issue, but what if (contrary to Ockhamism) God's belief in the past turned out to be a hard, nonrelational fact about the past? The Ockhamist claims that all hard facts about the past are now fixed. But interestingly enough, some philosophers have insisted that not even *hard* facts about the past are now fixed. I shall in the next section develop an argument that, again,

17. See M. Adams, 1967; Fischer, 1983a; and Hoffman and Rosenkrantz, 1984.

has the same sort of structure as the arguments developed above—it uses the principle of the transfer of powerlessness to argue that we are not free. But this time the threat comes not from foreknowledge, but from causal determinism, and the argument raises the question of whether even indisputably hard facts about the past are fixed. Again, the aim of the argument is to show that, quite alarmingly, under conditions less bizarre and unusual than those involving electronic stimulation, brainwashing, and so on, we would totally lack freedom to do otherwise—the future would not be a "garden of forking paths."

### Causal Determinism

It might well be true that everything that happens is caused to happen by previous occurrences. Furthermore, whereas we do not presently know what the causal laws that govern the universe are, there may *be* such laws, and these laws might be, for all we know, deterministic. The doctrine of causal determinism may well be true; that is, very roughly, it might be the case that the truths about the *genuine* facts about a time, together with the laws of nature, entail all truths about what happens after that time. And even if no one actually knows such truths, they are in principle knowable (if determinism is true); if one had a sufficiently great capacity for information (like LaPlace's demon or some sort of tremendous "supercomputer"), one could, it seems, predict with accuracy all future events.

We can construct an argument, parallel to the argument from foreknowledge, that, if causal determinism is true, no one is free to do other than what he does.[18] If causal determinism is true, and you go to the movies Thursday, then genuine conditions obtaining in the past, together with the laws of nature, imply that you go to the movies Thursday. But since you have no control over genuine features of the past, and you have no control over the laws of nature, it follows (given the transfer principle) that you have no control over your actions— you are not free to refrain from going to the movies Thursday. Since you are not free so to act that hard facts about the past would be different or the laws would be different, you are not free to do otherwise than you actually do. The conclusion of the argument, then, is that freedom to do otherwise is incompatible with causal determinism. Again, the principle of transfer of powerlessness leads to what

18. For such arguments, see Ginet, 1966 and 1980; Wiggins, 1973; Lamb, 1977; and van Inwagen, 1975 and 1983.

might be a surprising result—that, under determinism, we would be no different from (say) a drug addict with respect to freedom to do otherwise.

Let's state the argument a bit more precisely. We can define the doctrine of causal determinism as follows:

> Causal determinism is the thesis that, for any given time, a complete statement of the hard facts about the world at that time, together with a complete statement of the laws of nature, entails every truth as to what happens after that time.

Now again imagine that you go to the movies on Thursday. Then if causal determinism obtains, it follows that there exists a proposition describing the hard facts about the world in (say) the year 1000 (call this proposition $b$), that, together with the laws of nature, entails that you go to the movies on Thursday. Since you have no control over hard facts about the past,

(9) $N_{\text{Thursday}}^{\text{you}}\ b$.

And since you have no control over the laws of nature,

(10) $N_{\text{Thursday}}^{\text{you}}$ (If $b$, then you go to the movies on Thursday.)

And from the principle of transfer of powerlessness, it follows that

(11) $N_{\text{Thursday}}^{\text{you}}$ (You go to the movies on Thursday.)

The argument has precisely the same structure as the ones discussed previously. However, the justification for the premises may be interestingly different. Here, the fixity-of-the-past premise concerns indisputably hard facts. And the second premise is (unlike the corresponding premises in the other arguments) based on a fixity-of-the-laws claim. As we shall see, these differences may allow one to respond differently to the various arguments.

We have already discussed an argument showing that the conditional analysis of freedom is inadequate. And the conditional analysis is a *compatibilist* analysis of freedom. To see this point, imagine that I go to a baseball game. Now, if determinism is true, then conditions in the past $C$ together with laws $L$ imply that I go to the game. If I was nevertheless free to stay home instead, and the conditional analysis of my freedom were correct, then my freedom consists in the truth of a conditional such as "If I had chosen to stay home, I would have stayed home." As things actually happen, $C$ and $L$ imply that I choose to go to the game and do go. But if I had chosen to stay home, either $C$ or $L$ *wouldn't* have obtained, and I would have stayed home. Whereas conditions in the world as it actually is imply that I go to the game, it needn't follow that I was not free to do otherwise (according to the compatibilist), and had I done otherwise, conditions would have been different.

As we have noted, the conditional analysis is inadequate. But this situation leaves it open that some *other* compatibilist analysis is correct—the compatibilist needn't be a conditional analyst.[19] And even if no compatibilist *analysis* were correct, it still wouldn't follow that compatibilism is false, since it might turn out that freedom is unanalyzable into more basic concepts and yet still is consistent with causal determinism. But the general argument for the incompatibility of causal determinism and freedom to do otherwise just presented would show (if it is sound) that *no* compatibilist analysis is correct and that even an unanalyzed freedom to do otherwise is not consistent with causal determinism. Since we presumably don't know that causal determinism is false, we are again threatened with an epidemic of powerlessness.

The argument for incompatibilism is a powerful and worrying argument, and it is highly controversial. There are various different ways in which one might challenge the argument, and I will not explore them all here. I shall simply pick out a few salient strategies of response. Note also that the issue here is not whether causal determinism is actually true; rather, the issue is whether, if it were true, that would rule out human freedom to do otherwise. The issue is the compatibility claim.

One kind of response to the argument might be called multiple-pasts compatibilism.[20] Suppose that determinism is true and you go to the movies on Thursday. This kind of compatibilist starts by asserting that a certain kind of "backtracking conditional" would be true. That is, it is true that if (contrary to fact) you did not go to the movies on Thursday, then the past would have been different insofar as $b$ *wouldn't* have obtained.

---

19. For an alternative compatibilist account of freedom, a "possible-worlds approach," see Lehrer, 1976. For discussions of this approach, see Horgan, 1977; Audi, 1978; and Fischer, 1979.

20. For a discussion of this sort of approach (or similar approaches), see Saunders, 1968; Narveson, 1977; Gallois, 1977; Foley, 1979; Lehrer, 1980; Fischer, 1983b; and Davies, 1983.

Now, the "multiple pasts" compatibilist distinguishes between two ways in which we might be thought to be powerless over the past. Suppose proposition $b$ says that some event $e_1$ occurred at time $t_1$. The compatibilist wishes to distinguish two ways in which an agent might be said to be powerless to affect $b$:

(FP$_1$) If $e_1$ occurred at $t_1$, then no agent can at any time later than $t_1$ initiate a causal sequence issuing in $e_1$'s *not* occurring at $t_1$.

(FP$_2$) If $e_1$ occurred at $t_1$, then no agent can at any time later than $t_1$ perform an action such that if he were to perform it, $e_1$ would not have occurred at $t_1$.

The multiple-pasts compatibilist claims that, whereas (FP$_1$) is valid, it is not equally clear that (FP$_2$) is valid. The multiple-pasts compatibilist takes the (FP$_2$) sense to be the pertinent sense, and in this sense, he points out that the fixity-of-the past premise, (9), is *false*.

The point here is that there are two ways in which one might be able to "affect" the past: causally and noncausally. The compatibilist says that, whereas we can't affect the past causally, we can "affect" it noncausally; that is, I might be able to do something now such that, if I were to do it, the past would have been different from the way it actually was.

The compatibilist's point is that there does not seem to be anything incoherent about asserting both a "can claim" (that you can on Thursday refrain from going to the movies) and a "backtracker" (if you were to refrain from going to the movies, $b$ wouldn't have obtained). All this sort of compatibilist need be committed to is thus an (allegedly) innocuous claim about our power over the past: a conjunction of a "can claim" and a "backtracker."

On the other hand, an incompatibilist might reject the claim that we have even this weaker sort of power over the past. His claim is that if the backtracking conditional really is true, then the can claim must be false. So, for instance, if it really were true that, if I were now to do some act, John F. Kennedy wouldn't have been assassinated, then I simply *can't* do that act. The incompatibilist claims that hard facts about the past are fixed even in the weaker sense, so that both (FP$_1$) and (FP$_2$) are valid. The incompatibilist here claims that the plausibility of (FP$_2$) does not come from conflating it with (FP$_1$)—it is, according to the incompatibilist, independently plausible.[21]

Now let us consider another kind of compatibilist response to the

21. Ginet, 1983.

basic argument for incompatibilism.[22] This kind of compatibilist asserts that the "local miracle" conditional (rather than the "backtracking" conditional) would be true if determinism obtained. So imagine again that causal determinism obtains and that you do in fact go to the movies Thursday. The "local-miracle compatibilist" asserts that, if (contrary to fact) you were to refrain from going to the movies on Thursday, then the past would have been exactly as it actually was but some law that actually obtained wouldn't have obtained.

The local-miracle compatibilist distinguishes two senses in which we might lack power over the laws of nature:

(FL$_1$) No agent can ever perform an act that itself would be or would cause a law-breaking event.

(FL$_2$) No agent can ever so act that a law-breaking event would (at some point) have occurred.

The local-miracle compatibilist points out that whereas (FL$_1$) is valid, (FL$_2$) is not obviously valid, and although compatibilism (of this sort) must deny (FL$_2$), it needn't deny (FL$_1$). The local-miracle compatibilist takes (FL$_2$) to be the pertinent sense, and he points out that, in this sense, the fixity-of-the-laws premise, (10), is false.

The local-miracle compatibilist points out that, if you go to the movies on Thursday, your going to the movies needn't itself be or cause any law-breaking event; after all, we do not envisage that you will go to the movies in a spacecraft that travels faster than the speed of light! And although it is quite clear that no human being can perform an act that would be or would cause a law-breaking event, it might be that a human can so act that a "small miracle" would have occurred (immediately prior to his action).

The compatibilist's point here is that it doesn't seem to be incoherent to assert both a "can claim" (that you can on Thursday refrain from going to the movies) and a "local-miracle conditional" (that if you were to refrain from going to the movies, a law that actually held wouldn't have held). So all this compatibilist need be committed to is an (allegedly) innocuous claim about our power over the laws.

But the incompatibilist will presumably reject the claim that we have even this weaker sort of power over the laws. His claim is that, if it is a necessary condition of doing something that a law of nature be

___

22. The classic presentation of this view is Lewis, 1981. Also see Fischer, 1983b and forthcoming; cf. Ginet, 1983.

false, then one simply *cannot* do that thing. For the incompatibilist, if ($FL_1$) is plausible, then so is ($FL_2$); what difference does it make, the incompatibilist asks, whether the violation of natural law is taken to occur during or after the act in question, or immediately prior?[23]

This may be a good place to stop and compare the corresponding premises of the arguments for the incompatibility of divine fore-knowledge and human freedom to do otherwise and the incompatibility of causal determinism and freedom to do otherwise. I have pointed out that there is controversy over whether God's belief at a time is a hard fact about that time. If not, then the fixity-of-the-past assumption of the argument from divine foreknowledge is *less* plausible than that of the argument from causal determinism, and someone who holds that genuine facts about the past are fixed could reject the premise of the argument from divine foreknowledge while accepting the premise of the argument from causal determinism. This reasoning opens the possibility of being a compatibilist with respect to divine foreknowledge and freedom and an incompatibilist about causal determinism and freedom. But if God's belief at a time is a hard fact about that time (or relevantly similar to a hard fact), then the two arguments are on a par with respect to the fixity of the past.

Furthermore, since God is essentially omniscient, it doesn't seem as though one could reject the second premise of the argument from divine foreknowledge—one has no control over the fact that, if God believes that *p*, *p* is true. But I have pointed out that one might deny the corresponding premise of the argument from causal determinism and adopt "local miracle compatibilism." This move opens the possibility of being a compatibilist about causal determinism and freedom to do otherwise but an incompatibilist about divine foreknowledge and freedom to do otherwise. Such a theorist would hold that all hard facts about the past are fixed and that God's belief is such a fact but that the natural laws needn't be fixed.

Now I shall consider one more strategy for blocking the incompatibilist's argument. This strategy accepts the premises but denies that the conclusion follows from them—it thus rejects the principle of transfer of powerlessness.[24] I believe that this strategy is best analyzed by comparing it with a parallel argument concerning *knowledge*.

Just as we intuitively believe that we are often faced with alternative paths to the future, we think that we often *know* things about the world (though perhaps fewer things than we'd like!). But there is a

---

23. For this sort of worry, see Ginet, 1983; and Fischer, forthcoming.
24. For an interesting development of this approach, see Slote, 1982.

challenge to our confidence in our claims to knowledge that parallels
the challenge issued by the incompatibilist to our claims to freedom,
and the challenges rest on a similar principle. It seems plausible to
suppose that knowledge is transferred by known implication; that is,
it appears that, if I know that $p$, and I know that p implies $q$, I know
that $q$. (Of course, knowledge needn't be transferred by mere implication; what is required is *known* implication. So if I know that $p$, and $p$
[unbeknownst to me] implies $q$, it *doesn't* follow that I know that $q$.)
The principle of transfer of knowledge (by known implication) is
often called the principle of "closure of knowledge under known
implication." Let us now interpret $N$ as knowledge (or "epistemic
necessity"), so that "$N^S\ p$" shall abbreviate "$S$ knows that $p$." Now the
principle of closure of knowledge under known implication can be
exhibited as structurally parallel to the principle of transfer of
powerlessness:
From

(12) $N^S\ p$

and

(13) $N^S$ (If $p$, then $q$.)

Infer

(14) $N^S\ q$.

An argument for a kind of skepticism—the claim that we don't know
any proposition about the external world—can be constructed, using
the closure principle. Suppose that you know some ordinary proposition about the external world. So

(15) $N^{You}$ (There exist rocks.)

But you also know that, if these are rocks, then you are not being
deceived (say, by an evil scientist—with a National Science Founda-
tion grant—manipulating your brain) into falsely believing that there
are rocks. So

(16) $N^{You}$ (If there are rocks, then you are not being deceived into believing that there are rocks).

But given the closure principle, we can infer from (15) and (16) that

(17) $N^{You}$ (You are not being deceived into falsely believing that there are rocks).

But (17) seems to be false; the skeptic claims that you *don't* know (for instance) that you are not being subtly manipulated into falsely believing that there are rocks. So it follows (according to the skeptic) that (15) is false. And in general, if the closure principle is valid, we don't know anything about the external world.

The challenge of skepticism rests on a principle similar to the principle of transfer of powerlessness—the closure principle. One way to block the skeptic's argument would be to claim that (17) is true. But some philosophers wish to block the argument for skepticism by *rejecting the closure principle*. How exactly could one justify rejecting the closure principle? Here is a kind of situation in which some philosophers would claim that it can be seen that closure fails.[25]

You are in an ordinary zoo looking at what seems to be a zebra in front of you. So you know that it is a zebra in front of you. That is,

(18) $N^{You}$ (There is a zebra in front of you.)

But presumably it is also true that

(19) $N^{You}$ (If it is a zebra, it is not a cleverly disguised mule in front of you.)

Now, if the closure principle is valid, we could infer from (18) and (19) that

(20) $N^{You}$ (It is not a cleverly disguised mule in front of you.)

But intuitively you *don't* know that it is not a cleverly disguised mule in front of you. So it might be argued that there are possible situations in which (18) and (19) are true but (20) is false, and thus the principle of closure of knowledge under known implication is invalid. And just as one might deny the closure principle for knowledge, one might deny the corresponding principle of transfer of powerlessness.

The denial of the closure principle is highly controversial. Whereas

25. The following example is due to Fred Dretske, 1970. Robert Nozick also denies the principle of closure of knowledge under known implication, in Nozick, 1981, pp. 197–247.

some philosophers believe that the truth of (18) and (19) is consistent with the falsity of (20), others (including skeptics) believe that if (20) is false, (18) must be false. That is, the proponent of the closure principle will insist that, if you don't know that it is not a cleverly disguised mule in front of you, then it follows that you don't know that it is a zebra! So, on this view, we *don't* have here a counterexample to the closure principle.

It seems to me that skepticism and incompatibilism are on a par. They are both challenges to the conventional wisdom, and they have considerable bite, because they rest on principles that seem intuitively attractive. Whereas these parallel principles don't seem obviously valid, they also don't seem obviously invalid; it is hard to see how one could either conclusively prove or disprove them.[26] So whereas one might attempt to block the incompatibilist's argument by rejecting the transfer principle, this strategy is certainly controversial.

We started with certain cases in which it seemed that we lacked freedom of a certain sort—freedom to do otherwise. It also seemed as though, in those cases, the individuals could not legitimately be held morally responsible for their actions. But underlying the clear cases of powerlessness was a principle that seemed to threaten an epidemic of powerlessness. Perhaps we don't know that God doesn't exist, or that causal determinism doesn't obtain. And parallel arguments can be constructed (using the principle of transfer of powerlessness) purporting to show that, if God exists or causal determinism is true, no human would ever be free to do otherwise. Whereas the arguments are controversial in various interesting ways, it is not obvious that they are bad arguments. And so, if moral responsibility requires freedom to do otherwise, the epidemic of powerlessness threatens an epidemic of *blamelessness*. The arguments might shake our confidence in the appropriateness of a range of attitudes and activities about which we *care* deeply. Since it is not easy absolutely to dismiss the incompatibilist arguments, but it seems unthinkable to abandon moral responsibility, perhaps we ought to consider whether moral responsibility requires freedom of the sort described so far—freedom to do otherwise.

*Acting Freely*

We have seen that, in certain cases, the discovery that an agent lacks freedom of action convinces us that the agent is not an appropriate candidate for reactive attitudes. The cases seem to suggest that an

26. For a systematic discussion of the closure principle, see Brueckner, 1985.

individual can properly be praised or blamed only if he *controls* his action in the sense that he determines which course of action he takes, where there is more than one course of action open to him. Otherwise, it might be supposed, the individual is compelled to do what he does—someone or something else controls his behavior, or perhaps there is no locus of control at all. Now, it is quite clear that, when a person does not, in this sense, control his action—when he is not free to do otherwise—he lacks an important kind of freedom, but we must inquire more closely whether it is a necessary condition of moral responsibility that an individual have this sort of freedom, and in so doing, it will be important to distinguish carefully among various different kinds of freedom.

Let's consider two cases. In both cases, a man walks along a beach and, noting that there is a child drowning, dives into the water and rescues the child. In both cases, the man is, evidently, a hero. But in the first case, White (who rescues the child) has had the sort of extraordinary device discussed above implanted in his brain and has been subjected to direct electronic stimulation by the scientists in California. His decision to save the child (and the subsequent rescue) are the result of direct manipulation. White obviously lacks control over his actions, and he doesn't deserve credit for saving the child. Though we might feel relieved and happy that the child has been saved, and we might even praise the scientists for their activity, it would be ridiculous to praise White.

The second case is different in an interesting way. Though Green (the man who rescues the child) has also had a device implanted in his brain, the device does not play any role in Green's decision to save the child (and his subsequent action). That is, the device monitors Green's brain activity but does not actually intervene in it. Let us suppose that this is because the scientists can see that Green is about to decide to save the child and to act accordingly. But let's also suppose that the scientists would have intervened to bring about a decision to save the child if Green had shown an inclination to decide to refrain from saving the child. That is, were Green inclined to decide on his own not to save the child, the scientists would ensure electronically that he decide to save the child and also that he act to carry out this decision. This kind of case—involving a fail-safe arrangement that plays no actual role but the presence of which nevertheless *ensures* the result— was presented and discussed in a series of fascinating essays by Harry Frankfurt.

Now, it is clear that Green can't refrain from saving the child. It isn't up to him whether or not he rescues the child. But there seems to be a perfectly good sense in which he *freely* rescues the child; after all, he chooses and acts on his own, in just the way he would have, had the device not been implanted in his brain. The circumstances that make it the case that Green is not free to do otherwise play no role in his actual decision and action. It seems that, whereas both White and Green lack freedom to do otherwise, Green displays a kind of freedom that White lacks. White is a mere marionette manipulated by someone else, whereas Green is not (although he would be, under other circumstances).

Similarly, consider two different drug addicts. One is unaware that he is an addict; he takes the drug because he "really wants" to take it. Although (being an addict) he in fact has an irresistible desire for the drug, the irresistibility of the desire plays no role in his decision to take the drug. Contrast this "happy addict" with an addict who struggles with his desire to take the drug but must finally give in—he takes the drug despite the fact that he doesn't really want to. Both persons are addicts—both have irresistible desires for the drug and thus are unable to avoid taking it. But the first addict does so freely. He may be responsible for taking it insofar as his addiction plays no role in his decision and action; he would have done exactly the same thing had he not been an addict.

A theory of moral responsibility needs to explain why we don't think it fitting to subject White and the unhappy addict to praise or blame for their actions. The traditional explanation—that they lack the freedom to do otherwise, that they are not the locus of control—is too strong, since it implies that Green is also not responsible for his actions. We might want a theory of moral responsibility that is capable of making more nuanced discriminations than the traditional one.

What cases such as those of White and Green show, I believe, is that we need to abandon the traditional model of moral responsibility, which requires control in the sense of freedom to do otherwise. We need what might be called an "actual-sequence" model of responsibility, a model that focuses on the actual sequence of events leading to behavior. Green's situation shows that the actual sequence issuing in an action can be of the sort that properly grounds responsibility ascriptions, even if, had things been otherwise, the sequence that would have occurred would not have been of the sort that renders the agent accessible to praise or blame. There may be various paths to an action; on some paths, there may be coercive or compulsive mechanisms, mechanisms that undermine responsibility, while on other paths there may be mechanisms suitable to responsibility.

The cases of Green and the happy addict suggest that in some situations an agent lacks freedom to do otherwise (and in this sense, lacks control) but is nevertheless morally responsible for what he does. This opens the possibility that we can develop a theory of moral responsibility that shows responsibility to be compatible with causal determinism and with divine foreknowledge, even if causal determinism and divine foreknowledge were incompatible with freedom to do otherwise. It is natural to think that incompatibilist positions should hang together. If one is an incompatibilist about (say) divine foreknowledge and freedom to do otherwise, then it might be thought that one ought to be an incompatibilist about divine foreknowledge and moral responsibility. But we are beginning to see reason to reject this assimilation of doctrines—the case for incompatibilism about divine foreknowledge (or causal determinism) and freedom to do otherwise might be fundamentally different from the case for incompatibilism about divine foreknowledge (or causal determinism) and moral responsibility.

I have suggested that it would be desirable to have a theory of responsibility that would explain why such agents as Green and the "happy addict" are responsible for their actions, although they couldn't have done otherwise. One such theory has been developed by Harry Frankfurt, and it will be useful to sketch out some aspects of Frankfurt's theory here.[27]

On Frankfurt's theory, some organisms have not only "first-order" desires (desires for courses of action or perhaps states of affairs) but also "second-order desires" (desires that have as their objects first-order desires). Desires on a particular level may conflict, so I may have a first-order desire to smoke a cigarette but also a first-order desire to remain healthy and thus a first-order desire not to smoke. Furthermore, since I want to be the sort of person who acts on his desire to remain healthy, I may have a second-order desire to *act* on my first-order desire to refrain from smoking. On Frankfurt's theory, the first-order desire on which I am actually moved all the way to act is my "will."

Frankfurt distinguishes two sorts of second-order desires. I may have a second-order desire to *have* a particular first-order desire but not to *act* on this first-order desire. This would be a "mere second-order desire." For instance, I may be studying a certain sort of eating disorder, so I may want to have a desire to overeat but not to be

27. Frankfurt's model of acting freely (and moral responsibility) is "hierarchical," positing levels of preferences. There are developments of similar kinds of hierarchical accounts in Dworkin, 1970a and 1976; Jeffrey, 1974; and Neely, 1974. There is an excellent survey and discussion of hierarchical theories in Shatz, 1985.

moved all the way to action by the desire to "binge." In contrast, when I have a second-order desire that I *act* on a certain first-order desire— that is, when I have a second-order desire that a particular first-order desire be my *will*—this second-order desire is a "second-order volition." My second-order desire to act on my desire not to smoke is a second-order volition. Note that, on Frankfurt's "hierarchical" view, it is possible for an individual to have third-order (and higher) desires and volitions. For instance, one might not want to be the sort of person who is quite so preoccupied with health, and so one might have a third-order desire not to have the second-order volition to act on the first-order desire not to smoke and so on.

On Frankfurt's view, it is logically possible that a being have second-order desires but *no* second-order volitions. Also, of course, a being may have first-order desires but no second-order desires of any kind. Frankfurt calls an organism with no second-order volitions a "wanton"; a wanton is "passive" with respect to his impulses and doesn't care which of his urges lead him to action. For Frankfurt, a "person"—an organism accessible to the reactive attitudes—is an organism with second-order volitions. Since such a being *cares* which impulses he acts on, the task of securing conformity between his second-order volitions and his will can be a *problem* for him; in Frankfurt's words, a person is an organism for whom *freedom of the will* can be a problem.

Let us distinguish now between various kinds of freedom. On Frankfurt's theory, when one has freedom of action, one has the power to do what one wants.[28] Frankfurt's view is that when one has such freedom, one is free to do otherwise (that is, one could have translated a different want into action). Frankfurt believes that many creatures—even nonhuman animals—have this sort of freedom. But whereas freedom of action is an important sort of freedom, it is not the only sort.

Parallel to freedom of action, one has freedom of the will when one has the power to will what one wants to will, that is, when one has the power to make *any* of his first-order desires the one that moves him all the way to action (or perhaps the power to make *some* first-order desire [other than his actual will] the one that moves him to action). Again, as with freedom of action, Frankfurt's view is that one has

28. Notice that this formulation needn't imply that, when one has freedom of action, one has freedom to do otherwise. There is a sense of "having the power to do what one wants" on which one would have this power insofar as one had the power to do what one *actually* wants (but nothing else). But Frankfurt has in mind a more robust sense. (The same point applies to Frankfurt's explanation of freedom of the will.)

freedom of the will only if one could have "willed otherwise" (that is, only if one could have made any [or perhaps some] other first-order desire his will).[29] It is clear how an individual could have freedom of the will without freedom of action; he may be able to make any first-order desire the one that *moves* him to action, but he may not be able to translate his will *successfully* into action. So a man who is locked in a room may will to leave and actually attempt to leave; whereas he may have freedom of the will, he lacks freedom of action (since he can't actually leave).

The relationship between freedom of action and freedom of the will, on Frankfurt's approach, is a bit complicated. Frankfurt says, "We do not suppose that animals enjoy freedom of the will, although we recognize that an animal may be free to run in whatever direction it wants. Thus, having the freedom to do what one wants to do is not a sufficient condition for having freedom of the will."[30] But one might wonder how this is possible. If an organism has freedom of action, then he has freedom to do otherwise and therefore freedom to make at least some other desire (than the one which actually moves him) his will. So whereas it is relatively clear that having a free will doesn't require having freedom of action, it is not so clear that having freedom of action doesn't require having freedom of the will. One could perhaps justify Frankfurt's assertion that freedom of action does not imply freedom of the will by understanding freedom of the will to involve the power to make another first-order desire one's will *as a result of a second-order volition.*

Also, to clarify Frankfurt's view of freedom of the will further, note that he believes that an addict who struggles against his irresistible desire for a drug *lacks* freedom of the will. One might have thought that this sort of addict would be like the man locked in a room; his *will* might seem to be free, though he does not have the power to translate his will successfully into action. Why is the will of the addict not free but the will of the man locked in the room free? (Note that, if—contrary to Frankfurt's intention—the will of the man locked in the room is deemed *unfree,* then it is hard to see how Frankfurt could maintain his claim that having freedom of the will does not imply having freedom of action.)

29. Frankfurt says, "The willing addict's will is not free, for his desire to take the drug will be effective regardless of whether or not he wants this desire to constitute his will" (Chapter 1, below, p. 79). He is not explicit about whether freedom of the will requires the capacity to make *some* other first-order desire one's will or *any* other first-order desire one's will.
30. Frankfurt, Chapter 1, below, p. 74.

I believe Frankfurt would say that the drug addict, although he struggles against his irresistible urge, is *moved* (when he takes the drug) *by his desire for the drug.* To be sure, he has a desire to refrain from taking the drug, but this desire is not the one that motivates him when he acts. And furthermore, the irresistibility of his urge to take the drug implies that he doesn't have the power to avoid being moved by that desire in acting. In contrast, when the man who is locked in the room attempts unsuccessfully to leave, he is moved to action by a desire to leave the room. Indeed, he may have both the capacity to be moved by a desire to leave the room and a desire to stay in the room. So this man has a capacity that the addict lacks. This sort of account explains Frankfurt's claim that the drug addict *lacks* freedom of the will (and it is compatible with also saying that the man locked in the room *has* freedom of the will thus avoiding a collapse of freedom of the will into freedom of action).

We have distinguished and discussed two sorts of freedom: freedom of the will and freedom of action. The traditional approach to moral responsibility demands both sorts of freedom. But Frankfurt rejects the traditional approach, arguing that all that's required for moral responsibility is "acting freely" (where acting freely does not require freedom of action or freedom of the will). This sort of approach may be able to distinguish between such agents as the unhappy and happy addict and White and Green.

I shall now sketch in a preliminary way Frankfurt's account of acting freely; this account is suggested by one of Frankfurt's formulations, although it will be seen below that it is not Frankfurt's considered view. Frankfurt suggests that a person acts freely insofar as he performs an act (at least partly) because he "really wants" to. That is, the suggestion is that, when one "secures conformity of one's second-order volition and one's will," one acts freely. So it seems that Frankfurt's view is that, when one's act is caused (in an appropriate way) by one's second-order volition, this constitutes a sufficient condition for acting freely and for moral responsibility.[31] The interesting claim here is that the condition sufficient for moral responsibility is acting freely *and* that conforming the second-order volition to the will is *sufficient* for acting freely.

This theory certainly is promising. It implies that Green is morally responsible for his action of saving the child, although he couldn't

31. These suggestions are found in Frankfurt, Chapter 1, below, pp. 75 and 79. When Frankfurt says, "It is in securing the conformity of his will to his second-order volitions, then, that a person exercises freedom of the will" (p. 75), I take it that he also means to say that an agent who secures such a conformity would be *acting freely.*

have done otherwise, and it implies that the "happy addict" is morally responsible for taking the drug, although he couldn't have done otherwise (and lacked freedom of the will). On the other hand, the "unhappy addict" who struggles against his addiction does *not* act freely— he acts on a desire that is discordant with his second-order volition. This theory promises to give us an explanation of moral responsibility that allows us to *separate* the question of the compatibility of (say) causal determinism with responsibility from that of the compatibility of causal determinism with freedom to do otherwise. This feature is desirable insofar as one is inclined to accept the fixity of the past, the fixity of the laws, and the principle of transfer of powerlessness but is also inclined to cling to moral responsibility (even in the absence of confidence that causal determinism is *false*).

We considered above the natural supposition that a person is different from (say) a rat insofar as a person often has freedom to do otherwise, whereas a rat never does. On Frankfurt's approach, another feature differentiates a person from a rat: the structure and complexity of the motivational states that issue in action. There is one sense of "control" according to which an individual who cannot do otherwise lacks control. But Frankfurt's theory seems to show that there is another sense of "control"; in this sense, one can control an outcome if the "actual sequence" proceeds in a certain way even if one couldn't have done otherwise. For example, a pilot may turn a plane westward by moving the steering apparatus appropriately, thus causing the plane to turn westward. If, unbeknownst to him, the plane would have turned westward even if he had tried to cause it to fly in any other direction (perhaps because of a malfunction or a strong wind or something else), the pilot still might be said to "control" the plane insofar as he actually guides it westward. Frankfurt's claim is that this sort of control provides a sufficient condition for moral responsibility.

Frankfurt's "hierarchical" model of personhood and moral responsibility meets with various objections.[32] The articles in Part 1 of this anthology discuss some of these objections as well as developing other interesting approaches. I shall here mention three sorts of worries about the claim that securing conformity between one's second-order volition and one's will is a sufficient condition for acting freely and moral responsibility.

One is put forward by Gary Watson in "Free Agency." His point

32. A classic attack on hierarchical theories can be found in Thalberg, 1978; a response to some of Thalberg's worries is D. Zimmerman, 1981. Also see Shatz, 1985.

can be put as follows. If action on a first-order desire isn't sufficient for acting freely, then how can action on a second-order volition be sufficient? Why stop at the second level? Suppose, for instance, that one is a "wanton at the third level"—one doesn't care which second-order desires (or volitions) one has. Why would one here be acting freely simply in virtue of acting on a *second*-order volition? How can adding the second level make the crucial difference, even in the absence of an appropriate third level? Partly because of this sort of problem, Watson rejects the hierarchical model; instead, he develops an account of free action that posits different *sources* of desires (rather than different *levels* of desires).

Consider the following response to Watson's objection. One might say that one acts freely insofar as one's act issues from a "totally integrated preference structure."[33] Thus, one acts freely in doing $X$ insofar as (a) one acts on a second-order volition to do $X$ (that is, a second-order desire that one's first-order desire to do $X$ move him to action), and (b) for any $n$th order volition to do $X$, there exists an $(n + 1)$th order volition to do $X$. Unfortunately, this approach demands too much; it is implausible to suppose that any human agent has indefinitely many levels of preference (even if these preferences needn't be construed as explicit, conscious episodes). So either there will be too few levels or too many.

Here is another problem for the claim that conformity between one's second-order volition and one's will is a sufficient condition for acting freely. Just as one can have conflicting first-order desires, one can have conflicting higher-order desires (and volitions). Why should acting on a second-order volition to do $X$ be sufficient for acting freely even if one also has a second-order volition to *refrain* from doing $X$? It is logically possible for someone to have a totally integrated preference structure on behalf of doing $X$ and *also* such a structure on behalf of refraining from doing $X$; so even if an agent could have such a structure on behalf of $X$, why would this be sufficient for doing $X$ freely?

I said above that Frankfurt's approach seems to involve a twofold claim: (a) that the "freedom-relevant" condition sufficient for moral responsibility is "acting freely" and (b) that conformity between the second-order volition and the will is sufficient for acting freely. The sorts of problems discussed above (and others) force a retreat from (b). Frankfurt's considered view is something like what follows. When one *identifies* (or perhaps "identifies decisively") with the first-order

---

33. Lehrer employs this term for a similar notion that he develops in Lehrer, 1980.

desire on which one acts, this constitutes a sufficient condition for acting freely. In general, a person is an organism for which it can be a problem to achieve harmony between the desires with which he *identifies* and those that issue in action. Sometimes it is (partly) through the formation of a second-order volition that one identifies with a particular first-order desire, but this does not provide a sufficient condition for identification.

On Frankfurt's view, when one (decisively) identifies with a first-order desire, one commits oneself to it (and the course of action it recommends). As he puts it, "When a person identifies himself *decisively* with one of his first-order desires, this commitment 'resounds' throughout the potentially endless array of higher orders. . . . The fact that his second-order volition to be moved by this desire is a decisive one means that there is no room for questions concerning the pertinence of volitions of higher orders."[34]

Of course, this sort of move leaves (as yet) unexplained the crucial notions of "identification" and "resonance." In order better to understand and evaluate Frankfurt's theory, we will need more explicit accounts of these notions.[35] For instance, can an "identification" be caused by direct electronic stimulation or hypnosis? Can it be causally determined?

Let us now consider another apparent problem for Frankfurt's theory, even on the "refined" version, according to which it is "identification" that is sufficient for responsibility. Consider a bank teller who is held up at gunpoint and is told, "Your money or your life!" (Don Locke and Michael Slote discuss this example and others.) And suppose that this teller considers the situation and is not overwhelmed by an irresistible urge to comply with the threat. He believes that he *could* resist the robber but decides that it would be unreasonable to sacrifice his life in order to save the money, and so he calmly hands over the money. Now, Frankfurt's theory seems to imply that the teller *freely* hands over the money; after all, given the situation, the teller identifies with the desire to give the robber the money (and thus to save his life). But is it plausible to think that the teller hands over the money freely?

Slote believes that the teller does *not* hand over the money freely, and he suggests a revision of the hierarchical theory that would accommodate this view. But Slote thinks that, nevertheless, the teller can be held morally responsible for his action. Thus Slote believes that

---

34. Frankfurt, Chapter 1, below, p. 76.
35. Frankfurt undertakes more explicitly to explain "identification," "decisiveness," and the "resonance effect" in Frankfurt, forthcoming.

acting freely is not necessary for moral responsibility. Frankfurt and Locke both hold that the teller acts freely. On Frankfurt's theory, the teller acts freely and is morally responsible for his act. Of course, it does not follow, on Frankfurt's account, that the teller is *blameworthy* for what he does. The teller's action is something for which he is morally accountable (in a way in which a hypnotized person would not be accountable), but it doesn't follow that he is actually blameworthy. Locke wishes to say that, whereas the teller acts freely, he is not morally responsible because he is not blameworthy. This approach doesn't distinguish (as does Frankfurt's) between the claim that an agent is an *appropriate candidate* for blame on the basis of an action and the claim that he ought to be blamed for the action. But although Frankfurt and Locke seem to be operating with different conceptions of moral responsibility, and Frankfurt and Slote are operating with different conceptions of acting freely, they needn't differ with respect to the claims that the teller is a rational candidate for the reactive attitudes and that in fact he should not be punished for his behavior.

There is a third objection to Frankfurt's hierarchical approach that I wish to consider. (Again, both Locke and Slote discuss this kind of example.) Remember the possibility I raised, that your best friend is being manipulated (unbeknownst to him). Of course, his higher-level volitions and "identifications" may also be directly induced. But this sort of agent does not act freely (insofar as acting freely suffices for moral responsibility). He is not a rational candidate for the reactive attitudes.

Again, this kind of problem appears to show that conformity between a second-order volition and the will does not suffice for acting freely.[36] Also, it threatens to show that "identification" does not suffice for acting freely. Frankfurt might wish to respond in one of two ways. First, he may want to say that it is essential to an identification that it not be produced in the way imagined—say, by hypnosis or electronic stimulation and so forth. But then we need an account of identification that would explain why. And the question would arise as to whether this explanation would allow for causally determined identifications. If not, then Frankfurt's theory would not be able to reconcile determinism with acting freely and moral responsibility (independently of a reconcilation of determinism with freedom to do otherwise). This approach would need to explain why certain mechanisms issuing in mental events are inconsistent with identification,

---

36. Of course, this sort of example is a problem not only for the hierarchical approach but also for "multiple-source" views such as that of Watson.

whereas certain other mechanisms (even causally deterministic ones) *may* result in identification. This approach involves looking carefully at the *history* of a particular act in order to determine whether it is performed freely.

Another possible response would be to claim that the manipulated agent does act freely, although he is not responsible for the fact that he acts freely. On this approach, the history of the "identification" is not relevant to whether the act is performed freely. But it is clear that this approach severs acting freely from moral responsibility; surely even if the agent is said to be acting freely he cannot be thought to be morally responsible for his act. So on this approach, we would not (as yet) have a reconciliation of causal determinism with *moral responsibility.*

We started this section with the idea that a theory of moral responsibility should distinguish between such agents as the unhappy and happy addicts and White and Green and that it should allow that Green be morally responsible, although he couldn't have done otherwise. (Remember that Green acts to save the child without any manipulation, although he could not have done otherwise.) So far we have looked at a theory that proposes to explain how an agent can be morally responsible in virtue of properties of the actual sequence of events leading to an action. The hierarchical model that we have been investigating is an "actual sequence" model of moral responsibility. A problem with this approach, which we have just discussed, is that, whereas it can distinguish the happy and unhappy addicts, it may not be able to distinguish White and Green; that is, it may be that a directly manipulated agent (such as White) must be said to act freely. But there is another sort of worry about the claims that Green is morally responsible for his action, although he couldn't have done otherwise, and that, in general, we can separate the issue of moral responsibility from the issue of freedom to do otherwise. In the next section I shall consider this worry.

*Moral Responsibility and Alternate Possibilities*

Some philosophers worry that examples such as that of Green do *not* successfully separate responsibility from freedom to do otherwise. One development of this objection is given by Peter van Inwagen in "Ability and Responsibility." Van Inwagen points out that we must distinguish among various sorts of things for which an agent might be morally responsible: actions, omissions, particular events, states of affairs, and so forth. His claim is that, when one considers the purported examples in which an agent is morally responsible for something to which there is no alternative, one will find that: (a) the thing for which the agent is in fact morally responsible is something to which there *is an alternate possibility* and (b) the agent is *not* responsible for the thing to which there is no alternate possibility. Van Inwagen's basic idea is that, if we are sufficiently careful about specifying what the agent is allegedly morally responsible for (the "content" of moral responsibility), then we will see that moral responsibility *does* require the existence of genuine alternatives.

Consider again the case of Green, who actually saves the drowning child. Unbeknownst to him, he would have been caused to do so by the scientists had he been inclined not to. Now, let's distinguish between two different things: the actual concrete event of the child's being saved and the state of affairs, "that the child is saved." As opposed to the concrete "event particular," let us suppose that the *same* state of affairs would have taken place had the child been saved in another way (say, by another person and so forth). So a state of affairs here is taken to be a "universal"—it (the very same state of affairs) can be "realized" in various different ways.

To focus on the difference between event particulars and universals (states of affairs), suppose you are skiing down a slope and you come to a fork in the trail; unbeknownst to you, both forks end up at the lodge. The state of affairs "that you ski to the lodge" can be realized by your going left or right; the two ways of realizing the same state of affairs are two different event particulars (or perhaps sequences of event particulars). Intuitively, van Inwagen's idea is that when you voluntarily decide to take the left fork, you are responsible for the *particular* event of your taking the left fork, but of course, there is an alternative. But you are not morally responsible for the thing to which there is no alternative—the fact that you end up at the lodge. (We can assume here that you never had an option as to whether you end up at the fork in the trail and so forth.)

Now let's apply this sort of strategy to the example of Green. Van Inwagen claims that Green *is* morally responsible for the *particular* event of the child's being saved, but there *is* an alternate possibility, because had the scientists intervened, a different event particular would have occurred—a *different* particular event of the child's being saved. And although there is no alternative to the fact that the child is saved (in some way or other), Green is *not* morally responsible for this fact—perhaps it is the scientists who have "set up" the apparatus who are responsible for this fact. Either way, there is no thing of which both of the following are true: (a) the agent is morally responsible for *it* and (b) there is no genuine alternative to *it*.

More carefully, van Inwagen's argument can be put as follows. Frankfurt might seem to have produced counterexamples to the traditionally accepted "Principle of Alternate Possibilities."

(PAP) A person is morally responsible for what he has done only if he could have done otherwise.

But there is a trio of principles to which he has not produced a convincing counterexample:

A person is morally responsible for failing to perform a given act only if he could have performed it.

A person is morally responsible for a certain event-particular only if he could have prevented it.

A person is morally responsible for a certain state of affairs only if (that state of affairs obtains and) he could have prevented it from obtaining.

Van Inwagen's claim is that if the principles are indeed valid, then it follows that moral responsibility for *anything* (even for actions) requires the existence of the appropriate alternate possibilities.

Van Inwagen's strategy is certainly tempting. Think, for instance, about omissions or failures to perform actions. Suppose Brown does not have any sort of fancy device implanted in his brain. He is walking along the beach and sees a child struggling in the water. He knows that he can swim and believes he could save the child, but he simply decides not to bother; he continues walking along the beach, and the baby drowns. Unbeknownst to Brown, there is a school of hungry sharks swimming under the water, and they would have eaten him had he tried to save the child. Now, is Brown morally responsible for failing to save the child? It seems *not;* there is a strong intuitive temptation here to say that he is morally responsible for an omission to which there is a genuine alternative: failing to try to save the child (failing to jump into the water and so forth). When one is careful about specifying what the agent is morally responsible for, it is thus not so obvious that there are counterexamples to the principle that an agent is morally responsible for failing to perform an act only if he could have performed it. Again, careful specification of the content of moral responsibility might lead to preserving the association of responsibility with freedom to do otherwise. If this association is preserved, then the traditional questions about the compatibility of determinism with freedom to do otherwise remain pressing, and we have not successfully separated these questions from the issue of the compatibility of determinism with responsibility.

In "Responsibility and Control," I argue against certain aspects of van Inwagen's strategy. Let's consider the principle about event particulars:

> A person is morally responsible for a certain event particular only if he could have prevented it.

Van Inwagen points out that the example of Green is not clearly a case in which the *same* event particular would have occurred in the alternate sequence as in the actual sequence. Thus, Frankfurt-type examples wouldn't show the principle false in virtue of exhibiting cases in which the same event would have occurred even had the agent been inclined to do otherwise. But I argue that there may be another way in which the examples show the principle false; it is not clear that the only way in which one could show the falsity of the principle would be in the way envisaged by van Inwagen. I argue that, whereas it might be true that a different event particular would have occurred in the alternate sequence, still, Green didn't have the sort of freedom required by a defender of the principle. One who believes in associating responsibility with alternate possibilities will insist on some such interpretation of the principle:

> A person is morally responsible for a certain event particular only if he could have brought about an event particular of a different type (as a result of an intention to do so).

Now, the Frankfurt-style examples *do* seem to show this kind of principle false. Consider Green again. He does seem to be morally responsible for saving the child. But he *didn't* have the pertinent sort of "deliberate control" over the event of the child's being saved: he couldn't have brought about an event of the type "the child's not being saved." Think of the issue in the following way. The alternate-possibilities theorist believes that, if Green is morally responsible for saving the child, then he must have had more than one genuine opportunity; that is, there must be more than one genuine, open possibility in which he acts freely. But note that in the example there is only *one* path along which Green acts freely, and it is just this sort of situation that the alternate-possibilities theorist finds antithetical to moral responsibility.

Even if Frankfurt has successfully separated moral responsibility from freedom to do otherwise (and this is obviously controversial), I also argue that this dissociation in itself does not establish the consistency of moral responsibility and causal determinism.[37] Let's consider the problem for Frankfurt's approach. Frankfurt points out that, in cases such as Green's, the fact that he couldn't have done otherwise *plays no role* in his actual decision and action. Because of this irrelevance of the lack of alternate possibilities, one could say that Green can be held morally responsible, although he couldn't have done otherwise. But causal determinism is a doctrine about how the "actual sequence" proceeds; if an action is causally determined, then perhaps the fact that the agent couldn't have done otherwise *does* actually "play a role" in the decision and action. This is because the fact that an action results from a causally deterministic sequence seems to be a fact about how the action comes about. Interestingly, the fact that God knew in advance that an action would take place does *not* seem to be this sort of fact. Thus, it might be that causal determinism (but not divine fore-knowledge) rules out moral responsibility even though moral responsibility does not require freedom to do otherwise.

Perhaps the explanation of the consistency of Green's moral responsibility with his lack of freedom to do otherwise needs to be refined. In Green's case, instead of saying that he is morally responsible insofar as the fact that he couldn't have done otherwise plays no role in his decision and action, we might say that he is morally responsible insofar as the "responsibility-undermining factor" occurs in the *alternate* sequence rather than in the actual sequence. Then the question of whether causal determinism is consistent with moral responsibility would boil down to the question: Is causal determinism a responsibility-undermining factor independent of its ruling out freedom to do otherwise? That is, the challenge that Frankfurt-type cases pose to the incompatibilist (who accepts the dissociation of responsibility from freedom to do otherwise) is to explain why causally deterministic sequences rule out moral responsibility but *not* in virtue of ruling out freedom to do otherwise.

*Freedom and Unfreedom*

Both P. S. Greenspan's "Behavior Control and Freedom of Action" and Gert and Duggan's "Free Will as the Ability to Will" address certain questions about free action independently of the traditional

---

37. See also M. J. Zimmerman, 1982. Frankfurt considers the problem raised in this paragraph in Chapter 6, pp. 151–152. He here refines the explanation of the consistency of Green's moral responsibility with his lack of freedom to do otherwise.

questions about (say) the compatibility of causal determinism and freedom to do otherwise; in this respect, their approaches are similar to that of Frankfurt, and they offer illuminating accounts of various different kinds of unfreedom.

We have discussed cases in which it is allegedly true that an agent acts freely (and is morally responsible for his action), although he could not have done otherwise. Greenspan discusses cases in which, although the agent is free to do otherwise, the act is "unfree."[38] Suppose that, because of some sort of conditioning, an agent would experience intense discomfort if he were to try to do otherwise. Greenspan claims that his act would be unfree if it would be "unreasonable" (relative to some standard) to expect him to do otherwise even if he literally *could* do otherwise (and suffer). So when Alex (in *A Clockwork Orange*) refrains from violent acts, his acts (or omissions) are unfree, and this claim is not dependent upon a decision about whether Alex has freedom to do otherwise. Greenspan offers an account of the sort of unfreedom involved in certain kinds of conditioning and "manipulation" that distinguishes this sort of unfreedom from "psychological compulsion" or the lack of genuine alternatives.

Greenspan points out that, when one is *unaware* of certain sorts of conditioning or manipulation, this might render one unfree in some important sense, even though one does have the power to do otherwise. Lack of knowledge of the factors producing one's behavior might render one unfree without literally stripping one of the power to do otherwise.[39]

It is interesting to consider the relationship between the sort of unfreedom Greenspan discusses and moral responsibility. If someone's commission of a crime was "unfree" (on Greenspan's account), then it was unreasonable to expect him to do otherwise (in virtue of certain sorts of considerations). So perhaps he is "exculpated" in the sense of not being blameworthy for his action. But he still might be morally responsible for his behavior, in the sense that he is a rational candidate for praise or blame (in a way in which, for example, a directly electronically stimulated agent is not). It might be claimed, then, that moral responsibility is still associated with freedom to do otherwise even if actual blameworthiness is ruled out by its being unreasonable to expect the agent to do otherwise. Whereas certain sorts of unfreedom might be understood independently of questions about freedom to do otherwise, it is thus not clear that Greenspan's

38. See also Locke, Chapter 3, below, p. 108.
39. Nozick also makes this sort of point in Nozick, 1981, pp. 348–52.

considerations show that moral responsibility can be ascribed independently of the ascription of freedom to do otherwise (and Greenspan doesn't claim that they do).

Gert and Duggan provide an account of what they call "free actions," actions performed by an agent who is "acting intentionally, voluntarily, and freely." Free actions are those for which we can be held "fully responsible," and it is not required, on their account of free action, that the agent could literally have performed some other particular act.

Particularly interesting in Gert and Duggan's approach is their claim that a person has "Free Will" insofar as he has the "Ability to Will." To have the Ability to Will an $X$-type act, on their approach, is (roughly) to have the ability to believe that there might be both coercive and noncoercive reasons to do an $X$-type act and also not to do an $X$-type act and to have the ability to act on both the reasons to do an $X$-type act and not to do such acts. On this account, one must be "receptive" to reasons in the appropriate way and also "responsive" to them. And we can illuminate certain sorts of unfreedom in terms of different ways in which one might lack the ability to will. Those who cannot "believe" (those who are not receptive to reasons) are in this respect like delusional psychotics, and those who are not appropriately affected by their beliefs (those who are not responsive to reasons) are like compulsive or phobic neurotics. These two different sorts of defects correspond roughly to the two ways of developing an "insanity" defense, as discussed above.

Note that there is an interesting tension in Gert and Duggan's formulation of their position. On the one hand, they say that an act done by a person who lacks the Ability to Will is "unvoluntary" and thus is not a free action. On the other hand, they say that an act that is *due to* a person's lack of Ability to Will is unvoluntary. If one believes that the Frankfurt-type examples (or obvious extensions of them) show that one could be fully responsible for acting although one *lacks* the Ability to Will, one will want to accept the second formulation, according to which an act is unvoluntary insofar as it is *due* to a person's lack of the Ability to Will.

One might believe (à la Frankfurt) that, when the "volitional lack" is *irrelevant* to one's action, then one can be fully responsible, although one lacks the Ability to Will. This possibility suggests that the Gert-Duggan approach might be employed as an account of the kind of mechanism that *must actually operate* in cases of voluntary action rather than as an account of an ability an agent must possess if his act is to be voluntary. That is, in Frankfurt-type cases, one might want to say that the agent acts voluntarily insofar as the mechanism that actually operates is a receptive and responsive mechanism, although *another* sort of mechanism would have operated in the alternative scenario. Thus, the actual deliberative mechanism that issues in the action might have the appropriate "reasons sensitivity" even though an "insensitive" mechanism would have operated in the alternative sequence (or various alternative sequences), and thus the agent lacks the Ability to Will.[40]

Remember Green. He actually saves the child as a result of the operation of a "normal," unimpaired human deliberative mechanism; this mechanism seems to be receptive and responsive, even though the scientists would have intervened in the alternative sequence and would thus have caused an insensitive mechanism to operate. This approach might offer some hope of explaining what properties must be exhibited by the actual course of events if an agent is to be held responsible for an act that he couldn't have avoided performing.

*Asymmetrical Approaches*

Relying on a view like Gert and Duggan's that connects free will with the ability to act in accordance with reasons of a certain sort, Susan Wolf (in "Asymmetrical Freedom") offers a theory of responsibility that appears to depart both from the traditional approach to responsibility (which always requires freedom to do otherwise) and from those approaches that never require freedom to do otherwise (but only "acting freely"). She suggests an "asymmetrical" approach, on which an agent *can* be morally responsible for a *good* action that he couldn't have avoided doing, but *cannot* legitimately be held morally responsible for a *bad* action that he couldn't have avoided doing. Wolf presents interesting cases in which one might be held responsible for (good) acts that do not issue from receptive and responsive mechanisms.

She says that "an agent's action is *psychologically determined* if his action is determined by his interests—that is, his values or desires—and his interests are determined by his heredity or environment." She argues that, in order for an agent to be morally responsible for a bad act, it

40. For a development of a similar approach, see Nozick, 1981, pp. 317–52. The distinction between the properties of the actual-sequence mechanism and the alternative-sequence mechanism is parallel to such a distinction in epistemology. That is, a "sensitive" mechanism (a mechanism that "tracks truth") may actually operate when I know some proposition, although an insensitive mechanism would have operated in the alternative scenario: Nozick, 1981, pp. 179–86. Here is another parallel between epistemology and moral responsibility.

must not have been psychologically determined. But moral responsibility for a good act is consistent with psychological determination.

Note that Wolf's definition of psychological determination is not the same as the standard sort of definition of causal determination. Thus, an action may be psychologically undetermined, in Wolf's sense, but causally determined. (This would be the case if there were no psychological explanation of the action but there were a "subpsychological or physiological" explanation.) Thus, Wolf's argument for her asymmetry thesis may not translate readily into an argument for an asymmetrical approach to moral responsibility and causal determinism.

As I pointed out above, van Inwagen claims that it is impossible to produce an example in which a person is morally responsible for failing to do something that he *can't* do. He combines this view with other considerations to reach the result that moral responsibility for *anything* requires the existence of an alternative possibility. In contrast, one might believe that moral responsibility for doing something does not require freedom to refrain from doing it, whereas moral responsibility for failing to do something *does* require freedom to do it.[41] Wolf's asymmetry thesis concerns good and bad acts, whereas this assymmetry thesis concerns actions and omissions.

The intuitive support for such a thesis (about actions and omissions) comes from considering the following two cases. In the first, Green saves the child (though, unbeknownst to him, the scientists would have intervened had he been inclined to do otherwise and so forth). Intuitively, Green seems responsible for *saving the child*, although he couldn't have done otherwise. But remember Brown, who decides not to jump into the water (because he doesn't wish to be inconvenienced). Unbeknownst to him, a school of sharks would have eaten him had he jumped in. Brown, it seems, is morally responsible for failing to *try* to save the child, but he doesn't appear to be morally responsible for failing to *save* the child. Similarly, he wouldn't be morally responsible for failing to save the child if the child had *died* at the same moment that he jumped in!

Of course, much more would need to be said on behalf of this sort of asymmetrical approach in order to render it plausible. Also note that our intuitive conception of moral responsibility clearly includes moral responsibility for bad acts and for omissions, and on the asymmetrical approaches, responsibility for bad acts and for omissions requires freedom to do otherwise. So an asymmetrical theorist would still need to show that causal determinism doesn't rule out freedom to

41. I develop this sort of asymmetric theory in Fischer, 1985–1986.

do otherwise, in order to establish that causal determinism doesn't threaten moral responsibility, as normally understood.

### Transfer of Blamelessness

We don't know for certain whether causal determinism is false. And if we are not convinced that causal determinism is consistent with freedom to do otherwise, we are not certain that we are ever free to do otherwise. Now, if moral responsibility requires freedom to do otherwise, we don't know whether we are morally responsible—our most basic and deeply valued attitudes and activities are threatened.

One way to "save" moral responsibility is to deny that moral responsibility requires freedom to do otherwise; this strategy has been explored above. But there is another sort of threat to our moral responsibility. This threat is more "direct"; it does *not* claim that moral responsibility is ruled out by determinism because determinism rules out freedom to do otherwise. Rather, it proposes a plausible principle that might directly show determinism to be incompatible with responsibility.

In "The Incompatibility of Responsibility and Determinism," van Inwagen offers us what might be called the "principle of transfer of blamelessness":[42] if you are not morally responsible for one thing, and you are not morally responsible for that thing's leading to another, you are not morally responsible for the other. Now, an argument clearly parallel to the arguments discussed above can be generated to show that causal determinism rules out moral responsibility. Given that you are not morally responsible for the past, and you are not morally responsible for the laws of nature, and assuming the principle of transfer of blamelessness, causal determinism seems to rule out moral responsibility.

Again, the argument is controversial. One way to reject the argument is to reject the principle of transfer of blamelessness. And it seems that Frankfurt-style examples may provide the justification for such a rejection. After all, Green is not morally responsible for the fact that the scientists are ready to intervene, and he is not responsible for the fact that, if they are so ready, he will save the child. But he *does* seem to be morally responsible for saving the child. Thus, Frankfurt-style examples may be plausible counterexamples to the principle of transfer of blamelessness. Note that they are not counterexamples to

---

42. I borrow this term from John Taurek (Taurek, 1972). Here I shall be understanding "blamelessness" to mean *inaccessibility* to the reactive attitudes.

the principle of transfer of powerlessness. So a compatibilist about determinism and moral responsibility *might* accept the fixity of the past [in both the $(FP_1)$ and $(FP_2)$ senses], the fixity of the laws [in both the $(FL_1)$ and $(FL_2)$ senses], and the principle of transfer of powerlessness but might reject the principle of transfer of blamelessness.

But notice that this way of saving moral responsibility is also not uncontroversial. It is true that, given that the scientists are "standing by," Green will save the baby. But Green still seems to be morally responsible for saving the baby "on his own" (or not as a result of the scientists' manipulation). So it might be claimed that he *is* morally responsible for the fact that, if the scientists are ready, then he saves the baby *on his own*. But if this claim is correct, then Frankfurt-style examples do not show the principle of transfer of blamelessness to be false. That is, just as above, the van Inwagen-style response is to insist on a careful specification of what the agent is responsible for—the "content" of moral responsibility. Upon such specification, he will insist that we do not have a counterexample to the principle of transfer of blamelessness.

# I

## ACTING FREELY AND MORAL RESPONSIBILITY

# 1

# Freedom of the Will and the
# Concept of a Person

## HARRY G. FRANKFURT

What philosophers have lately come to accept as analysis of the concept of a person is not actually analysis of *that* concept at all. Strawson, whose usage represents the current standard, identifies the concept of a person as "the concept of a type of entity such that *both* predicates ascribing states of consciousness *and* predicates ascribing corporeal characteristics . . . are equally applicable to a single individual of that single type."[1] But there are many entities besides persons that have both mental and physical properties. As it happens— though it seems extraordinary that this should be so—there is no common English word for the type of entity Strawson has in mind, a type that includes not only human beings but animals of various lesser species as well. Still, this hardly justifies the misappropriation of a valuable philosophical term.

Whether the members of some animal species are persons is surely not to be settled merely by determining whether it is correct to apply to them, in addition to predicates ascribing corporeal characteristics,

"Freedom of the Will and the Concept of a Person" originally appeared in the *Journal of Philosophy*, 68 (January 1971), 5–20, © 1971 by the *Journal of Philosophy*, and is reprinted here with permission from Harry G. Frankfurt and from the *Journal of Philosophy*.
1. P. F. Strawson, *Individuals* (London: Methuen, 1959), pp. 101–102. Ayer's usage of 'person' is similar: "it is characteristic of persons in this sense that besides having various physical properties . . . they are also credited with various forms of consciousness" [A. J. Ayer, *The Concept of a Person* (New York: St. Martin's, 1963), p. 82]. What concerns Strawson and Ayer is the problem of understanding the relation between mind and body, rather than the quite different problem of understanding what it is to be a creature that not only has a mind and a body but is also a person.

predicates that ascribe states of consciousness. It does violence to our language to endorse the application of the term 'person' to those numerous creatures which do have both psychological and material properties but which are manifestly not persons in any normal sense of the word. This misuse of language is doubtless innocent of any theoretical error. But although the offense is "merely verbal," it does significant harm. For it gratuitously diminishes our philosophical vocabulary, and it increases the likelihood that we will overlook the important area of inquiry with which the term 'person' is most naturally associated. It might have been expected that no problem would be of more central and persistent concern to philosophers than that of understanding what we ourselves essentially are. Yet this problem is so generally neglected that it has been possible to make off with its very name almost without being noticed and, evidently, without evoking any widespread feeling of loss.

There is a sense in which the word 'person' is merely the singular form of 'people' and in which both terms connote no more than membership in a certain biological species. In those senses of the word which are of greater philosophical interest, however, the criteria for being a person do not serve primarily to distinguish the members of our own species from the members of other species. Rather, they are designed to capture those attributes which are the subject of our most humane concern with ourselves and the source of what we regard as most important and most problematical in our lives. Now these attributes would be of equal significance to us even if they were not in fact peculiar and common to the members of our own species. What interests us most in the human condition would not interest us less if it were also a feature of the condition of other creatures as well.

Our concept of ourselves as persons is not to be understood, therefore, as a concept of attributes that are necessarily species-specific. It is conceptually possible that members of novel or even of familiar nonhuman species should be persons; and it is also conceptually possible that some members of the human species are not persons. We do in fact assume, on the other hand, that no member of another species is a person. Accordingly, there is a presumption that what is essential to persons is a set of characteristics that we generally suppose— whether rightly or wrongly—to be uniquely human.

It is my view that one essential difference between persons and other creatures is to be found in the structure of a person's will. Human beings are not alone in having desires and motives, or in making choices. They share these things with the members of certain other species, some of whom even appear to engage in deliberation and to make decisions based upon prior thought. It seems to be peculiarly characteristic of humans, however, that they are able to form what I shall call "second-order desires" or "desires of the second order."

Besides wanting and choosing and being moved *to do* this or that, men may also want to have (or not to have) certain desires and motives. They are capable of wanting to be different, in their preferences and purposes, from what they are. Many animals appear to have the capacity for what I shall call "first-order desires" or "desires of the first order," which are simply desires to do or not to do one thing or another. No animal other than man, however, appears to have the capacity for reflective self-evaluation that is manifested in the formation of second-order desires.[2]

## I

The concept designated by the verb 'to want' is extraordinarily elusive. A statement of the form "*A* wants to *X*"—taken by itself, apart from a context that serves to amplify or to specify its meaning—conveys remarkably little information. Such a statement may be consistent, for example, with each of the following statements: (a) the prospect of doing *X* elicits no sensation or introspectible emotional response in *A;* (b) *A* is unaware that he wants to *X;* (c) *A* believes that he does not want to *X;* (d) *A* wants to refrain from *X*-ing; (e) *A* wants to *Y* and believes that it is impossible for him both to *Y* and to *X;* (f) *A* does not "really" want to *X;* (g) *A* would rather die than *X;* and so on. It is therefore hardly sufficient to formulate the distinction between first-order and second-order desires, as I have done, by suggesting merely that someone has a first-order desire when he wants to do or not to do such-and-such, and that he has a second-order desire when he wants to have or not to have a certain desire of the first order.

As I shall understand them, statements of the form "*A* wants to *X*" cover a rather broad range of possibilities.[3] They may be true even

2. For the sake of simplicity, I shall deal only with what someone wants or desires, neglecting related phenomena such as choices and decisions. I propose to use the verbs 'to want' and 'to desire' interchangeably, although they are by no means perfect synonyms. My motive in forsaking the established nuances of these words arises from the fact that the verb 'to want', which suits my purposes better so far as its meaning is concerned, does not lend itself so readily to the formation of nouns as does the verb 'to desire'. It is perhaps acceptable, albeit graceless, to speak in the plural of someone's "wants." But to speak in the singular of someone's "want" would be an abomination.

3. What I say in this paragraph applies not only to cases in which 'to *X*' refers to a possible action or inaction. It also applies to cases in which 'to *X*' refers to a first-order desire and in which the statement that '*A* wants to *X*' is therefore a shortened version of a statement—"*A* wants to want to *X*"—that identifies a desire of the second order.

when statements like (a) through (g) are true: when $A$ is unaware of any feelings concerning $X$-ing, when he is unaware that he wants to $X$, when he deceives himself about what he wants and believes falsely that he does not want to $X$, when he also has other desires that conflict with his desire to $X$, or when he is ambivalent. The desires in question may be conscious or unconscious, they need not be univocal, and $A$ may be mistaken about them. There is a further source of uncertainty with regard to statements that identify someone's desires, however, and here it is important for my purposes to be less permissive.

Consider first those statements of the form "$A$ wants to $X$" which identify first-order desires—that is, statements in which the term 'to $X$' refers to an action. A statement of this kind does not, by itself, indicate the relative strength of $A$'s desire to $X$. It does not make it clear whether this desire is at all likely to play a decisive role in what $A$ actually does or tries to do. For it may correctly be said that $A$ wants to $X$ even when his desire to $X$ is only one among his desires and when it is far from being paramount among them. Thus, it may be true that $A$ wants to $X$ when he strongly prefers to do something else instead; and it may be true that he wants to $X$ despite the fact that, when he acts, it is not the desire to $X$ that motivates him to do what he does. On the other hand, someone who states that $A$ wants to $X$ may mean to convey that it is this desire that is motivating or moving $A$ to do what he is actually doing or that $A$ will in fact be moved by this desire (unless he changes his mind) when he acts.

It is only when it is used in the second of these ways that, given the special usage of 'will' that I propose to adopt, the statement identifies $A$'s will. To identify an agent's will is either to identify the desire (or desires) by which he is motivated in some action he performs or to identify the desire (or desires) by which he will or would be motivated when or if he acts. An agent's will, then, is identical with one or more of his first-order desires. But the notion of the will, as I am employing it, is not coextensive with the notion of first-order desires. It is not the notion of something that merely inclines an agent in some degree to act in a certain way. Rather, it is the notion of an *effective* desire—one that moves (or will or would move) a person all the way to action. Thus the notion of the will is not coextensive with the notion of what an agent intends to do. For even though someone may have a settled intention to do $X$, he may nonetheless do something else instead of doing $X$ because, despite his intention, his desire to do $X$ proves to be weaker or less effective than some conflicting desire.

Now consider those statements of the form "$A$ wants to $X$" which identify second-order desires—that is, statements in which the term 'to $X$' refers to a desire of the first order. There are also two kinds of situation in which it may be true that $A$ wants to want to $X$. In the first place, it might be true of $A$ that he wants to have a desire to $X$ despite the fact that he has a univocal desire, altogether free of conflict and ambivalence, to refrain from $X$-ing. Someone might want to have a certain desire, in other words, but univocally want that desire to be unsatisfied.

Suppose that a physician engaged in psychotherapy with narcotics addicts believes that his ability to help his patients would be enhanced if he understood better what it is like for them to desire the drug to which they are addicted. Suppose that he is led in this way to want to have a desire for the drug. If it is a genuine desire that he wants, then what he wants is not merely to feel the sensations that addicts characteristically feel when they are gripped by their desires for the drug. What the physician wants, insofar as he wants to have a desire, is to be inclined or moved to some extent to take the drug.

It is entirely possible, however, that, although he wants to be moved by a desire to take the drug, he does not want this desire to be effective. He may not want it to move him all the way to action. He need not be interested in finding out what it is like to take the drug. And insofar as he now wants only to *want* to take it, and not to *take* it, there is nothing in what he now wants that would be satisfied by the drug itself. He may now have, in fact, an altogether univocal desire *not* to take the drug; and he may prudently arrange to make it impossible for him to satisfy the desire he would have if his desire to want the drug should in time be satisfied.

It would thus be incorrect to infer, from the fact that the physician now wants to desire to take the drug, that he already does desire to take it. His second-order desire to be moved to take the drug does not entail that he has a first-order desire to take it. If the drug were now to be administered to him, this might satisfy no desire that is implicit in his desire to want to take it. While he wants to want to take the drug, he may have *no* desire to take it; it may be that *all* he wants is to taste the desire for it. That is, his desire to have a certain desire that he does not have may not be a desire that his will should be at all different than it is.

Someone who wants only in this truncated way to want to $X$ stands at the margin of preciosity, and the fact that he wants to want to $X$ is not pertinent to the identification of his will. There is, however, a second kind of situation that may be described by '$A$ wants to want to $X$'; and when the statement is used to describe a situation of this second kind, then it does pertain to what $A$ wants his will to be. In such cases the statement means that A wants the desire to X to be the desire that moves him effectively to act. It is not merely that he wants the desire to X to be among the desires by which, to one degree or another, he is moved or inclined to act. He wants this desire to be effective—that is, to provide the motive in what he actually does. Now when the statement that A wants to want to X is used in this way, it does entail that A already has a desire to X. It could not be true both that A wants the desire to X to move him into action and that he does not want to X. It is only if he does want to X that he can coherently want the desire to X not merely to be one of his desires but, more decisively, to be his will.[4]

Suppose a man wants to be motivated in what he does by the desire to concentrate on his work. It is necessarily true, if this supposition is correct, that he already wants to concentrate on his work. This desire is now among his desires. But the question of whether or not his second-order desire is fulfilled does not turn merely on whether the desire he wants is one of his desires. It turns on whether this desire is, as he wants it to be, his effective desire or will. If, when the chips are down, it is his desire to concentrate on his work that moves him to do what he does, then what he wants at that time is indeed (in the relevant sense) what he wants to want. If it is some other desire that actually moves him when he acts, on the other hand, then what he wants at that time is not (in the relevant sense) what he wants to want. This will be so despite the fact that the desire to concentrate on his work continues to be among his desires.

## II

Someone has a desire of the second order either when he wants simply to have a certain desire or when he wants a certain desire to be his will. In situations of the latter kind, I shall call his second-order desires "second-order volitions" or "volitions of the second order." Now it is having second-order volitions, and not having second-order

4. It is not so clear that the entailment relation described here holds in certain kinds of cases, which I think may fairly be regarded as nonstandard, where the essential difference between the standard and the nonstandard cases lies in the kind of description by which the first-order desire in question is identified. Thus, suppose that A admires B so fulsomely that, even though he does not know what B wants to do, he wants to be effectively moved by whatever desire effectively moves B; without knowing what B's will is, in other words, A wants his own will to be the same. It certainly does not follow that A already has, among his desires, a desire like the one that constitutes B's will. I shall not pursue here the questions of whether there are genuine counterexamples to the claim made in the text or of how, if there are, that claim should be altered.

desires generally, that I regard as essential to being a person. It is logically possible, however unlikely, that there should be an agent with second-order desires but with no volitions of the second order. Such a creature, in my view, would not be a person. I shall use the term 'wanton' to refer to agents who have first-order desires but who are not persons because, whether or not they have desires of the second order, they have no second-order volitions.[5]

The essential characteristic of a wanton is that he does not care about his will. His desires move him to do certain things, without its being true of him either that he wants to be moved by those desires or that he prefers to be moved by other desires. The class of wantons includes all nonhuman animals that have desires and all very young children. Perhaps it also includes some adult human beings as well. In any case, adult humans may be more or less wanton; they may act wantonly, in response to first-order desires concerning which they have no volitions of the second order, more or less frequently.

The fact that a wanton has no second-order volitions does not mean that each of his first-order desires is translated heedlessly and at once into action. He may have no opportunity to act in accordance with some of his desires. Moreover, the translation of his desires into action may be delayed or precluded either by conflicting desires of the first order or by the intervention of deliberation. For a wanton may possess and employ rational faculties of a high order. Nothing in the concept of a wanton implies that he cannot reason or that he cannot deliberate concerning how to do what he wants to do. What distinguishes the rational wanton from other rational agents is that he is not concerned with the desirability of his desires themselves. He ignores the question of what his will is to be. Not only does he pursue whatever course of action he is most strongly inclined to pursue, but he does not care which of his inclinations is the strongest.

Thus a rational creature, who reflects upon the suitability to his desires of one course of action or another, may nonetheless be a wanton. In maintaining that the essence of being a person lies not in reason but in will, I am far from suggesting that a creature without reason may be a person. For it is only in virtue of his rational capaci-

5. Creatures with second-order desires but no second-order volitions differ significantly from brute animals, and, for some purposes, it would be desirable to regard them as persons. My usage, which withholds the designation 'person' from them, is thus somewhat arbitrary. I adopt it largely because it facilitates the formulation of some of the points I wish to make. Hereafter, whenever I consider statements of the form "A wants to want to X," I shall have in mind statements identifying second-order volitions and not statements identifying second-order desires that are not second-order volitions.

ties that a person is capable of becoming critically aware of his own will and of forming volitions of the second order. The structure of a person's will presupposes, accordingly, that he is a rational being.

The distinction between a person and a wanton may be illustrated by the difference between two narcotics addicts. Let us suppose that the physiological condition accounting for the addiction is the same in both men, and that both succumb inevitably to their periodic desires for the drug to which they are addicted. One of the addicts hates his addiction and always struggles desperately, although to no avail, against its thrust. He tries everything that he thinks might enable him to overcome his desires for the drug. But these desires are too powerful for him to withstand, and invariably, in the end, they conquer him. He is an unwilling addict, helplessly violated by his own desires.

The unwilling addict has conflicting first-order desires: he wants to take the drug, and he also wants to refrain from taking it. In addition to these first-order desires, however, he has a volition of the second order. He is not a neutral with regard to the conflict between his desire to take the drug and his desire to refrain from taking it. It is the latter desire, and not the former, that he wants to constitute his will; it is the latter desire, rather than the former, that he wants to be effective and to provide the purpose that he will seek to realize in what he actually does.

The other addict is a wanton. His actions reflect the economy of his first-order desires, without his being concerned whether the desires that move him to act are desires by which he wants to be moved to act. If he encounters problems in obtaining the drug or in administering it to himself, his responses to his urges to take it may involve deliberation. But it never occurs to him to consider whether he wants the relations among his desires to result in his having the will he has. The wanton addict may be an animal, and thus incapable of being concerned about his will. In any event he is, in respect of his wanton lack of concern, no different from an animal.

The second of these addicts may suffer a first-order conflict similar to the first-order conflict suffered by the first. Whether he is human or not, the wanton may (perhaps due to conditioning) both want to take the drug and want to refrain from taking it. Unlike the unwilling addict, however, he does not prefer that one of his conflicting desires should be paramount over the other; he does not prefer that one first-order desire rather than the other should constitute his will. It would be misleading to say that he is neutral as to the conflict between his desires, since this would suggest that he regards them as equally acceptable. Since he has no identity apart from his first-order desires, it is true neither that he prefers one to the other nor that he prefers not to take sides.

It makes a difference to the unwilling addict, who is a person, which of his conflicting first-order desires wins out. Both desires are his, to be sure; and whether he finally takes the drug or finally succeeds in refraining from taking it, he acts to satisfy what is in a literal sense his own desire. In either case he does something he himself wants to do, and he does it not because of some external influence whose aim happens to coincide with his own but because of his desire to do it. The unwilling addict identifies himself, however, through the formation of a second-order volition, with one rather than with the other of his conflicting first-order desires. He makes one of them more truly his own and, in so doing, he withdraws himself from the other. It is in virtue of this identification and withdrawal, accomplished through the formation of a second-order volition, that the unwilling addict may meaningfully make the analytically puzzling statements that the force moving him to take the drug is a force other than his own, and that it is not of his own free will but rather against his will that this force moves him to take it.

The wanton addict cannot or does not care which of his conflicting first-order desires wins out. His lack of concern is not due to his inability to find a convincing basis for preference. It is due either to his lack of the capacity for reflection or to his mindless indifference to the enterprise of evaluating his own desires and motives.[6] There is only one issue in the struggle to which his first-order conflict may lead: whether the one or the other of his conflicting desires is the stronger. Since he is moved by both desires, he will not be altogether satisfied by what he does no matter which of them is effective. But it makes no difference *to him* whether his craving or his aversion gets the upper hand. He has no stake in the conflict between them and so, unlike the unwilling addict, he can neither win nor lose the struggle in which he is engaged. When a *person* acts, the desire by which he is moved is either the will he wants or a will he wants to be without. When a *wanton* acts, it is neither.

---

6. In speaking of the evaluation of his own desires and motives as being characteristic of a person, I do not mean to suggest that a person's second-order volitions necessarily manifest a *moral* stance on his part toward his first-order desires. It may not be from the point of view of morality that the person evaluates his first-order desires. Moreover, a person may be capricious and irresponsible in forming his second-order volitions and give no serious consideration to what is at stake. Second-order volitions express evaluations only in the sense that they are preferences. There is no essential restriction on the kind of basis, if any, upon which they are formed.

III

There is a very close relationship between the capacity for forming second-order volitions and another capacity that is essential to persons—one that has often been considered a distinguishing mark of the human condition. It is only because a person has volitions of the second order that he is capable both of enjoying and of lacking freedom of the will. The concept of a person is not only, then, the concept of a type of entity that has both first-order desires and volitions of the second order. It can also be construed as the concept of a type of entity for whom the freedom of its will may be a problem. This concept excludes all wantons, both infrahuman and human, since they fail to satisfy an essential condition for the enjoyment of freedom of the will. And it excludes those suprahuman beings, if any, whose wills are necessarily free.

Just what kind of freedom is the freedom of the will? This question calls for an identification of the special area of human experience to which the concept of freedom of the will, as distinct from the concepts of other sorts of freedom, is particularly germane. In dealing with it, my aim will be primarily to locate the problem with which a person is most immediately concerned when he is concerned with the freedom of his will.

According to one familiar philosophical tradition, being free is fundamentally a matter of doing what one wants to do. Now the notion of an agent who does what he wants to do is by no means an altogether clear one: both the doing and the wanting, and the appropriate relation between them as well, require elucidation. But although its focus needs to be sharpened and its formulation refined, I believe that this notion does capture at least part of what is implicit in the idea of an agent who *acts* freely. It misses entirely, however, the peculiar content of the quite different idea of an agent whose *will* is free.

We do not suppose that animals enjoy freedom of the will, although we recognize that an animal may be free to run in whatever direction it wants. Thus, having the freedom to do what one wants to do is not a sufficient condition of having a free will. It is not a necessary condition either. For to deprive someone of his freedom of action is not necessarily to undermine the freedom of his will. When an agent is aware that there are certain things he is not free to do, this doubtless affects his desires and limits the range of choices he can make. But suppose that someone, without being aware of it, has in fact lost or been deprived of his freedom of action. Even though he is no longer free to do what he wants to do, his will may remain as free as it was before. Despite the fact that he is not free to translate his desires into actions or to act according to the determinations of his will, he may still form those desires and make those determinations as freely as if his freedom of action had not been impaired.

When we ask whether a person's will is free we are not asking whether he is in a position to translate his first-order desires into actions. That is the question of whether he is free to do as he pleases. The question of the freedom of his will does not concern the relation between what he does and what he wants to do. Rather, it concerns his desires themselves. But what question about them is it?

It seems to me both natural and useful to construe the question of whether a person's will is free in close analogy to the question of whether an agent enjoys freedom of action. Now freedom of action is (roughly, at least) the freedom to do what one wants to do. Analogously, then, the statement that a person enjoys freedom of the will means (also roughly) that he is free to want what he wants to want. More precisely, it means that he is free to will what he wants to will, or to have the will he wants. Just as the question about the freedom of an agent's action has to do with whether it is the action he wants to perform, so the question about the freedom of his will has to do with whether it is the will he wants to have.

It is in securing the conformity of his will to his second-order volitions, then, that a person exercises freedom of the will. And it is in the discrepancy between his will and his second-order volitions, or in his awareness that their coincidence is not his own doing but only a happy chance, that a person who does not have this freedom feels its lack. The unwilling addict's will is not free. This is shown by the fact that it is not the will he wants. It is also true, though in a different way, that the will of the wanton addict is not free. The wanton addict neither has the will he wants nor has a will that differs from the will he wants. Since he has no volitions of the second order, the freedom of his will cannot be a problem for him. He lacks it, so to speak, by default.

People are generally far more complicated than my sketchy account of the structure of a person's will may suggest. There is as much opportunity for ambivalence, conflict, and self-deception with regard to desires of the second order, for example, as there is with regard to first-order desires. If there is an unresolved conflict among someone's second-order desires, then he is in danger of having no second-order volition; for unless this conflict is resolved, he has no preference concerning which of his first-order desires is to be his will. This condition, if it is so severe that it prevents him from identifying himself in a sufficiently decisive way with *any* of his conflicting first-order desires, destroys him as a person. For it either tends to paralyze his will and to keep him from acting at all, or it tends to remove him from his will so that his will operates without his participation. In both cases he becomes, like the unwilling addict though in a different way, a helpless bystander to the forces that move him.

Another complexity is that a person may have, especially if his second-order desires are in conflict, desires and volitions of a higher order than the second. There is no theoretical limit to the length of the series of desires of higher and higher orders; nothing except common sense and, perhaps, a saving fatigue prevents an individual from obsessively refusing to identify himself with any of his desires until he forms a desire of the next higher order. The tendency to generate such a series of acts of forming desires, which would be a case of humanization run wild, also leads toward the destruction of a person.

It is possible, however, to terminate such a series of acts without cutting it off arbitrarily. When a person identifies himself *decisively* with one of his first-order desires, this commitment "resounds" throughout the potentially endless array of higher orders. Consider a person who, without reservation or conflict, wants to be motivated by the desire to concentrate on his work. The fact that his second-order volition to be moved by this desire is a decisive one means that there is no room for questions concerning the pertinence of desires or volitions of higher orders. Suppose the person is asked whether he wants to want to want to concentrate on his work. He can properly insist that this question concerning a third-order desire does not arise. It would be a mistake to claim that, because he has not considered whether he wants the second-order volition he has formed, he is indifferent to the question of whether it is with this volition or with some other that he wants his will to accord. The decisiveness of the commitment he has made means that he has decided that no further question about his second-order volition, at any higher order, remains to be asked. It is relatively unimportant whether we explain this by saying that this commitment implicitly generates an endless series of confirming desires of higher orders, or by saying that the commitment is tantamount to a dissolution of the pointedness of all questions concerning higher orders of desire.

Examples such as the one concerning the unwilling addict may suggest that volitions of the second order, or of higher orders, must be formed deliberately and that a person characteristically struggles to ensure that they are satisfied. But the conformity of a person's will to his higher-order volitions may be far more thoughtless and spontaneous than this. Some people are naturally moved by kindness when they want to be kind, and by nastiness when they want to be nasty, without any explicit forethought and without any need for energetic self-control. Others are moved by nastiness when they want to be kind and by kindness when they intend to be nasty, equally without forethought and without active resistance to these violations of their higher-order desires. The enjoyment of freedom comes easily to some. Others must struggle to achieve it.

## IV

My theory concerning the freedom of the will accounts easily for our disinclination to allow that this freedom is enjoyed by the members of any species inferior to our own. It also satisfies another condition that must be met by any such theory, by making it apparent why the freedom of the will should be regarded as desirable. The enjoyment of a free will means the satisfaction of certain desires—desires of the second or of higher orders—whereas its absence means their frustration. The satisfactions at stake are those which accrue to a person of whom it may be said that his will is his own. The corresponding frustrations are those suffered by a person of whom it may be said that he is estranged from himself, or that he finds himself a helpless or a passive bystander to the forces that move him.

A person who is free to do what he wants to do may yet not be in a position to have the will he wants. Suppose, however, that he enjoys both freedom of action and freedom of the will. Then he is not only free to do what he wants to do; he is also free to want what he wants to want. It seems to me that he has, in that case, all the freedom it is possible to desire or to conceive. There are other good things in life, and he may not possess some of them. But there is nothing in the way of freedom that he lacks.

It is far from clear that certain other theories of the freedom of the will meet these elementary but essential conditions: that it be understandable why we desire this freedom and why we refuse to ascribe it to animals. Consider, for example, Roderick Chisholm's quaint version of the doctrine that human freedom entails an absence of causal determination.[7] Whenever a person performs a free action, according to Chisholm, it's a miracle. The motion of a person's hand, when the person moves it, is the outcome of a series of physical causes; but

7. "Freedom and Action," in K. Lehrer, ed., *Freedom and Determinism* (New York: Random House, 1966), pp. 11–44.

some event in this series, "and presumably one of those that took place within the brain, was caused by the agent and not by any other events" (18). A free agent has, therefore, "a prerogative which some would attribute only to God: each of us, when we act, is a prime mover unmoved" (23).

This account fails to provide any basis for doubting that animals of subhuman species enjoy the freedom it defines. Chisholm says nothing that makes it seem less likely that a rabbit performs a miracle when it moves its leg than that a man does so when he moves his hand. But why, in any case, should anyone *care* whether he can interrupt the natural order of causes in the way Chisholm describes? Chisholm offers no reason for believing that there is a discernible difference between the experience of a man who miraculously initiates a series of causes when he moves his hand and a man who moves his hand without any such breach of the normal causal sequence. There appears to be no concrete basis for preferring to be involved in the one state of affairs rather than in the other.[8]

It is generally supposed that, in addition to satisfying the two conditions I have mentioned, a satisfactory theory of the freedom of the will necessarily provides an analysis of one of the conditions of moral responsibility. The most common recent approach to the problem of understanding the freedom of the will has been, indeed, to inquire what is entailed by the assumption that someone is morally responsible for what he has done. In my view, however, the relation between moral responsibility and the freedom of the will has been very widely misunderstood. It is not true that a person is morally responsible for what he has done only if his will was free when he did it. He may be morally responsible for having done it even though his will was not free at all.

A person's will is free only if he is free to have the will he wants. This means that, with regard to any of his first-order desires, he is free either to make that desire his will or to make some other first-order desire his will instead. Whatever his will, then, the will of the person whose will is free could have been otherwise; he could have done otherwise than to constitute his will as he did. It is a vexed question just how 'he could have done otherwise' is to be understood in contexts such as this one. But although this question is important to the theory of freedom, it has no bearing on the theory of moral

8. I am not suggesting that the alleged difference between these two states of affairs is unverifiable. On the contrary, physiologists might well be able to show that Chisholm's conditions for a free action are not satisfied, by establishing that there is no relevant brain event for which a sufficient physical cause cannot be found.

responsibility. For the assumption that a person is morally responsible for what he has done does not entail that the person was in a position to have whatever will he wanted.

This assumption *does* entail that the person did what he did freely, or that he did it of his own free will. It is a mistake, however, to believe that someone acts freely only when he is free to do whatever he wants or that he acts of his own free will only if his will is free. Suppose that a person has done what he wanted to do, that he did it because he wanted to do it, and that the will by which he was moved when he did it was his will because it was the will he wanted. Then he did it freely and of his own free will. Even supposing that he could have done otherwise, he would not have done otherwise; and even supposing that he could have had a different will, he would not have wanted his will to differ from what it was. Moreover, since the will that moved him when he acted was his will because he wanted it to be, he cannot claim that his will was forced upon him or that he was a passive bystander to its constitution. Under these conditions, it is quite irrelevant to the evaluation of his moral responsibility to inquire whether the alternatives that he opted against were actually available to him.[9]

In illustration, consider a third kind of addict. Suppose that his addiction has the same physiological basis and the same irresistible thrust as the addictions of the unwilling and wanton addicts, but that he is altogether delighted with his condition. He is a willing addict, who would not have things any other way. If the grip of his addiction should somehow weaken, he would do whatever he could to reinstate it; if his desire for the drug should begin to fade, he would take steps to renew its intensity.

The willing addict's will is not free, for his desire to take the drug will be effective regardless of whether or not he wants this desire to constitute his will. But when he takes the drug, he takes it freely and of his own free will. I am inclined to understand his situation as involving the overdetermination of his first-order desire to take the drug. This desire is his effective desire because he is physiologically addicted. But it is his effective desire also because he wants it to be. His will is outside his control, but, by his second-order desire that his desire for the drug should be effective, he has made this will his own. Given that it is therefore not only because of his addiction that his desire for the drug is effective, he may be morally responsible for taking the drug.

9. For another discussion of the considerations that cast doubt on the principle that a person is morally responsible for what he has done only if he could have done otherwise, see Chapter 6, pp. 143–152.

My conception of the freedom of the will appears to be neutral with regard to the problem of determinism. It seems conceivable that it should be causally determined that a person is free to want what he wants to want. If this is conceivable, then it might be causally determined that a person enjoys a free will. There is no more than an innocuous appearance of paradox in the proposition that it is determined, ineluctably and by forces beyond their control, that certain people have free wills and that others do not. There is no incoherence in the proposition that some agency other than a person's own is responsible (even *morally* responsible) for the fact that he enjoys or fails to enjoy freedom of the will. It is possible that a person should be morally responsible for what he does of his own free will and that some other person should also be morally responsible for his having done it.[10]

On the other hand, it seems conceivable that it should come about by chance that a person is free to have the will he wants. If this is conceivable, then it might be a matter of chance that certain people enjoy freedom of the will and that certain others do not. Perhaps it is also conceivable, as a number of philosophers believe, for states of affairs to come about in a way other than by chance or as the outcome of a sequence of natural causes. If it is indeed conceivable for the relevant states of affairs to come about in some third way, then it is also possible that a person should in that third way come to enjoy the freedom of the will.

10. There is a difference between being *fully* responsible and being *solely* responsible. Suppose that the willing addict has been made an addict by the deliberate and calculated work of another. Then it may be that both the addict and this other person are fully responsible for the addict's taking the drug, while neither of them is solely responsible for it. That there is a distinction between full moral responsibility and sole moral responsibility is apparent in the following example. A certain light can be turned on or off by flicking either of two switches, and each of these switches is simultaneously flicked to the "on" position by a different person, neither of whom is aware of the other. Neither person is solely responsible for the light's going on, nor do they share the responsibility in the sense that each is partially responsible; rather, each of them is fully responsible.

# 2

## Free Agency

---

### GARY WATSON

In this essay I discuss a distinction that is crucial to a correct account of free action and to an adequate conception of human motivation and responsibility.

## I

According to one familiar conception of freedom, a person is free to the extent that he is able to do or get what he wants. To circumscribe a person's freedom is to contract the range of things he is able to do. I think that, suitably qualified, this account is correct, and that the chief and most interesting uses of the word 'free' can be explicated in its terms. But this general line has been resisted on a number of different grounds. One of the most important objections—and the one upon which I shall concentrate in this paper—is that this familiar view is too impoverished to handle talk of free actions and free will.

Frequently enough, we say, or are inclined to say, that a person is not in control of his own actions, that he is not a "free agent" with respect to them, even though his behavior is intentional. Possible examples of this sort of action include those which are explained by addictions, manias, and phobias of various sorts. But the concept of free action would seem to be pleonastic on the analysis of freedom in

"Free Agency" originally appeared in the *Journal of Philosophy*, 72 (April 1975), 205–20, © 1975 by the *Journal of Philosophy*, and is reprinted here with permission from Gary Watson and from the *Journal of Philosophy*.

I have profited from discussions with numerous friends, students, colleagues, and other audiences, on the material of this essay; I would like to thank them collectively. However, special thanks are due to Joel Feinberg, Harry Frankfurt, and Thomas Nagel.

terms of the ability to get what one wants. For if a person does something intentionally, then surely he was able at that time to do it. Hence, on this analysis, he was free to do it. The familiar account would not seem to allow for any further questions, as far as freedom is concerned, about the action. Accordingly, this account would seem to embody a conflation of free action and intentional action.

Philosophers who have defended some form of compatibilism have usually given this analysis of freedom, with the aim of showing that freedom and responsibility are not really incompatible with determinism. Some critics have rejected compatibilism precisely because of its association with this familiar account of freedom. For instance, Isaiah Berlin asks: if determinism is true,

> . . . what reasons can you, in principle, adduce for attributing responsibility or applying moral rules to [people] which you would not think it reasonable to apply in the case of compulsive choosers—kleptomaniacs, dipsomaniacs, and the like?[1]

The idea is that the sense in which actions would be free in a deterministic world allows the actions of "compulsive choosers" to be free. To avoid this consequence, it is often suggested, we must adopt some sort of "contracausal" view of freedom.

Now, though compatibilists from Hobbes to J. J. C. Smart have given the relevant moral and psychological concepts an exceedingly crude treatment, this crudity is not inherent in compatibilism, nor does it result from the adoption of the conception of freedom in terms of the ability to get what one wants. For the difference between free and unfree actions—as we normally discern it—has nothing at all to do with the truth or falsity of determinism.

In the subsequent pages, I want to develop a distinction between wanting and valuing which will enable the familiar view of freedom to make sense of the notion of an unfree action. The contention will be that, in the case of actions that are unfree, the agent is unable to get what he most wants, *or values,* and this inability is due to his own "motivational system." In this case the obstruction to the action that he most wants to do is his own will. It is in this respect that the action is unfree: the agent is obstructed in and by the very performance of the action.

I do not conceive my remarks to be a defense of compatibilism. This point of view may be unacceptable for various reasons, some of

1. *Four Essays on Liberty* (New York: Oxford, 1969), pp. xx–xxi.

which call into question the coherence of the concept of responsibility. But these reasons do not include the fact that compatibilism relies upon the conception of freedom in terms of the ability to get what one wants, nor must it conflate free action and intentional action. If compatibilism is to be shown to be wrong, its critics must go deeper.

## II

What must be true of people if there is to be a significant notion of free action? Our talk of free action arises from the apparent fact that what a person most wants may not be what he is finally moved to get. It follows from this apparent fact that the extent to which one wants something is not determined solely by the *strength* of one's desires (or "motives") as measured by their effectiveness in action. One (perhaps trivial) measure of the strength of the desire or want is that the agent acts upon that desire or want (trivial, since it will be nonexplanatory to say that an agent acted upon that desire because it was the strongest). But, if what one most wants may not be what one most strongly wants, by this measure, then in what sense can it be true that one most wants it?[2]

To answer this question, one might begin by contrasting, at least in a crude way, a humean with a platonic conception of practical reasoning. The ancients distinguished between the rational and the irrational parts of the soul, between Reason and Appetite. Hume employed a superficially similar distinction. It is important to understand, however, that (for Plato at least) the rational part of the soul is not to be identified with what Hume called "Reason" and contradistinguished from the "Passions." On Hume's account, Reason is not a source of motivation, but a faculty of determining what is true and what is false, a faculty concerned solely with "matters of fact" and "relations among ideas." It is completely dumb on the question of what to do. Perhaps Hume could allow Reason this much practical voice: given an initial set of wants and beliefs about what is or is likely to be the case, particular desires are generated in the process. In other words, a humean might allow Reason a crucial role in deliberation. But its essential role would not be to supply motivation—Reason is not that kind of thing—but rather to calculate, within a context of

2. I am going to use 'want' and 'desire' in the very inclusive sense now familiar in philosophy, whereby virtually any motivational factor that may figure in the explanation of intentional action is a want; 'desire' will be used mainly in connection with the appetites and passions.

desires and ends, how to fulfill those desires and serve those ends. For Plato, however, the rational part of the soul is not some kind of inference mechanism. It is itself a source of motivation. In general form, the desires of Reason are desires for "the Good."

Perhaps the contrast can be illustrated by some elementary notions from decision theory. On the Bayesian model of deliberation, a preference scale is imposed upon various states of affairs contingent upon courses of action open to the agent. Each state of affairs can be assigned a numerical value (initial value) according to its place on the scale; given this assignment, and the probabilities that those states of affairs will obtain if the actions are performed, a final numerical value (expected desirability) can be assigned to the actions themselves. The rational agent performs the action with the highest expected desirability.

In these terms, on the humean picture, Reason is the faculty that computes probabilities and expected desirabilities. Reason is in this sense neutral with respect to actions, for it can operate equally on any given assignment of initial values and probabilities—it has nothing whatsoever to say about the assignment of initial values. On the platonic picture, however, the rational part of the soul itself determines what has *value* and how much, and thus is responsible for the original ranking of alternative states of affairs.

It may appear that the difference between these conceptions is merely a difference as to what is to be called "Reason" or "rational," and hence is not a substantive difference. In speaking of Reason, Hume has in mind a sharp contrast between what is wanted and what is thought to be the case. What contrast is implicit in the platonic view that the ranking of alternative states of affairs is the task of the rational part of the soul?

The contrast here is not trivial; the difference in classificatory schemes reflects different views of human psychology. For one thing, in saying this (or what is tantamount to this) Plato was calling attention to the fact that it is one thing to think a state of affairs good, worth while, or worthy of promotion, and another simply to desire or want that state of affairs to obtain. Since the notion of value is tied to (cannot be understood independently of) those of the good and worthy, it is one thing to value (think good) a state of affairs and another to desire that it obtain. However, to think a thing good is at the same time to desire it (or its promotion). Reason is thus an original spring of action. It is because valuing is essentially related to thinking or *judging* good that it is appropriate to speak of the wants that are (or perhaps arise from) evaluations as belonging to, or originating in, the rational (that is, *judging*) part of the soul; values provide *reasons* for action. The contrast is with desires, whose objects may not be thought good and which are thus, in a natural sense, blind or irrational. Desires are mute on the question of what is good.[3]

Now it seems to me that—given the view of freedom as the ability to get what one wants—there can be a problem of free action only if the platonic conception of the soul is (roughly) correct. The doctrine I shall defend is platonic in the sense that it involves a distinction between valuing and desiring which depends upon these being independent sources of motivation. No doubt Plato meant considerably more than this by his parts-of-the-soul doctrine; but he meant at least this. The platonic conception provides an answer to the question I posed earlier (207): in what sense can what one most wants differ from that which is the object of the strongest desire? The answer is that the phrase 'what one most wants' may mean either "the object of the strongest desire" or "what one most *values*." This phrase can be interpreted in terms of strength or in terms of ranking order or preference. The problem of free action arises because what one desires may not be what one values, and what one most values may not be what one is finally moved to get.[4]

The tacit identification of desiring or wanting with valuing is so common[5] that it is necessary to cite some examples of this distinction

3. To quote just one of many suggestive passages: "We must . . . observe that within each one of us there are two sorts of ruling or guiding principle that we follow. One is an innate desire for pleasure, the other an acquired judgment that aims at what is best. Sometimes these internal guides are in accord, sometimes at variance; now one gains the mastery, now the other. And when judgment guides us rationally toward what is best, and has the mastery, that mastery is called temperance, but when desire drags us irrationally toward pleasure, and has come to rule within us, the name given to that rule is wantonness" (*Phaedrus,* 237e–238e; Hackforth trans.). For a fascinating discussion of Plato's parts-of-the-soul doctrine, see Terry Penner's "Thought and Desire in Plato," in Gregory Vlastos, ed., *Plato: A Collection of Critical Essays,* vol. II (New York: Anchor, 1971). As I see it (and here I have been influenced by Penner's article), the distinction I have attributed to Plato was meant by him to be a solution to the socratic problem of *akrasia.* I would argue that this distinction, though necessary, is insufficient for the task, because it does not mark the difference between ("mere") incontinence or weakness of will and psychological compulsion. This difference requires a careful examination of the various things that might be meant in speaking of the strength of a desire.

4. Here I shall not press the rational/nonrational contrast any further than this, though Plato would have wished to press it further. However, one important and anti-Humean implication of the minimal distinction is this: it is not the case that, if a person desires to do *X,* he therefore has (or even regards himself as having) a reason to do *X.*

5. For example, I take my remarks to be incompatible with the characterization of value R. B. Perry gives in *General Theory of Value* (Cambridge, Mass.: Harvard, 1950). In ch. v, Perry writes: "This, then, we take to be the original source and constant feature of all value. That which is an object of interest is *eo ipso* invested with value." And 'interest' is characterized in the following way: ". . . liking and disliking, desire and aversion, will and refusal, or seeking and avoiding. It is to this all-pervasive characteristic of the motor-affective life, this *state, act, attitude* or *disposition of favor* or disfavor, to which we propose to give the name of 'interest'."

in order to illustrate how evaluation and desire may diverge. There seem to be two ways in which, in principle, a discrepancy may arise. First, it is possible that what one desires is not *to any degree* valued, held to be worth while, or thought good; one assigns *no* value whatever to the object of one's desire. Second, although one may indeed value what is desired, the strength of one's desire may not properly reflect the degree to which one values its object; that is, although the object of a desire is valuable, it may not be deemed the most valuable in the situation and yet one's desire for it may be stronger than the want for what is most valued.

The cases in which one in no way values what one desires are perhaps rare, but surely they exist. Consider the case of a woman who has a sudden urge to drown her bawling child in the bath; or the case of a squash player who, while suffering an ignominious defeat, desires to smash his opponent in the face with the racquet. It is just false that the mother values her child's being drowned or that the player values the injury and suffering of his opponent. But they desire these things nonetheless. They desire them in spite of themselves. It is not that they assign to these actions an initial value which is then outweighed by other considerations. These activities are not even represented by a positive entry, however small, on the initial "desirability matrix."

It may seem from these examples that this first and radical sort of divergence between desiring and valuing occurs only in the case of momentary and inexplicable urges or impulses. Yet I see no conclusive reason why a person could not be similarly estranged from a rather persistent and pervasive desire, and one that is explicable enough. Imagine a man who thinks his sexual inclinations are the work of the devil, that the very fact that he has sexual inclinations bespeaks his corrupt nature. This example is to be contrasted with that of the celibate who decides that the most fulfilling life for him will be one of abstinence. In this latter case, *one* of the things that receive consideration in the process of reaching his all-things-considered judgment is the value of sexual activity. There is something, from his point of view, to be said for sex, but there is more to be said in favor of celibacy. In contrast, the man who is estranged from his sexual inclinations does not acknowledge even a prima facie reason for sexual activity; that he is sexually inclined toward certain activities is not even *a* consideration. Another way of illustrating the difference is to say that, for the one man, forgoing sexual relationships constitutes a *loss*, even if negligible compared with the gains of celibacy; whereas from the standpoint of the other person, no loss is sustained at all.

Now, it must be admitted, any desire may provide the basis for a reason insofar as nonsatisfaction of the desire causes suffering and hinders the pursuit of ends of the agent. But it is important to notice that the reason generated in this way by a desire is a reason for *getting rid* of the desire, and one may get rid of a desire either by satisfying it or by eliminating it in some other manner (by tranquilizers, or cold showers). Hence this kind of reason differs importantly from the reasons based upon the evaluation of the activities or states of affairs in question. For, in the former case, attaining the object of desire is simply a means of eliminating discomfort or agitation, whereas in the latter case that attainment is the end itself. Normally, in the pursuit of the objects of our wants we are not attempting chiefly to relieve ourselves. We aim to satisfy, not just eliminate, desire.

Nevertheless, aside from transitory impulses, it may be that cases wherein nothing at all can be said in favor of the object of one's desire are rare. For it would seem that even the person who conceives his sexual desires to be essentially evil would have to admit that indulgence would be pleasurable, and surely that is something. (Perhaps not even this should be admitted. For indulgence may not yield pleasure at all in a context of anxiety. Furthermore, it is not obvious that pleasure is intrinsically good, independently of the worth of the pleasurable object.) In any case, the second sort of divergence between evaluation and desire remains: it is possible that, in a particular context, what one wants most strongly is not what one most values.

The distinction between valuing and desiring is not, it is crucial to see, a distinction among desires or wants according to their content. That is to say, there is nothing in the specification of the objects of an agent's desires that singles out some wants as based upon that agent's values. The distinction in question has rather to do with the *source* of the want or with its role in the total "system" of the agent's desires and ends. It has to do with why the agent wants what he does.

Obviously, to identify a desire or want simply in terms of its content is not to identify its source(s). It does not follow from my wanting to eat that I am hungry. I may want to eat because I want to be well-nourished; or because I am hungry; or because eating is a pleasant activity. This single desire may have three independent sources. (These sources may not be altogether independent. It may be that eating is pleasurable only because I have appetites for food.) Some specifications of wants or desires—for instance, as cravings—pick out (at least roughly) the source of the motivation.

It is an essential feature of the appetites and the passions that they engender (or consist in) desires whose existence and persistence are independent of the person's judgment of the good. The appetite of hunger involves a desire to eat which has a source in physical needs and physiological states of the hungry organism. And emotions such as anger and fear partly consist in spontaneous inclinations to do various things—to attack or to flee the object of one's emotion, for example. It is intrinsic to the appetites and passions that appetitive and passionate beings can be motivated in spite of themselves. It is because desires such as these arise independently of the person's judgment and values that the ancients located the emotions and passions in the irrational part of the soul;[6] and it is because of this sort of independence that a conflict between valuing and desiring is possible.[7]

These points may suggest an inordinately dualistic view according to which persons are split into inevitably alien, if not always antagonistic, halves. But this view does not follow from what has been said. As central as it is to human life, it is not often noted that some activities are valued only to the extent that they are objects of the appetites. This means that such activities would never be regarded as valuable constituents of one's life were it not for one's susceptibility to "blind" motivation—motivation independent of one's values. Sexual activity and eating are again examples. We may value the activity of eating to the degree that it provides nourishment. But we may also value it because it is an enjoyable activity, even though its having this status depends upon our appetites for food, our hunger. In the case of sex, in fact, if we were not erotic creatures, certain activities would not only lose their value to us, they might not even be physiologically possible.

These examples indicate, not that there is no distinction between desiring and valuing, but that the value placed upon certain activities depends upon their being the fulfillment of desires that arise and persist independently of what we value. So it is not that, when we value the activity of eating, we think there are reasons to eat no matter what other desires we have; rather, we value eating when food appeals to us; and, likewise, we value sexual relationships when we are aroused. Here an essential part of the *content* of our evaluation is that the activity in question be motivated by certain appetites. These ac-

6. Notice that most emotions differ from passions like lust in that they involve beliefs and some sort of valuation (cf. resentment). This may be the basis for Plato's positing a third part of the soul which is in a way partly rational—viz. *Thumos.*

7. To be sure, one may attempt to cultivate or eliminate certain appetites and passions, so that the desires that result may be in this way dependent upon one's evaluations. Even so, the resulting desires will be such that they can persist independently of one's values. It is rather like jumping from an airplane.

tivities may have value for us only insofar as they are appetitively motivated, even though to have these appetites is not *ipso facto* to value their objects.

Part of what it means to value some activities in this way is this: we judge that to cease to have such appetites is to lose something of worth. The judgment here is not merely that, if someone has these appetites, it is worth while (*ceteris paribus*) for him to indulge them. The judgment is rather that it is of value to have and (having them) to indulge these appetites. The former judgment does not account for the eunuch's loss or sorrow, whereas the latter does. And the latter judgment lies at the bottom of the discomfort one may feel when one envisages a situation in which, say, hunger is consistently eliminated and nourishment provided by insipid capsules.

It would be impossible for a non-erotic being or a person who lacked the appetite for food and drink fully to understand the value most of us attach to sex and to dining. Sexual activity must strike the non-erotic being as perfectly grotesque. (Perhaps that is why lust is sometimes said to be disgusting and sinful in the eyes of God.) Or consider an appetite that is in fact "unnatural" (i.e., acquired): the craving for tobacco. To a person who has never known the entice-ment of Lady Nicotine, what could be more incomprehensible than the filthy practice of consummating a fine meal by drawing into one's lungs the noxious fumes of a burning weed?

Thus, the relationship between evaluation and motivation is intri-cate. With respect to many of our activities, evaluation depends upon the possibility of our being moved to act independently of our judg-ment. So the distinction I have been pressing—that between desiring and valuing—does not commit one to an inevitable split between Reason and Appetite. Appetitively motivated activities may well con-stitute for a person the most worth-while aspects of his life.[8] But the distinction does commit us to the possibility of such a split. If there are sources of motivation independent of the agent's values, then it is possible that sometimes he is motivated to do things he does not deem worth doing. This possibility is the basis for the principal problem of free action: a person may be obstructed by his own will.

A related possibility that presents considerable problems for the understanding of free agency is this: some desires, when they arise, may "color" or influence what appear to be the agent's evaluations, but only temporarily. That is, when and only when he has the desire,

---

8. It is reported that H. G. Wells regarded the most important themes of his life to have been (1) the attainment of a World Society, and (2) sex.

is he inclined to think or say that what is desired or wanted is worth while or good. This possibility is to be distinguished from another, according to which one thinks it worth while to eat when one is hungry or to engage in sexual activity when one is so inclined. For one may think this even on the occasions when the appetites are silent. The possibility I have in mind is rather that what one is disposed to say or judge is temporarily affected by the presence of the desire in such a way that, both before and after the "onslaught" of the desire, one judges that the desire's object is worth pursuing (in the circumstances) whether or not one has the desire. In this case one is likely, in a cool moment, to think it a matter for regret that one had been so influenced and to think that one should guard against desires that have this property. In other cases it may not be the desire itself that affects one's judgment, but the set of conditions in which those desires arise—e.g., the conditions induced by drugs or alcohol. (It is noteworthy that we say: "under the influence of alcohol.") Perhaps judgments made in such circumstances are often in some sense self-deceptive. In any event, this phenomenon raises problems about the identification of a person's values.

Despite our examples, it would be mistaken to conclude that the only desires that exhibit an independence of evaluation are appetitive or passionate desires. In Freudian terms, one may be as dissociated from the demands of the super-ego as from those of the id. One may be disinclined to move away from one's family, the thought of doing so being accompanied by compunction; and yet this disinclination may rest solely upon acculturation rather than upon a current judgment of what one is to do, reflecting perhaps an assessment of one's "duties" and interests. Or, taking another example, one may have been habituated to think that divorce is to be avoided in all cases, so that the aversion to divorce persists even though one sees no justification for maintaining one's marriage. In both of these cases, the attitude has its basis solely in acculturation and exists independently of the agent's judgment. For this reason, acculturated desires are irrational (better: nonrational) in the same sense as appetitive and passionate desires. In fact, despite the inhibitions acquired in the course of a puritan up-bringing, a person may deem the pursuit of sexual pleasure to be worth while, his judgment siding with the id rather than the super-ego. Acculturated attitudes may seem more akin to evaluation than to appetite in that they are often expressed in evaluative language ("divorce is wicked") and result in feelings of guilt when one's actions are not in conformity with them. But, since conflict is possible here, to want something as a result of acculturation is not thereby to value it, in the sense of 'to value' that we want to capture.

It is not easy to give a nontrivial account of the sense of 'to value' in question. In part, to value something is, in the appropriate circumstances, to want it, and to attribute a want for something to someone is to say that he is disposed to try to get it. So it will not be easy to draw this distinction in behavioral terms. Apparently the difference will have to do with the agent's attitude toward the various things he is disposed to try to get. We might say that an agent's values consist in those principles and ends which he—in a cool and non-self-deceptive moment—articulates as definitive of the good, fulfilling, and defensible life. That most people have articulate "conceptions of the good," coherent life-plans, *systems* of ends, and so on, is of course something of a fiction. Yet we all have more or less long-term aims and normative principles that we are willing to defend. It is such things as these that are to be identified with our values.

*The valuational system* of an agent is that set of considerations which, when combined with his factual beliefs (and probability estimates), yields judgments of the form: the thing for me to do in these circumstances, all things considered, is $a$. To ascribe free agency to a being presupposes it to be a being that makes judgments of this sort. To be this sort of being, one must assign values to alternative states of affairs, that is, rank them in terms of worth.

*The motivational system* of an agent is that set of considerations which move him to action. We identify his motivational system by identifying what motivates him. The possibility of unfree action consists in the fact that an agent's valuational system and motivational system may not completely coincide. Those systems harmonize to the extent that what determines the agent's all-things-considered judgments also determines his actions.

Now, to be sure, since to value is also to want, one's valuational and motivational systems must to a large extent overlap. If, in appropriate circumstances, one were never inclined to action by some alleged evaluation, the claim that that was indeed one's evaluation would be disconfirmed. Thus one's valuational system must have some (considerable) grip upon one's motivational system. The problem is that there are motivational factors other than valuational ones. The free agent has the capacity to translate his values into action; his actions flow from his evaluational system.

One's evaluational system may be said to constitute one's standpoint, the point of view from which one judges the world. The important feature of one's evaluational system is that one cannot coherently dissociate oneself from it *in its entirety*. For to dissociate oneself from the ends and principles that constitute one's evaluational system is to disclaim or repudiate them, and any ends and principles so disclaimed (self-deception aside) cease to be constitutive of one's valuational system. One can dissociate oneself from one set of ends and principles only from the standpoint of another such set that one does not disclaim. In short, one cannot dissociate oneself from all normative judgments without forfeiting all standpoints and therewith one's identity as an agent.

Of course, it does not follow from the fact that one must assume some standpoint that one must have only one, nor that one's standpoint is completely determinate. There may be ultimate conflicts, irresolvable tensions, and things about which one simply does not know what to do or say. Some of these possibilities point to problems about the unity of the person. Here the extreme case is pathological. I am inclined to think that when the split is severe enough, to have more than one standpoint is to have none.

This distinction between wanting and valuing requires far fuller explication than it has received so far. Perhaps the foregoing remarks have at least shown *that* the distinction exists and is important, and have hinted at its nature. This distinction is important to the adherent of the familiar view—that talk about free action and free agency can be understood in terms of the idea of being able to get what one wants—because it gives sense to the claim that in unfree actions the agents do not get what they really or most want. This distinction gives sense to the contrast between free action and intentional action. Admittedly, further argument is required to show that such unfree agents are *unable* to get what they want; but the initial step toward this end has been taken.

At this point, it will be profitable to consider briefly a doctrine that is in many respects like that which I have been developing. The contrast will, I think, clarify the claims that have been advanced in the preceding pages.

### III

In an important and provocative article,[9] Harry Frankfurt has offered a description of what he takes to be the essential feature of "the

---

9. "Freedom of the Will and the Concept of a Person," included as Chapter 1 of the present volume.

concept of a person," a feature which, he alleges, is also basic to an understanding of "freedom of the will." This feature is the possession of higher-order volitions as well as first-order desires. Frankfurt construes the notion of a person's will as "the notion of an *effective* desire—one that moves (or will or would move) a person all the way to action" (68). Someone has a second-order volition, then, when he wants "a certain desire to be his will." (Frankfurt also considers the case of a second-order desire that is not a second-order volition, where one's desire is simply to have a certain desire and not to act upon it. For example, a man may be curious to know what it is like to be addicted to drugs; he thus desires to desire heroin, but he may not desire his desire for heroin to be effective, to be his will. In fact, Frankfurt's actual example is somewhat more special, for here the man's desire is not simply to have a desire for heroin: he wants to have a desire for heroin which has a certain source, i.e., is addictive. He wants to know what it is like to *crave* heroin.) Someone is a *wanton* if he has no second-order volitions. Finally, "it is only because a person has volitions of the second order that he is capable both of enjoying and of lacking freedom of the will" (74).

Frankfurt's thesis resembles the platonic view we have been unfolding insofar as it focuses upon "the structure of a person's will" (66). I want to make a simple point about Frankfurt's paper: namely that the "structural" feature to which Frankfurt appeals is not the fundamental feature for either free agency or personhood; it is simply insufficient to the task he wants it to perform.

One job that Frankfurt wishes to do with the distinction between lower and higher orders of desire is to give an account of the sense in which some wants may be said to be more truly the agent's own than others (though in an obvious sense all are wants of the agent) the sense in which the agent "identifies" with one desire rather than another and the sense in which an agent may be unfree with respect to his own "will." This enterprise is similar to our own. But we can see that the notion of "higher-order volition" is not really the fundamental notion for these purposes, by raising the question: Can't one be a wanton, so to speak, with respect to one's second-order desires and volitions?

In a case of conflict, Frankfurt would have us believe that what it is to identify with some desire rather than another is to have a volition concerning the former which is of higher order than any concerning the latter. That the first desire is given a special status over the second is due to its having an $n$-order volition concerning it, whereas the second desire has at most an $(n - 1)$-order volition concerning it. But why does one necessarily care about one's higher-order volitions? Since second-order volitions are themselves simply desires, to add them to the context of conflict is just to increase the number of contenders; it is not to give a special place to any of those in contention. The agent may not care which of the second-order desires win out. The same possibility arises at each higher order.

Quite aware of this difficulty, Frankfurt writes:

> There is no theoretical limit to the length of the series of desires of higher and higher orders; nothing except common sense and, perhaps, a saving fatigue prevents an individual from obsessively refusing to identify himself with any of his desires until he forms a desire of the next higher order (76).

But he insists that

> It is possible . . . to terminate such a series of acts [i.e., the formation of ever higher-order volitions] without cutting it off arbitrarily. When a person identifies himself *decisively* with one of his first-order desires, this commitment "resounds" throughout the potentially endless array of higher orders. . . . The fact that his second-order volition to be moved by this desire is a decisive one means that there is no room for questions concerning the pertinence of volitions of higher orders . . . The decisiveness of the commitment he has made means that he has decided that no further question about his second-order volition, at any higher order, remains to be asked (ibid.).

But either this reply is lame or it reveals that the notion of a higher-order volition is not the fundamental one. We wanted to know what prevents wantonness with regard to one's higher-order volitions. What gives these volitions any special relation to "oneself"? It is unhelpful to answer that one makes a "decisive commitment," where this just means that an interminable ascent to higher orders is not going to be permitted. This *is* arbitrary.

What this difficulty shows is that the notion of orders of desires or volitions does not do the work that Frankfurt wants it to do. It does not tell us why or how a particular want can have, among all of a person's "desires," the special property of being peculiarly his "own." There may be something to the notions of acts of identification and of decisive commitment, but these are in any case different notions from that of a second- (or *n*-) order desire. And if these are the crucial notions, it is unclear why these acts of identification cannot be themselves of the first order—that is, identification with or commitment to courses of action (rather than with or to desires)—in which case, no ascent is necessary, and the notion of higher-order volitions becomes superfluous or at least secondary.

In fact, I think that such acts of "identification and commitment" (if one goes for this way of speaking) are generally to courses of action, that is, are first-order. Frankfurt's picture of practical judgment seems to be that of an agent with a given set of (first-order) desires concerning which he then forms second-order volitions. But this picture seems to be distorted. As I see it, agents frequently formulate values concerning alternatives they had not hitherto desired. Initially, they do not (or need not usually) ask themselves which of their desires they want to be effective in action; they ask themselves which course of action is most worth pursuing. The initial practical question is about courses of action and not about themselves.

Indeed, practical judgments are connected with "second-order volitions." For the same considerations that constitute one's on-balance reasons for doing some action, $a$, are reasons for wanting the "desire" to do $a$ to be effective in action, and for wanting contrary desires to be ineffective. But in general, evaluations are prior and of the first order. The first-order desires that result from practical judgments generate second-order volitions because they have this special status; they do not have the special status that Frankfurt wants them to have because there is a higher-order desire concerning them.

Therefore, Frankfurt's position resembles the platonic conception in its focus upon the structure of the "soul."[10] But the two views draw their divisions differently; whereas Frankfurt divides the soul into higher and lower orders of desire, the distinction for Plato—and for my thesis—is among independent sources of motivation.[11]

## IV

In conclusion, it can now be seen that one worry that blocks the acceptance of the traditional view of freedom—and in turn, of com-

---

10. Frankfurt's idea of a wanton, suitably construed, can be put to further illuminating uses in moral psychology. It proves valuable, I think, in discussing the problematic phenomenon of psychopathy or sociopathy.

11. Some very recent articles employ distinctions, for similar purposes, very like Frankfurt's and my own. See, for example, Richard C. Jeffrey, "Preferences among Preferences," *Journal of Philosophy*, LXXI, 13 (July 18, 1974): 377–391. In "Freedom and Desire," *Philosophical Review*, LXXXIII, 1 (January 1974): 32–54, Wright Neely appeals to higher-order desires, apparently unaware of Frankfurt's development of this concept.

patibilism—is unfounded. To return to Berlin's question (see above), it is false that determinism entails that all our actions and choices have the same status as those of "compulsive choosers" such as "kleptomaniacs, dipsomaniacs, and the like." What is distinctive about such compulsive behavior, I would argue, is that the desires and emotions in question are more or less radically independent of the evaluational systems of these agents. The compulsive character of a kleptomaniac's thievery has nothing at all to do with determinism. (His desires to steal may arise quite randomly.) Rather, it is because his desires express themselves independently of his evaluational judgments that we tend to think of his actions as unfree.

The truth, of course, is that God (traditionally conceived) is the only free agent, *sans phrase*. In the case of God, who is omnipotent and omniscient, there can be no disparity between valuational and motivational systems. The dependence of motivation upon evaluation is total, for there is but a single source of motivation: his presumably benign judgment.[12] In the case of the Brutes, as well, motivation has a single source: appetite and (perhaps) passion. The Brutes (or so we normally think) have no evaluational system. But human beings are only more or less free agents, typically less. They are free agents only in some respects. With regard to the appetites and passions, it is plain that in some situations the motivational systems of human beings exhibit an independence from their values which is inconsistent with free agency; that is to say, people are sometimes moved by their appetites and passions in conflict with their practical judgments.[13]

As Nietzsche said (probably with a rather different point in mind): "Man's belly is the reason why man does not easily take himself for a god."[14]

12. God could not act *akratically*. In this respect, Socrates thought people were distinguishable from such a being only by ignorance and limited power.
13. This possibility is a definitive feature of appetitive and passionate wants.
14. *Beyond Good and Evil*, section 141.

# 3

# Three Concepts of Free Action: I

## DON LOCKE

The free will problem is one of the hardy perennials of philosophy. Milton chose it when he wanted to provide his fallen angels with some never-ending topic of discussion with which to while away the hours of eternity, and the status of the issue has not changed much since Milton's day. Indeed the fact that the problem continues to bloom vigorously, down the centuries, with no generally agreed solution, suggests that it has been misconstrued in some crucial way, that the answer to the question of whether the will be free or no is that there is no answer, because the question itself is based on an error. But unfortunately this attempt to dissolve rather than solve the problem has a history almost as long as the problem itself. The problem of whether there genuinely is or is not a free will problem also continues to bloom vigorously, down the centuries, with no generally agreed solution.

A partial explanation of this unsatisfactory state of affairs, I believe, is that the various parties to the dispute tend to be operating with differing conceptions of free action, in some of which it is clear that there are free actions and that there need be no conflict between this freedom and causal determinism, in others of which this is by no means clear. In this paper I want to concentrate on three leading concepts of free action, associated classically with the names of Locke, Hobbes and Moore. I am concerned here with free *action*, with what it is for an agent to act freely, rather than with free will, which might well be different, or with any other of the many possible applications and senses of freedom. There is, after all, much more to human

"Three Concepts of Free Action: I" originally appeared in *Proceedings of the Aristotelian Society*, supp. vol. IL (1975), 95–112, © The Aristotelian Society 1975, and is reprinted here by courtesy of the Editor.

freedom than freedom of action in the technical, philosophical sense, a sense which we will see to be far from clear.

I

The first concept of free action construes free action as willing action. This is the idea we meet in Locke, that to act freely is to act as you want to: the man who wants to get out of a locked room does not remain there freely but, Locke insists, a man who wants to stay there, to speak to a friend, does stay freely, even if the door is locked.

There are, however, difficulties with this formulation, due to the notorious obscurity, ambiguity even, of the notion of wanting. A man may do something because he thinks he ought to, but do it with great reluctance in that he finds it unpleasant or inconvenient. Does he want to do it? In one way obviously not; but in another obviously so, for if he did not want to do as he ought then his acting as he does would be bizarre, to say the least. There are conflicting interpretations here of what it is to want to do something. In a relatively strong sense a man wants to do something if he looks forward to it with pleasure, or expects to enjoy doing it; it is in this sense that the man just cited does not want to do as he ought. In a weaker sense a man wants to perform some action simply in so far as he thinks that, for whatever reason, it is the thing for him to do; it is in this sense that the man does want to do as he ought, just because he thinks he ought to do it. But in which interpretation, if either, is a man who does as he wants acting willingly and hence, according to the present concept of free action, freely?

First of all, it seems that acting willingly cannot be identified with acting in the expectation of pleasure or enjoyment, or even with acting in the non-expectation of pain and discomfort. There seems no reason why a man should not willingly do what he dislikes or expects to suffer from doing: I may expect nothing but trouble and ridicule from taking a stand on some disputed point, but still do it willingly. Even more obviously, acting willingly cannot be identified with doing what you have reason to do, for it often happens that a man both has reason for acting in a certain way and has reason for not acting in that way, and hence simultaneously wants to do it and wants not to do it. Precisely this happens in our example, but it would be odd to describe the man's behavior as both willing and unwilling, let alone both free and unfree.

One way around this latter point might be to distinguish between what a man *wants* and what he *wills*, where what he wills to do is what his different and perhaps conflicting wants actually motivate him to do, or at least attempt. A man may have conflicting wants, but he can have only one will; we may say, perhaps tautologically, that the strongest want determines the will. A willing action, then, might be one where the agent does as he wills. But this would mean, in effect, that all intentional actions are willing actions, and hence that the behaviour of the bridegroom threatened with the shotgun, or of an alcoholic, kleptomaniac or half-crazed drug addict, will to the extent that it is intentional, be willing and hence free.

What, then, is it to act willingly? One approach might be to distinguish between those wants which a man has naturally, which he chooses for himself or which arise from his intrinsic nature, and external or artificial wants, which are imposed on him from outside or formed for him by his circumstances or community. But the distinction is hard to draw, if it can be drawn at all, for how are we to tell whether the desire e.g., to own a car or marry a certain sort of girl, is a desire which truly springs from his own nature, rather than being a product of his particular upbringing or various social pressures? The distinction presupposes some theory of human nature, of what a man truly is or ought to be, such as might be proposed by an Aristotle or a Marx, so that we can then separate those wants which are genuine from those which are merely artificial. But any such theory will be highly controversial, and any account of free action which it generates will be theory-laden in the extreme.

A more profitable approach might be to distinguish between those wants, whatever their source, that a man identifies with and accepts as his own, and those which while being wants that he has are nevertheless wants which he would prefer to be without and regards as not truly in accordance with what he is or would hope to be. Thus (following Dworkin, "Acting Freely") we might say that a man acts willingly, and so freely, when he acts from wants he wants to have, or reasons he does not mind having. More formally (following Frankfurt, "Freedom of the Will and the Concept of a Person," Chapter 1 of the present volume), we might distinguish between first- and second-level wants or desires. A man who has a want without wanting that want, e.g., a smoker trying to kill his desire for cigarettes, has the first-level want but not the second-level want; a man who wants a want he does not have, i.e., wishes he felt some desire he does not feel, has the second-level want but not the first-level want. And the suggestion is that a man really acts as he wants to, acts willingly, when he has both the first- and the second-level wants. The difference between a willing and an unwilling drug addict, for example, is that although both share a desire for their daily dose, the willing addict wants that desire and the unwilling addict does not.

This account has, however, to be understood in a certain sort of way. The pilot of the hi-jacked airliner who flies to Havana because he wants to avoid being shot both has that want and also, not being suicidally-inclined, wants that want. What he does not want is that the first-level want, his desire not to get shot, should have any relevance to his present situation and conduct. Understood in this way he lacks the relevant second-level want, and so flies unwillingly to Cuba. But if Havana happened to be the home of his mistress, so that he is glad of any excuse to spend the night there, then he may want the desire not to get shot to apply to his situation, since it gives him just the excuse he needs, and so he flies willingly to Cuba, despite being forced to.

The suggestion so far is that to act willingly is to act in accordance with both a first- and a second-level desire or want. But consider now the case of someone who wants a certain desire, without wanting it ever to motivate his behaviour: a saint seeking to understand the sinner, perhaps, or a researcher anxious to understand the psychology of drug addiction. It is certainly possible that having acquired that desire he finds that, contrary to his wishes, it does motivate him after all: he is driven, unwillingly, to do something which in a definite sense he does not want to do, despite having the first- and second-level desires. To handle this case we need to introduce Frankfurt's further distinction between first- and second-level willing or volition. A man may have a certain will, be motivated in a certain way, yet wish that were not his will, want not to be motivated in that way, as when the smoker finally succumbs to his desire for another cigarette: this is his first-level will but he lacks the appropriate second-level volition. Conversely a man may want a certain will yet lack it, as when he wishes he were more highly motivated in some respect: he has the second-level volition but not the appropriate first-level one. We have seen, too, that someone may have a certain second-level desire while lacking the appropriate second-level volition, i.e., want the desire without wanting it to motivate him. And conversely a man may have the second-level volition without having the second-level desire, interpreted as we have interpreted it. The pilot of the hi-jacked airliner, we said, lacks the second-level desire in that he does not want the wish not to get shot to be relevant to his present conduct; but unless he is positively suicidal, he certainly wants that want to be his will, to motivate him.

This last example shows that the relevant second-level volition is not, by itself, sufficient for willing action, but the earlier example, of the man motivated by a desire which he wants to have but does not want to be motivated by, suggests that it is at least necessary. To act willingly, therefore, is to act in accordance with both a second-level want and a second-level volition. Acting unwillingly, on the other hand, requires not merely the absence of the relevant second-level desire and volition, but the presence of opposed ones. If I want a drink and get one, just because I feel thirsty, without either wanting that want or wanting not to have it and without either wanting to be so motivated or wanting not to be, then I do not get my drink either willingly or unwillingly. It is only if I positively want not to have that want, or want it not to motivate me, *e.g.*, because it breaks my concentration on some difficult problem, then I get my drink unwillingly, though still wanting a drink. Similarly, a creature incapable of second-level wants or volitions will equally be incapable of acting either willingly or unwillingly, though it may or may not do as it wants to. This, at any rate, is how I prefer to understand these terms, though I can see some case for a weaker, looser sense of 'willingly' in which it means merely 'not unwillingly'.

It emerges, therefore, that to act freely, in accordance with this first concept of free action is to act in accordance with both a second-level desire and a second-level volition. Unfortunately, however, such willingness seems to be neither a necessary nor a sufficient condition of free action in any obvious or natural sense. For on the one hand it provides for a distinction, so far as freedom of action is concerned, between the willing and the unwilling drug addict, which seems implausible given that both are equally addicts. What might be argued with more plausibility is that the willing addict is responsible for his behaviour in a way that the unwilling addict is not (see Frankfurt, "Freedom of the Will," Chapter 1 above, pp. 79–80). But while I can see a respect in which the willing addict might be regarded as more reprehensible, in that his desires are as depraved as his actions, this does not seem to me to make any difference to his responsibility for his behaviour. Again, they may differ in their responsibility for not trying to kick the habit, but so far as the actual taking of drugs is concerned, the willing and the unwilling addict seem to me equally responsible and blameworthy, if responsible and blameworthy at all, and assuming no crucial difference in the way they came originally to be addicts. Similarly it would be as odd to suggest that the pilot who flies willingly to Cuba, glad of any excuse to spend the night in Havana, bears some responsibility for flying there that the pilot who obeys unwillingly does not, as it would be to suggest that the former acts freely while the latter does not.

On the other hand there is the case with which we began, of the man who feels he ought to do something and to that extent wants to do it, but at the same time heartily wishes that no such moral requirement applied. His position is precisely analogous with the pilot forced unwillingly to Cuba: he does not want that want, or at least does not want it to apply to his present situation, but given that it does apply, then, being a moral man, he wants it to motivate him, to be his will. He does his duty unwillingly—he has the second-level volition but lacks the second-level desire—but it would be implausible to suggest that he therefore acts unfreely, let alone that he lacks responsibility for doing as he does.

Moreover, just as a man may both want to do something and also want not to do it, so he may both want a certain desire or volition and not want it. In such a case he will, by our definition, act both willingly and unwillingly. This is what happens in the difficult example (suggested by Dworkin, p. 379) of the kleptomaniac who is kept from indulging his obsession by the fear of being discovered and punished, and is moreover glad and grateful that this constraint inhibits him from giving in to his anti-social desires: he both wants the fear of punishment to apply to his situation and wants it not to; he both wants that fear to motivate him and wants it not to; and hence he acts both willingly and unwillingly. This is not, I think, counterintuitive; but the further consequence, that he therefore acts both freely and unfreely, is.

Finally there is the implication of this account (see Fain, "Prediction and Constraint") that we can get a man to act freely merely by persuading him to do willingly what he has no option but to do: "there would seem to be two ways of freeing the prisoner. One would be to remove the chains; the other would be to present the prisoner with a copy of Epictetus" (Fain, p. 372). For all these reasons, then, it seems implausible to identify free action with willing action.

## II

We turn now to the second, Hobbesian concept of free action. As the first concept began from the idea that an agent acts freely when he acts as he wants to, so the second concept begins from the idea that he acts freely when he is not made to act as he does. A free action, that is, is one where the agent is not subject to such things as compulsion, coercion, constraint or duress; nothing and no-one forces him to act, or prevents him from acting differently. On this interpretation, therefore, neither drug addict and neither pilot acts freely, given that both are equally subject to compulsion or coercion. Nor for that matter does the man in Locke's example: even if he wants to stay in the room he does not do so freely, not if the door is locked. We need, then, some account of what it is for behaviour to be subject to compulsion, coercion, constraint and the rest. Of course these all differ among themselves, but the suggestion is that they share some common feature which conflicts with an action's being free. For convenience let us call any action which has this feature a 'C-action'. What we are looking for is some characterisation of a C-action, and hence of its opposite, a free action in this second sense.

Hobbes' position, in effect, was that a C-action is an action which results from factors which operate regardless of what the agent himself is, wants or does: liberty consists in "the absence of all impediments to action which are not contained in the nature and intrinsical quality of the agent". But this seems too restrictive, leaving no room for psychological compulsions, or even straight-forward coercion: Hobbes explicitly says that the man who acts from fear is as free as the man who acts from covetousness. Another suggestion might be that a C-action is one which results from factors which the agent does not want to motivate him. But this seems too generous, amounting in effect to an identification of C-action with unwilling action, and hence of the second concept with the first: it would mean that the willing drug addict is not compelled to take drugs while the unwilling addict is, when it is surely obvious that no distinction can be drawn between the two in this respect. A third suggestion (see Frankfurt, "Coercion and Moral Responsibility") might be that a C-action is one where the agent is motivated by a desire he cannot control, one which he cannot prevent from determining his response. But this means that if the pilot makes a calculated decision to submit to the hi-jacker then his flying to Havana is not a C-action; it will be a C-action only if he reacts from sheer uncontrollable terror. But hi-jacking is surely as clear a case of coercion as we might hope to find (Frankfurt's error appears to be an explicit equation of coercion with compulsion in a strong sense; the example shows that a man may be coerced—and in a way which absolves him of responsibility, which is Frankfurt's main concern—without being literally compelled to act as he does).

A fourth suggestion (which might be derived from Nozick, "Coercion") is that a C-action is one where the agent cannot reasonably be expected to act otherwise, as the drug addict cannot reasonably be expected to withstand his desire for drugs and the pilot cannot reasonably be expected to ignore the hi-jacker's demands, whether they want to or not. Yet there are cases where an agent cannot reasonably be expected to act otherwise, without its being the case that he is coerced, compelled, constrained or the like, in any way which conflicts with freedom of action. If I am offered £10 for some useless piece of junk it would be as unreasonable to expect me to refuse as it would if I were threatened with a loaded shot-gun, yet the latter is seen as a case of coercion in a way that the former is not. Nor is this simply a consequence of the important distinction between an offer and a threat (interestingly discussed in both Nozick, "Coercion," and Frankfurt, "Coercion and Moral Responsibility"), for our concern here is not with coercion as such but with C-action, action which is seen as coerced or compelled or something of the sort, in a way which infringes freedom of action, and offers may do this as easily as threats. Indeed one familiar way of making a man do as you wish is precisely to make him an offer he cannot refuse. If I am offered £1000 for some item dear to me, but whose sentimental value really cannot justify my passing up the desperately-needed £1000, then we may well allow that I am forced to let the item go, I have no choice. Nevertheless the difference between this case of C-action, and the case where I simply get rid of a piece of junk at a more-than-reasonable price, does not consist in whether or not it would be reasonable to expect me to act otherwise. If anything it would be less reasonable to expect me to act otherwise in the latter case than in the former.

Rather, the difference between the two offers appears to be that one of £ 10, while one I cannot reasonably be expected to refuse, is probably not one which I would accept even if I were unwilling to sell. An offer of £1000, on the other hand, probably is an offer I would accept even if I were unwilling to sell; it is an offer I cannot refuse; and hence an offer which makes me sell, forces me to sell, much as a threat might do. Again if we return to the two drug addicts, the crucial similarity seems to be that their willingness or unwillingness can make no difference to how they actually behave. The drug addict will succumb to his need for drugs whether he wants to or not; otherwise he is not strictly an addict. And similarly with psychological compulsions. It seems, therefore, that a C-action will be not one performed unwillingly, but rather one which would be performed whether the agent were willing or not. In the terminology of the previous section, a C-action is one which is not dependent on the relevant second-level wants and volitions; and a free action, by contrast, will be one that is.

According to this second concept, then, a free action is an action performed only because the agent is willing, i.e., one dependent on the appropriate second-level wants and volitions. The definition differs in two respects from Frankfurt's similar definition of acting of your own free will, which he distinguishes both from acting freely and from having a free will, in "Freedom of the Will" (Chapter 1 above). For Frankfurt refers only to second-level volitions; and requires only that they be sufficient, not that they be necessary, for the agent's acting as he does. Thus on Frankfurt's account the willing drug addict does act of his own free will, while on the present account neither drug addict and neither hi-jacked pilot acts freely, nor does the man in the locked room. Moreover the question of whether the kleptomaniac, in Dworkin's puzzling example, freely refrains from stealing becomes, most plausibly, the question of whether his fear of the consequences of stealing would continue to motivate him even if he did not want that fear, or did not want it to motivate him.

Nevertheless freedom from compulsion, constraint and the rest seems, no more than acting willingly, to be a necessary or sufficient condition of free action in any obvious or natural sense. On the one hand there remains the case of the reluctant moralist who does as he ought despite his unwillingness, despite lacking the relevant second-order desire. There is also the man we might call the dedicated moralist, who willingly does as he ought but would still do it even if he were unwilling, and so does not act just because he is willing. By our definition both men are, in a sense, compelled to act as they do, and there is, after all, such a thing as moral compulsion, the feeling that we have to do something just because we ought to do it, whether we want to or not. But although such moral compulsion infringes our freedom of action to the extent that we feel we are not free to act in any other way, it is I think counter-intuitive to conclude that we are therefore not acting freely.

On the other hand there appear to be cases where a man is not compelled or coerced in our present sense, yet does not act freely. In an early work called *Problems of Mind and Matter* (p. 116) John Wisdom considered the predicament of a man, the precise extent of whose desires has been fixed by the Devil. Richard Taylor has a similar example in his *Metaphysics* (pp. 45–6), with the Devil replaced by his modern secular counterpart, a neurologist who manipulates our desires by manipulating the state of our brain. Wisdom reports that he himself, and most of those he has questioned, and especially those who are not philosophers, are inclined to say that such a person is not responsible for what he does. Our concern here is with free action, not moral responsibility, but it may seem equally plausible to insist, with Taylor, that he is not acting freely either.

Nevertheless the example is not entirely convincing. The plain fact is that many of our preferences in such matters as food, drink or sex are set for us, as brute facts about ourselves over which we have little or no direct control, as surely as if they were fixed by a Devil/neurologist; but that of itself does not seem to conflict with freedom of action. I personally happen to prefer beer to whisky, and this is not a preference I can change 'at will', simply by making up my mind. No doubt I could follow some course of education, therapy or behaviour-modification aimed at altering my preferences in this respect, but if at the moment I should want a drink it is in no way up to me whether I will prefer beer or whisky. Of course not all preferences are like this: when it comes to choosing between two brands of beer, that may very well be a matter of my simply making up my mind which to have. But faced with a choice between beer and whisky, my natural God-given (or for that matter Devil- or neurology-given) preference is for beer. Yet this surely does not conflict with any freedom of choice I have between the two.

It seems that what counts, so far as freedom of choice and action is concerned, is not what wants the agent has, but his being motivated by them. It would not matter if all my desires were fixed by the Devil/neurologist, so long as it remained up to me, within my control, which of those desires is actually going to motivate me. My preference for beer over whisky is not something I can directly control, but I can decide, for whatever reason, to have whisky rather than beer, despite the fact that this is not my true preference. Whether that want becomes my will *is* something which depends on me, and in particular on my second-level volitions. So I freely choose beer over whisky inasmuch as I do so only because I want my natural preference for beer, rather than any other consideration, to motivate me. The example seems only to confirm the identification of free action with actions performed only because the agent is willing.

Nevertheless we have now only to extend the original example, so that the Devil/neurologist manipulates not only the first-level wants but also the second-level desires and volitions, and in such a way as to ensure that we act because we want the wants which motivate us, and want to be motivated by them. Here the Devil/neurologist ensures that we act in a certain way, while also ensuring that we act freely, on the current definition. He does not, I think, compel or force us to act as we do; certainly we are not made to act against our will. But in so far as we act in that way only because the Devil/neurologist has ensured that we will want to, it is difficult to see this as a free action in any full or important sense. What seems to be lacking here is the idea that it is up to the agent, within his control, not merely what he does but also which wants, and in particular which second-level volitions, he has. It is to the extent that he interferes with this freedom that the Devil/neurologist interferes with our freedom of action. And this freedom, the freedom to want, will and do things other than those we actually want, will and do, is the freedom expressed in our third concept. To it we must now turn.

## III

The third concept of free action begins from the idea that an agent acts freely when his action is avoidable or alterable by the agent himself: we lack freedom of action to the extent that we cannot help doing what we do. So for an action to be free it must be within the agent's power either to do that thing or not, as he pleases; and we thus arrive at the Moorean definition, that an agent acts freely so long as he could have acted differently if he had chosen to, or wanted to, or some such. The analysis of this 'could have done otherwise' is a notoriously vexed and complex matter, and in the time that remains I can only be brief and dogmatic (I have discussed these points also in my "Natural Powers and Human Abilities," and "The 'Can' of Being Able").

First, the 'can' in question is clearly not the 'can' of power or ability that we find in 'I can swim' or 'I can ride a bike'. To say that an agent acted freely is not merely to say that he possessed abilities he was not at that time exercising, or else a man acts freely in falling down stairs, inasmuch as falling down stairs is compatible with possessing the ability to drive a car or sing in tune. It is rather to say that he was able to act differently. Second, the 'can' in question is to be interpreted categorically, as asserting that the agent actually was able, at the time and on the occasion in question. To say that he acted freely is not merely to say that there are some circumstances in which he could have acted differently; it is to say that he could actually have acted differently, there and then. And finally, the 'can' in question is not to be analysed wholly hypothetically, in terms of what the agent would do in different circumstances, precisely because that analysis makes nonsense of the claim that he could have acted differently in these very circumstances. For according to the analysis this is to say that he would have acted differently in different circumstances in these circumstances, which means either that he would have acted differently in different circumstances—which is not equivalent to the claim that he could have acted differently in *these* circumstances—or means nothing very clear at all. Similarly, according to the analysis, the claim that he could have acted differently in different circumstances means that he would have acted differently in different circumstances in different circumstances, which if it means anything at all means that he would have acted differently in different circumstances, and this again is not equivalent to the claim that he *could have* acted differently in different circumstances.

Thus according to our third concept of free action, an agent acts freely when, in the circumstances where he acts as he does, he is categorically able, it is categorically possible for him, to act in some other way, if he wants to. But once again it can be argued that this account, like the others, provides neither a necessary nor a sufficient condition of free action in any natural or obvious sense. For on the one hand there seem to be cases where an agent could have acted differently, without our wanting to say that he therefore acted freely. The bank clerk faced with an armed raider does not hand over the money freely, despite the fact that he could refuse if he wished—and get shot for his pains. This is certainly a possible course of action open to him, albeit not one which might reasonably be expected of him (and in that sense, perhaps, he can do no other; see Nesbitt and Candlish, "On Not Being Able to Do Otherwise"). All this might suggest that the test of a free action is not whether the agent can act differently, but whether he can reasonably be expected to. But against that there is the example where I am offered £10 for the useless piece of junk: I cannot reasonably be expected to refuse such a generous offer, but it scarcely follows that I do not sell it freely.

On the other hand it might be argued that a man acts freely even though he cannot act in any other way, so long as his doing what he does is in no way determined by the fact that it is the only alternative open to him. Suppose a man firmly intends to do something but someone else, who is very desirous that he should do it, so arranges things that if he changes his mind he will find that he is not in fact able to act in any other way; nevertheless the man sticks to his original intention and acts, as we say, of his own free will, without the external constraint needing to be brought into play. Here the agent can do no other, but does this really mean that he is not acting freely, when what he does results from his own free decision, is his doing and his responsibility? This time the example suggests that the test of a free action is not whether the agent could have acted differently, but whether he acted as he did *only because* he could not act differently (Frankfurt, "Alternate Possibilities and Moral Responsibility," Chapter 6 in the present volume, offers this not as a test of free action, but as a test of moral responsibility). But this has the consequence, once again, that the willing drug addict acts freely (or is responsible for his drug-taking), since he does not do it only because it is impossible for him not to: he would continue to take drugs even if he could stop himself.

But personally I am not persuaded by these counter-examples to our third concept of free action. After all the simplest example of the man who can do no other, without acting as he does *because* he can do no other, is the man who stays in the room because he wants to, but is locked in to make assurance double sure. It does not seem to me that he stays there freely, despite the fact that his staying there is not determined by the fact that it is the only alternative open to him. There is, moreover, some reason to insist that the bank clerk does act freely, even when faced with a loaded shot-gun. It is his decision and his decision alone whether to hand over the funds or risk his life, and which he does will depend on him, his wishes and his preferences, not on anyone else, not even on the raider. The reason for denying that he acts freely is that we do not blame him for giving the money to the raider, even though, strictly, he could have refused. But we do not have to tie free action to moral responsibility. Indeed I believe that one main source of difficulty and slow progress in this area is precisely that philosophers tend to approach the free will problem with one eye cast backwards at questions of responsibility, praise and blame, instead of confronting it directly as an issue in the theory of action. Certainly freedom of action is not a necessary condition of moral responsibility: if I drive at 50 mph in a 30 mph area and hit a child who runs out from behind a parked car, then while I freely drive at that speed I do not freely hit the child; nevertheless I am morally accountable not only for driving at that speed but also for its consequence, hitting the child.

This is not, however, to argue that our third concept captures the idea of free action in some 'obvious or natural' sense; very likely there is no such sense. It is only to suggest that this third concept provides the most plausible interpretation, as it is also the most interesting.

IV

We can now return to the key questions of whether there are free actions, and whether this freedom of action is compatible with an agent's being caused to act as he does. These questions are, of course, connected, in that the main motive for insisting that we never perform free actions is precisely that this is ruled out by our actions' being caused, whereas the main motive for insisting that some of our actions are free is precisely that there need to be no such conflict between free action and causal determinism. Now if an action is free in the sense that the agent acts willingly, or alternatively that he acts as he does only because he is willing, then it is surely obvious both that there are such free actions, and that there need be no incompatibility between an action's being free, in these senses, and its having a cause. Indeed these accounts fit naturally, as they are meant to, with the self-determinist conception of free action as action determined by the agent's wants and volitions. Free action, of this sort, will be denied only by those who maintain, most implausibly, that our behaviour is caused by factors which have nothing to do with our various wants and intentions, so that we would continue to act as we do even if our desires and volitions were different.

But on the other hand, if an action is free in the sense that the agent can act differently from the way in which he actually does act, then it follows that nothing causes him to act as he does. It is, I believe, a necessary—though not a sufficient—condition of an agent's being able to perform a certain action that it be empirically, both physically and psychologically, possible for him to act in that way: if it is empirically impossible for $A$ to do $x$, then $A$ is unable to do $x$. Consequently, if the circumstances are such as to make it empirically impossible for $A$ to do $x$, then in those particular circumstances $A$ is unable to do $x$, whatever might be possible in different circumstances. And finally, on any understanding of causation, if circumstances $C$ are such as to cause $E$ to occur, then the non-occurrence of $E$ given $C$ is an empirical impossibility. This will hold true even if causation is analysed by reference to empirical regularities, since a parallel analysis will also be given for empirical possibility, and it will remain the case that if $C$ causes $E$ then the conjunction of $C$ and not $E$ is an impossibility of the analysed sort. Causal possibility is, after all, a prime form of empirical possibility. Thus a free action, in the sense of one where the agent is able to act differently, will have to be one which lacks a determining cause.

Notice, however, that causal determinism will not be incompatible with free action if by the latter we mean that the agent could have acted differently *if he had wanted to* for, surprisingly perhaps, a distinction can be drawn between being able, and being able if you want to (see "The 'Can' of Being Able"). We know from Austin that "He can if he wants to" does not mean that he would have been able if he had wanted to, but neither does it mean that he was able, categorically and without qualification. Rather, as David Pears has shown ("Ifs and Cans, I"), it means that he is categorically able to perform a certain conditional task, to do it should he want to. A truck may be said to possess, categorically, the power to do 70 in certain conditions, *e.g.*, when unladen, and this power, the power of doing 70 when unladen, will be possessed by the truck even when that condition is not satisfied: even when fully laden the truck retains the power to do 70 when unladen. Similarly we may say of an agent that he is able to act differently if he wants to, and this conditional performance, acting differently if he wants to, is something which the agent is categorically able to do: even when he does not in fact want to act differently, nevertheless he is able to act differently should he want to. And just as there is a difference between asserting that the truck can do 70 when unladen, and asserting that it can do 70, categorically and without qualification, so too there is a difference between asserting that an agent is able to do something if he wants to, and asserting that he is able to do it, categorically and without qualification. This difference is easily concealed by our idiomatic tendency to equate 'He can do it' and 'He can do it if he wants to', and in just the same way truck salesmen, in particular, may say 'This truck can do 70', when strictly it can do 70 only when unladen.

Now if the circumstances are such that the agent is caused to act as he does then, I have argued, in those circumstances he is unable to act differently, inasmuch as it is in those circumstances impossible for him to do so. Nevertheless even in these circumstances he may still be able to act differently if he wants to, for even in circumstances where he is caused to act as he does it may still be true that he is able to act differently if he wants to. For he will be unable to act differently even if he wants to only if the causes of his behaviour would make it impossible for him to act differently even if he were motivated to. So insofar as the agent's motivation itself contributes to causing him to act as he does, it will not be the case that he cannot act differently if he wants to, even if it is true that he cannot act differently given the motivation that he has.

But once this distinction is drawn, the question arises whether free action, in any full and important sense, requires only that the agent be able to act differently if he wanted to, or whether it requires rather that he be able to do it, categorically and without qualification. Consider finally the case of a man suffering from psychological inhibitions or fixations which render him unable to perform, or alternatively refrain from, a certain action precisely because they ensure that nothing can motivate him to any such thing. It may be true of him that he could do it if he wanted to, so long as there is nothing which makes it impossible for him to succeed should he be motivated. But nevertheless he is unable to do it, since nothing could ever bring him to do it. Does he act freely? For myself I say not. In this final sense of free action, therefore, free action is after all incompatible with causal determinism: if all human behaviour is caused then we are never able to do other than what we do do, though it may often be true that we are able to act otherwise if we want to. The question of whether there are free actions in this sense then becomes the difficult and currently unanswerable question of whether there are human actions which lack a cause, an idea which is not, I believe, incoherent.

This conclusion is, of course, highly contentious, partly through the failure to distinguish different concepts of free action, partly through misunderstanding and misinterpretation of the claim that an agent could have acted otherwise. But I do not have time to defend it further here.

*References*
Gerald Dworkin, "Acting Freely," *Nous* 1970.
Hack Fain, "Prediction and Constraint," *Mind* 1956.
Harry G. Frankfurt, "Alternate Possibilities and Moral Responsibility," *Journal of Philosophy* 1969 (Chapter 6 of the present volume).
Harry G. Frankfurt, "Freedom of the Will and the Concept of a Person," *Journal of Philosophy* 1971 (Chapter 1 of the present volume).
Harry G. Frankfurt, "Coercion and Moral Responsibility," in T. Honderich, ed., *Essays on Freedom of Action*, Routledge and Kegan Paul 1973.
Don Locke, "Natural Powers and Human Abilities," *Proceedings of the Aristotelian Society* 1973–74.
Don Locke, "The 'Can' of Being Able," *Philosophia* 6 (March 1976).
Winston Nesbitt and Stewart Candlish, "On Not Being Able to Do Otherwise," *Mind* 1973.
Robert Nozick, "Coercion," in S. Morgenbesser, P. Suppes and M. White, eds., *Philosophy, Science and Method*, St. Martin's Press 1969.
David Pears, "Ifs and Cans," *Canadian Journal of Philosophy* 1971–72.
Richard Taylor, *Metaphysics*, Prentice-Hall 1963.
John Wisdom, *Problems of Mind and Matter*, Cambridge University Press 1934.

# 4

# Three Concepts of Free Action: II

## HARRY G. FRANKFURT

1. There are many situations in which a person performs an action because he prefers it to any other among those he thinks are available to him, or because he is drawn more strongly to it than to any other, and yet is reluctant nonetheless to describe himself without qualification as having acted willingly. He may acknowledge that he did what in *some* sense he wanted to do, and that he understood well enough what he wanted and what he did. But at the same time he may think it pertinent and justifiable to dissociate himself in a way from his action—perhaps by saying that what he did was not something he *really* wanted to do, or that it was not something he really *wanted* to do. Situations of this sort fall into several distinct types.

In situations of Type A, the person's feeling that he acted unwillingly derives from the fact that the external circumstances under which he acted were, as he perceived them, discordant with his desires. It is nearly always possible, of course, for a person to imagine being in a situation that he would like better than the one he is actually in. There is, however, a substantial difference—often easy enough to discern, though difficult to explicate precisely—between recognising that a state of affairs is less than ideal and being actively discontented by it or resistant to it. The discordance between reality and desire that characterises situations of Type A gives rise to the latter, and not merely to the former: it is not just that there is another imaginable situation in which the agent would prefer to be, but that he regrets or resents the state of affairs with which he must in fact contend.

"Three Concepts of Free Action: II" originally appeared in *Proceedings of the Aristotelian Society*, supp. vol. IL (1975), 113–25, © The Aristotelian Society 1975, and is reprinted by courtesy of the Editor.

Suppose someone's reason for having performed a certain action was that he regarded it as the least of various evils among which he had to choose. Given the alternatives he confronted, he preferred without reservation the one he pursued. That provides the warrant for describing him as having done what he wanted to do. But the alternatives he confronted comprised a set from which he did not want to have to choose; he was discontented with the necessity of having to make that choice. It is this discrepancy, between the world as it was and as he wanted it to be, that supports his claim that he did not act altogether willingly.

In situations of Type B, it is the inner circumstances of his action that are discordant with the agent's desires. What motivates his action is a desire by which, given the alternatives he confronts, he does not want to be moved to act. There is a conflict within him, between a first-order desire to do what he actually does and a second-order volition that this first-order desire not be effective in determining his action. In other words, he wants to be motivated effectively, with respect to the alternatives he faces, by some desire other than the one that actually moves him to act as he does.

This person's denial that he has acted altogether willingly reflects his sense that in the conflict from which his action emerged he was defeated by a force with which, although it issued from inside of him, he did not identify himself. For instance, he may have struggled un-successfully against a craving (effective first-order desire) to which he did not want to succumb (defeated second-order volition). Then his effort to dissociate himself from what he has done expresses his view of himself as having been helpless in the face of a desire that drove him unwillingly, regardless of his preference for another action, to do what he did.

Worldly misfortune and inner conflict, of the kinds in question here, bear differently upon the moral responsibilities of agents who are beset by them. In virtue of the discrepancy between the desire that motivates his action and the desire by which he wants to be motivated, the agent in a situation of Type B may not be morally responsible for what he does. The desire that moves him is in one way, to be sure, indisputably his. But it moves him to act against his own will, or against the will he wants. In this respect it is alien to him, which may justify regarding him as having been moved passively to do what he did by a force for which he cannot be held morally responsible.

On the other hand, the fact that someone confronts alternatives from which he does not want to have to choose has in itself no effect at all upon his moral responsibility for the action he elects to perform. There is no reason why a person should not be found meritorious or blameworthy—in other words, be considered morally responsible—for how he acts in situations he would prefer to have avoided, as well as for his behaviour in situations that he is pleased to be in. Thus the fact that a person acts in a situation of Type A provides no basis whatever for denying that he is morally responsible for what he does.

Situations of Type A include many in which the agent is threatened with a penalty, which will be imposed either by another person or by impersonal forces, unless he performs a certain action. Now if we assume that being *coerced* into doing something precludes being morally responsible for doing it, then a threat is not coercive when the threatened person believes correctly that he can defy it if he chooses to do so. For in that case the action he performs if he submits to the threat will be one to which he thinks he has an alternative; he performs it, therefore, because he himself decides to do so. And his action is consequently meritorious or blameworthy—that is, he *is* morally responsible for performing it—according to whether or not performing it is, given the circumstances in which he chooses to perform it, morally preferable to defiance.

Coercive threats, on the other hand, involve penalties that the recipient of the threat cannot effectively choose to incur. His inclination to avoid the undesirable consequence he faces is irresistible; it is impossible for him to bring himself to accept that consequence. When it is the irresistibility of this inclination or desire that accounts for the action he performs, then the recipient of a threat is not morally responsible for what he does—no more than someone is morally responsible for the performance of an action that is accounted for by an irresistible compulsion that originates within himself.

The situation of a person who succumbs to a threat because he is unable to defy it is not, accordingly, of Type A. Nor is it necessarily of Type B either, since there is no reason to assume that a person who acts because of the irresistibility of a desire would prefer, given his alternatives, to be motivated by some different desire. The situation is thus of a distinguishable type, C, whose special characteristic is that the agent acts because of the irresistibility of a desire without attempting to prevent that desire from determining his action. (The agent in a situation of Type C is in certain respects analogous to what I have elsewhere called a "wanton," which may in part account for the repugnance of coercion.) He is not defeated by the desire, as in situations of Type B, since he does not oppose a second-order volition to it. Nor is he autonomous within the limits of an unsatisfactory set of alternatives, as in situations of Type A, since his action does not result from an effective choice on his part concerning what to do.

In the light of some of Locke's remarks, two points need to be made particularly clear in connection with situations of Type C. First, a person may act to satisfy a desire that he cannot in fact resist, and yet it may not be the desire's irresistibility that accounts for his action. He may be unaware that the desire is irresistible, for instance, and perform for reasons unconnected with his inability to resist it the very action to which he would otherwise be driven. In that case, his situation is not of Type C. Second, the fact that someone acts because of the irresistibility of a desire does not mean that he acts in a panic or with a great rush of feeling. A person may believe of himself that he cannot resist a certain desire, and therefore proceed in calm resignation to satisfy it, without experiencing the uncontrollable compulsive thrust that he might indeed encounter if he should attempt to refuse it satisfaction.

Both in situations of Type B and of Type C, the agent is moved to act without the concurrence of a second-order volition: in the former case because his second-order volition is defeated, and in the latter because no second-order volition plays a role in the economy of his desires. On the other hand, the agent in a situation of Type A endorses the desire that moves him to act. Despite his dissatisfaction with a state of affairs in which he finds the desire to merit his endorsement, he is satisfied, given that state of affairs, to be moved by the desire. Thus his action is in accordance with a second-order volition, and the unwillingness with which he acts is of a different character than the unwillingness with which agents act in situations of Types B and C. This difference is reflected in the fact that he may be morally responsible for what he does, whereas they are not.

Let us consider whether it is possible to identify the class of free actions with the class—call it "W"—of actions that are *not* performed in situations of Type B or Type C, assuming that all actions in this class are performed with appropriate understanding and intent. Notice that W resembles the class of willing actions defined by Locke's notion of willingness. However W is broader than that class: it includes not only all members of the latter but also all actions performed in situations of Type A.

2. Because of this difference between the two classes, Locke's claim that willingness cannot be a *necessary* condition for free action has no force against the view that free actions must be members of W. In support of his claim Locke adduces the example of a person who acts in order to do what he takes to be his duty, but who wishes that the action he performs were not morally required of him. Locke observes that while this person acts unwillingly, "it would be implausible to

suggest that he therefore acts unfreely, let alone that he lacks responsibility for doing as he does." But since the situation of the reluctant moralist is of Type A, and not of Type B or Type C, his action belongs to $W$. Thus Locke's observation that he acts both freely and responsibly raises no difficulties for the view that membership in $W$ is a necessary condition for free action.

Locke also maintains that willingness cannot be a *sufficient* condition for free action. The support he provides for this claim loses none of its pertinence on account of the difference between his class of willing actions and $W$. He argues that if willingness is taken to be sufficient for free action—his point can be made equally if membership in $W$ is regarded as sufficient—then a willing addict acts freely when he takes the drug to which he is addicted while an unwilling addict does not. This conclusion does indeed follow, and Locke asserts that it is "implausible given that both are addicts."

But wherein lies its implausibility? The fact that both are addicts means just that neither can refrain from taking the drug or, if one likes, that neither is free to refrain from taking it. This hardly settles the question. For it is far from apparent that a person who is not free to refrain from performing a certain action cannot be free to perform it, or that he cannot perform it freely. Why, after all, should a person's freedom with respect to the performance of one action be thought to have anything essentially to do with his freedom with respect to the performance of another? Evidently, however, Locke takes it for granted that doing something freely entails being able to refrain from or to avoid doing it. Later in his essay he adopts this assumption more openly and makes it central to his own account of free action. Yet nowhere in his essay does he provide any argument to support it.

It is to my mind very implausible to maintain, as Locke also does, that the two addicts have equal moral responsibility for taking the drug. I believe it is decisive, in this connection, that the willing addict's addiction may play no role at all in the explanation of his action. What explains his taking the drug may in fact be, especially if he is unaware of being addicted, exactly the same as what explains the taking of a drug by a non-addict who takes it simply because he unreservedly likes taking it. In that case, surely, the moral responsibility of the willing addict for his action corresponds to that of the non-addict who takes the drug, rather than to that of the unwilling addict who takes it and whose taking it is explicable only in terms of his addiction.

What the willing addict's action reveals about him is the same as what is revealed by the action of the non-addict. It is not the same as what the action of the unwilling addict reveals. The moral significance of the willing addict's action is therefore the same as that of the non-addict's action, it seems to me, and different from the moral significance of what the unwilling addict does. Notice, by the way, that the actions of the willing addict and of the non-addict both belong to $W$, while that of the unwilling addict does not.

In evaluating the moral responsibilities of the willing and unwilling addicts, Locke tends to ignore the distinction between performing an action one is unable to avoid performing and performing an action *because* one is unable to avoid performing it. This is apparently what makes it possible for him erroneously to regard the problem of assessing moral responsibility in the case of the two addicts as a relevant analogue to the problem of assessing it in the case of the two hijacked pilots. His comment about the pilot—that it would be odd to ascribe to the willing pilot some responsibility for flying to Cuba that is not ascribable equally to the unwilling pilot—does not, as he thinks, support his claim that the responsibilities of the two addicts are the same.

Both pilots, as Locke describes them, act for the same reason—to avoid being shot—even though one of them is glad to have this reason for flying to Cuba while the other is not. Now it is precisely because they act for the same reason, or because their actions have the same explanation, that the pilots are equally responsible for what they do. In this crucial respect, of course, their case differs from the case of the two addicts; for what accounts for the action of the one addict is not what accounts for the action of the other. If we were to suppose that the willing pilot flew to Cuba because he wanted to see his mistress in Havana, and that the desire to avoid being shot was not what actually motivated him, then the case of the two pilots *would* be more pertinently like that of the two addicts. But then we would also, I believe, judge the responsibility of the willing pilot to differ from the responsibility of the unwilling one.

Locke's discussions of the addicts and pilots do not establish any basis for rejecting the identification of $W$ with the class of free actions, or for accepting his claim that free actions must be avoidable. It is clear that the unwilling addict acts neither freely nor responsibly, when he takes the drug, and that the willing addict is no more able than he is to avoid taking it. The two addicts differ, however, in what leads each of his action. In virtue of that difference, their moral responsibilities for those actions differ. The view that there is no difference in the freedom with which they act gains no support, therefore, from considerations having to do with moral responsibility.

3. It seems that actions belonging to $W$ might be performed by an individual whose mental life and physical behaviour were determined by some sort of manipulation of his physiological condition by Locke's Devil/neurologist. Identifying $W$ with the class of free actions would therefore apparently mean allowing that the D/n could ensure that his subject acted freely. Is this objectionable?

Let us distinguish two fundamentally different states of affairs, ignoring the difficult problems connected with the possibilities of mixed and borderline cases. In the first state of affairs the D/n manipulates his subject on a continuous basis, like a marionette, so that each of the subject's mental and physical states is the outcome of specific intervention on the part of the D/n. In that case the subject is not a person at all. His history is utterly episodic and without inherent connectedness. Whatever identifiable themes it may reveal are not internally rooted; they cannot be understood as constituting or belonging to the subject's own nature. Rather, they are provided gratuitously by an agency external to the subject. To be sure, the subject's instantaneous states of mind may be as rich as those of a person; they may include second-order desires and volitions, or have even more complex structures. But the subject has no character or dispositions of his own, and there is no reason to expect from him—except derivatively, insofar as there is reason to expect it from the D/n—even the minimum of continuity and intelligibility essential to being a person. Instances of his behaviour can reasonably be excluded from membership in $W$, I believe, on the ground that since he lacks all autonomy they cannot legitimately be ascribed to him as his actions.

The other possibility is that the D/n provides his subject with a stable character or program, which he does not thereafter alter too frequently or at all, and that the subsequent mental and physical responses of the subject to his external and internal environments are determined by this program rather than by further intervention on the part of the D/n. In that case there is no reason for denying that instances of the subject's behaviour may be members of $W$. Nor, in my opinion, are there compelling reasons either against allowing that the subject may act freely or against regarding him as capable of being morally responsible for what he does.

He may become morally responsible, assuming that he is suitably programmed, in the same way others do: by identifying himself with some of his own second-order desires, so that they are not merely desires that he happens to have or to find within himself, but desires that he adopts or puts himself behind. In virtue of a person's identification of himself with one of his own second-order desires, that desire becomes a second-order volition. And the person thereby *takes* responsibility for the pertinent first- and second-order desires and for the actions to which these desires lead him.

Locke suggests that the subject of a D/n cannot be regarded as acting freely because it is not up to the subject, or within the subject's control, what he does or what desires and second-order volitions he has. Evidently he construes the notions "up to $X$" and "within $X$'s control" in such a way that nothing is up to a person, or within that person's control, if someone else determines its occurrence. In my view these notions are to be construed differently, at least in the present context. What is at stake in their application is not so much a matter of the causal origins of the states of affairs in question, but $X$'s activity or passivity with respect to those states of affairs.

Now a person is active with respect to his own desires when he identifies himself with them, and he is active with respect to what he does when what he does is the outcome of his identification of himself with the desire that moves him in doing it. Without such identification the person is a passive bystander to his desires and to what he does, regardless of whether the causes of his desires and of what he does are the work of another agent or of impersonal external forces or of processes internal to his own body. As for a person's second-order volitions themselves, it is impossible for him to be a passive bystander to them. They *constitute* his activity—i.e., his being active rather than passive—and the question of whether or not he identifies himself with them cannot arise. It makes no sense to ask whether someone identifies himself with his identification of himself, unless this is intended simply as asking whether his identification is wholehearted or complete.

This notion of identification is admittedly a bit mystifying, and I am uncertain how to go about explicating it. In my opinion, however, it grasps something quite fundamental in our inner lives, and it merits a central role in the phenomenology and philosophy of human mentality. Instead of attempting to provide the analysis the notion requires, I shall limit myself to a declaration: to the extent that a person identifies himself with the springs of his actions, he takes responsibility for those actions and acquires moral responsibility for them; moreover, the questions of how the actions and his identifications with their springs are caused is irrelevant to the questions of whether he performs the actions freely or is morally responsible for performing them.

The fact that the D/n causes his subject to have and to identify with certain second-order desires does not, then, affect the moral significance of the subject's acquisition of the second-order volitions with which he is thereby endowed. There is no paradox in the supposition that a D/n might create a morally free agent. It might be reasonable, to be sure, to hold the D/n too morally responsible for what his free subject does, at least insofar as he can fairly be held responsible for anticipating the subject's actions. This does not imply, however, that full moral responsibility for those actions may not also be ascribable to the subject. It is quite possible for more than one person to bear full moral responsibility for the same event or action.

4. An action may belong to $W$ even when the agent performs it under duress—that is, in submission to a threat, but where the agent's submission does not result from the irresistibility of his desire to avoid the penalty with which he is threatened. If $W$ is identified with the class of free actions, then of course it follows that actions may be performed freely even when they are performed under duress. This has a rather jarring sound. It must be noted, however, that the consequence would evidently not be unacceptable to Locke.

He is prepared to allow that a bank clerk acts freely when, in order to avoid being shot, the clerk submits to the demands of an armed raider. And he explains that the clerk may be said to act freely because "it is his decision and his decision alone whether to hand over the funds or risk his life, and which he does will depend on him, his wishes and preferences, not on anyone else, not even on the raider." Locke apparently does not suppose that the clerk is stampeded by his desire to avoid being shot, or that his action derives from a belief that he cannot avoid succumbing to this desire. In other words, he construes the clerk's situation to be of Type A and his action to belong to $W$: the clerk acts under duress, but he is not coerced.

On this assumption the point of characterising the clerk as acting freely, even though he can hardly be said to act willingly, is just that the clerk's action is not due to his being inescapably forced to act as he does. His action results from a decision to which he has, or thinks he has, an available alternative. Thus it expresses a genuine choice on his part. It is plainly irrelevant to the genuineness of this choice whether or not the clerk is correct in his belief that he could refrain from or avoid handing over the funds if he preferred that alternative. Insofar as the freedom of the clerk's action rests upon its derivation from a genuine choice on his part, as Locke suggests, freedom of action appears not to require avoidability.

Although Locke regards the clerk as acting freely, he does not think him morally responsible for his action. In Locke's opinion, indeed, it is an error to suppose that there is any necessary connection at all between the concepts of free action and moral responsibility. His reasons for holding this opinion, however, are not convincing.

To support the position that acting freely is not a necessary condition for moral responsibility Locke claims that a speeding driver may be morally responsible for hitting a child who runs out from behind a parked car, despite the fact that the driver does not freely hit the child. But this claim seems incorrect. Other things being equal, the driver is no more blameworthy than if he had missed the child; and he is far less blameworthy than someone who freely hits a child with his car. These considerations indicate that the speeder is not morally responsible for hitting the child at all. What he is responsible for is something like driving recklessly, and there is no reason to doubt that he does this freely. The example does not, then, undermine the view that acting freely is a necessary condition for moral responsibility.

And what of the bank clerk? It is true that we would probably not blame him for submitting to the demands of the armed raider. Locke evidently supposes that this is because we do not think him morally responsible for his action, and that if free action were tied to moral responsibility we would consequently have to say (wrongly, in his judgment) that the clerk does not act freely. But assuming that we do regard the clerk as acting freely, the reason we refrain from blaming him is not that we think he bears no moral responsibility for his submission to the raider. It is that we judge him to act reasonably when he gives up the bank's money instead of his own life, and so we find nothing blameworthy in what he does. Thus the example does not show, as it is presumably intended to do, that a person may act freely without being morally responsible for what he does.

5. Given the roles played by freedom and related concepts in our general conceptual scheme, and the reflections of these roles in linguistic custom, it would not be unreasonable to require that the concept of free action be understood in such a way that a person can bear no moral responsibility except for what he has done freely. On the same basis, it would be equally reasonable to require that no action be construed as having been performed freely if it was performed under duress, or under duress of a certain degree of harshness. Locke's analysis, according to which free actions are those that are avoidable, satisfies neither of these requirements. Being able to avoid performing an action is not incompatible with performing the action

under duress, nor is it a necessary condition for being morally responsible for performing it.

This does not mean that avoidability has nothing whatever to do with freedom. It only means that a person may act freely when he is not free to act differently. From the fact that $X$ did $A$ freely, in other words, it does not follow that $X$ was free to refrain from doing $A$. Thus a person may be free to do what it happens that he wants to do, and do it freely, without enjoying freedom in the sense of being in a position to do whatever he might both want and be inherently able to do. It does not strike me as objectionable to say that a prisoner may come to act more freely—that is, to perform more of his actions freely—through having learned the lessons of Epictetus. But there will naturally remain as many things as before that he is not free to do, which he would be capable of doing if he were not imprisoned. Therefore it would not be correct to describe him as having been freed, or as having escaped the limitations of his imprisonment, by his study of Stoic philosophy.

Identifying $W$ with the class of free actions, since it allows that actions may be performed both freely and under duress, fails to satisfy one of the requirements that has been suggested. It does appear to satisfy the other: membership in $W$ is a necessary condition for a morally responsible action. In fact it is not possible to satisfy both requirements at once, because a person may be morally responsible for what he does under duress. Phrases like "did it freely" are actually used somewhat equivocally: at times they connote that the agent did what he did willingly, and at times they connote his moral responsibility for doing it. If we must have an established and univocal philosophical usage for "free action", we must decide whether it is preferable to satisfy the one requirement or to satisfy the other. So far as I can see, there is little to choose between these alternatives.

# 5

# Understanding Free Will

_____

## MICHAEL SLOTE

In recent years, Harry Frankfurt, Wright Neely, and Gary Watson have offered accounts of free will and free agency that play down the challenge of determinism and equate freedom with a kind of rationality in action.[1]

I believe that the approach taken by Frankfurt, Neely, and Watson (FNW, for short) represents, in its conceptual sophistication and explanatory power, a genuine advance over previous rationality theories of freedom like that of Spinoza. But I also believe that FNW have themselves misunderstood, or failed to see clearly, the nature and implications of their own theories, and that the theories they present must borrow ideas from Spinoza in order to escape implausibility and attain their fullest development. In the end, however, I shall argue that no available rationality conception fully captures our intuitions about what it is to act of one's own free will.

### I

Let me first give a rough sketch of some of the important features of FNW's approach, for the most part concentrating on Frankfurt's

"Understanding Free Will" originally appeared in the _Journal of Philosophy_, 77 (March 1980), 136–51, © 1980 by the _Journal of Philosophy_, and is reprinted here with permission from Michael Slote and from the _Journal of Philosophy_.
1. See Neely, "Freedom and Desire," _Philosophical Review_, LXXXIII, I (January 1974): 32–54; Watson, "Free Agency," Chapter 2 above; Frankfurt, "Freedom of the Will and the Concept of a Person," Chapter 1 above, and "Coercion and Moral Responsibility," in T. Honderich, ed., _Essays in Freedom of Action_ (London: Routledge & Kegan Paul, 1973), pp. 65–86; and "Three Concepts of Free Action: II," Chapter 4 above. Also cf. Gerald Dworkin, "Acting Freely," _Noûs_, IV, 4 (November 1970): 367–383, for a similar approach to freedom which I shall not specifically discuss.

theory, which has been the most elaborately and systematically developed, but indicating differences among the theories when it seems important to do so.

All three philosophers focus upon cases of irrational addiction as paradigms of unfreedom.[2] Frankfurt and Neely both characterize the typical unwilling addict as someone who (e.g.) has a second-order desire not to *desire* some drug and a second-order desire (or volition) not to *give in* to his (or her) first-order desire for the drug, but who (irrationally) gives in to his first-order desire for the drug, nonetheless.[3] In a slightly different vein, Watson characterizes the unwilling addict as someone who (e.g.) puts no (positive) value upon (getting) a certain drug, but who (irrationally) acts upon his strong desire for the drug, nonetheless. In the light of such examples, they then claim, roughly, that a person acts freely when and only when his actions flow from his higher-, or highest-, order desires/volitions, rather than opposing them; alternatively, in Watson's conception, a person acts freely when and only when his actions express his values and not just his (strongest) desires or wants. At this point, I think at least some of the connection between FNW's theories and Spinoza's rationality conception of freedom should be apparent: the addictive people that the former treat as unfree are clearly also cases of Spinozan "human bondage."

Frankfurt makes the further claim that a bank clerk who reluctantly hands over money to a holdup man who threatens him with a gun will typically count, on the account he has offered, as having acted freely.[4] Such a man, he says, would prefer not to have to make the choice that faces him; but, faced with that choice, he is satisfied to be moved by his desire to hand over the money and acts in accordance with a second-order volition. And although Frankfurt also holds that the clerk will resent the intruder and be actively discontented, presum-

2. The expressions 'freedom', 'free agency', '(acting) freely', and '(acting) of one's own free will' all occur in the papers of FNW. But among such expressions, the phrase 'of one's (his) own free will' has, for English-speaking philosophers, the distinct advantage of indicating that what one is saying is relevant to the traditional problem of free will. This particular phrase, then, will be canonical for the present essay, and any other expressions I use *in propria persona* will be merely stylistic variants. Although I shall often make use of FNW's particular terminologies in reporting their views, I believe that our own canonical phraseology can be used to report those views without undue distortion. After all, they too want their ideas to be relevant to the traditional problem of free will.

3. For Frankfurt, second-order volitions are a particular kind of second-order desire: desires that one or another first-order desire be (or not be) acted upon, i.e., effective in action. See Chapter 1 above, p. 68ff; and Chapter 4 above, p. 114.

4. Chapter 4 above, p. 113–116; and 121–122.

ably because he feels loyalty to the bank or to its clients, he seems to feel that such descriptions do not conflict with his characterization of the act as free by the lights of his own theory. To say that such a bank clerk acts freely has, Frankfurt admits, a jarring sound; and he thinks it a prima facie condition on the adequacy of a theory of free action that someone acting under duress in the manner of his bank clerk be judged not to have acted freely (or, presumably, of his own free will). But he attempts to mitigate the presumed implausibility of his theory not by modifying the theory, but by positing a second sense of 'free action' in which the bank clerk does *not* act freely. Neely makes the very same response to cases of duress: he does not see how his own theory can handle them and claims that there is another sense of 'free' that can.[5]

But it seems both ad hoc and self-indulgent to respond to the inability of an analysis to account for certain cases not by reformulating the analysis, but by holding on to it and claiming that the problem cases only demonstrate that there are two senses of the term or expression one is trying to define. Moreover, there is also good reason to believe that the difficulties Frankfurt and Neely think cases of duress present to their theories are themselves more imagined than real. I think it can be shown that Frankfurt and Neely's own theories, suitably supplemented, can actually *explain* why the everyday cases of duress they have in mind are not cases in which (it is natural to say that) a person acts of his own free will.

As Frankfurt and Neely describe the relevant cases of coercion, the person who reluctantly complies with a threat is reasonable to do so. So, given the emphasis their theories place on certain elements of rationality in the concept of free action, it might easily seem that they would be committed to saying that Frankfurt's bank clerk hands over the money of his own free will. But although it may be reasonable, or rational, for the clerk *to* comply with the robber's threat, he may not act rationally *in* complying with it. He may, for example, be overly frightened, or panicked; and he almost certainly will resent the intruder, if, as Frankfurt seems to assume, he has any loyalty either to the bank or to the people it serves. But does this resentment not signify a desire (or wish) for retaliation or defiance: that is, not merely a desire that the would-be robber should somehow be punished, but a desire to do something oneself to punish him or, at least, to show him what one thinks of him? Even if heroism is not widely treated as a moral obligation, most of us have a deep tendency to treat it as an

5. "Freedom and Desire," pp. 35, 50.

ideal to be emulated. And so I think that if the clerk resents the robber, he will have various momentary/fragmentary fantasies of heroic defiance, or foiling, or retaliation, with appropriate accompanying thoughts.

But then someone who fulfills Frankfurt's description of the bank clerk and about whom the above things are also true will qualify as *ambivalent,* if he ends up complying with the intruder's threat: ambivalent, in particular, about his own compliance. On the one hand, to the very extent that the afore-mentioned resentment, wishes, and fantasies exist, he will tend, both before and after the fact, to reproach himself for saving his own skin.[6] When he complies with the robber's threat, such a person acts from a desire by which he wishes not to be moved to act, even *given* the alternatives he confronts. There is in him a conflict between a first-order desire to comply (and play it safe) and an ultimately frustrated second-order volition that that desire not be effective and that, in particular, he should overcome that safe-playing desire through appropriate heroics or defiance. And so he will count at not having acted freely, on Frankfurt's own theory.[7] But, on the other hand, the bank clerk will also, presumably, have an opposing second-order volition that his desire to play it safe should be effective and his tendencies toward defiance and heroics restrained, based on the value he places on his own self-presevation. And it is just this conflict of second-order volitions that qualifies the clerk's attitude toward his compliance as ambivalence. Frankfurt ignores the possibility that his bank clerk might have to be ambivalent, given the descriptions he furnishes and normal human background assumptions. But once we recognize the ambivalence of the typical bank clerk in the situation imagined, we can see that there is no need to reformulate Frankfurt and Neely's theories or postulate a second meaning of 'freedom' in order to explain our reluctance to characterize most people who act under duress as acting freely.[8]

In saying that someone who is ambivalent about his own actions in

6. It is a psychological commonplace that anger or resentment against a given person tends to displace itself onto other (inappropriate) targets when it cannot be directed against its original object. So perhaps we can draw a more direct connection between the clerk's resentment of the intruder and his later self-reproach, by arguing that if he does hand over the money and has any compunction about blaming innocent associates, his unsatisfied anger at the intruder is apt to turn inward (*sub specie* his ideas of heroism). For more on how resentment against others may be turned against the self, compare Nietzsche's fascinating speculations in *The Genealogy of Morals, passim.*

7. Cf. Chapter 4 above, pp. 114, 116–117.

8. If we assume that no *given* act can really express an ambivalent person's values, then Watson too can account for the lack of free agency in typical cases of duress.

the way described above does not act freely—either on FNW's theories or in actual fact—I do not, however, mean to suggest that *whenever* we choose among desires that cannot, in certain circumstances, be jointly realized, we do not act of our own free will. The choice of one out of an incompatible set of alternatives need not involve one in ambivalence about one's choice. If, for example, I have a hankering for Italian food and a stronger hankering for Chinese food that eventually "wins out," I may not in any way wish that my desire for Chinese food had not been effective, even though my hankering for Italian food has not been satisfied or entirely disappeared. For simply to have a desire for something is not, automatically, to want (wish) that other, incompatible desires not exist or be fulfilled. In ambivalence, then, we have conflicting second-order desires/volitions about a first-level desire or want: wanting the first-level desire to exist or issue in action and, at the same time, wanting this not to be so. And there seems to be no reason to suppose that this phenomenon must be present when we (simply) choose between jointly unrealizable desires on the basis, say, of the greater strength of one of those desires.

Certain kinds of ambivalence, then, disqualify one from acting of one's own free will. But that is not to say that all cases of irrational, unfree action involve ambivalence. The heroin addict may not have conflicting second-order volitions in the manner of the bank clerk; he may desire heroin, wish that desire were not effective, and in no way want the desire to be effective or even to exist. To put the matter in Watson's terminology, he may place no value on realizing his desire for heroin, whereas the ambivalent bank clerk seems to place a value both on fulfilling his desire to take no chances and on overcoming that desire in heroism. However, the bank clerk and the addict do fail to act from one of their highest-order desires. And it is this common failure that makes them seem to fall short of rationality-in-action in a way that someone who merely acts from the strongest of his jointly unrealizable desires does not.[9]

## II

I have so far touched upon only one central case of acting under threat or duress. For ideological or personal reasons, however, some

---

9. Neely (*op. cit.,* p. 48f.) says that anyone with conflicting desires is to that extent less free; but this very statement gives us reason to suspect that he is characterizing not our ordinary concept of acting of one's own free will, but some other, related notion, or ideal, of freedom. I shall ignore this divergence in what follows.

bank clerk might be quite *willing* to hand over money to an armed robber. But then he would be unlikely to be ambivalent about handing over the money, and there would be little reason to deny that he did so of his own free will.

It also seems to be possible for someone to comply with an initially unwelcome threat without being ambivalent, and this fact must be accounted for and brought to bear on the theories of free agency we have been discussing. Consider a man told by a king whom he dislikes that if he does not visit him at the palace in a month's time, he will be sent to prison. Is it not possible that the man should reasonably decide that compliance was the sensible course of action under the circumstances and should reconcile himself to the visit—so that when the time came for him to go to the palace, he neither resented the king for forcing such a choice upon him nor wished, at some level, that he could somehow defy or disobey him? Such a person responds to the king's threat, calmly and unambivalently, as if it were some sort of *physical* obstacle, and that may give us reason to say that when he finally does visit the palace, he does so of his own free will.[10] For someone who (e.g.) comes to a large lake while on a long journey may well be faced with a choice—between detouring around the lake and turning back—that he would have preferred not to have to make. But typically, when faced with such a physical obstacle, a traveler will ungrumblingly and automatically adjust his plans; and we would normally think of such a traveler as going around the lake of his own free will, even though the location of the lake clearly does make his options worse than he might have expected. And if the man whom the king threatens has an "objective" and ungrumbling attitude toward the consequent deterioration of his options—I assume that he would generally prefer not to visit such a king, even if he knows he is in no danger in doing so—then I believe he too counts as acting of his own free will if and when he finally visits the palace on the appointed day.

10. It is less natural to say that he complies with the king's threat of his own free will than that he goes to the palace of his own free will. "Of his own free will" entails "knowingly" and "intentionally" and possesses the intensionality of these latter concepts; so although one may in doing $X$ also be doing $Y$, it can still be the case that one is doing $X$ of one's own free will but not doing $Y$ of one's own free will. It sounds somewhat odd to say that someone complies with a threat of his own free will, because it suggests that the person involved is consciously aware that he is acting as he does because of a threat; for this, in turn, suggests rather too much dwelling on the particular source of his action to make it plausible to think that he really is reconciled and "objective" about his situation or thus acting freely. It stands in favor of our account, of course, that it can explain our tendency to make these fine distinctions. But, for ease of exposition, I shall sometimes use phrases that suggest that 'of his own free will' is not intensional.

Certainly, there is a long tradition, exemplified by Spinoza, in which the ability to reconcile oneself to the inevitable without bitterness, or personalizing, or self-recrimination, is taken as a major aspect of what is involved in being a free person. Indeed, the ability to have such an attitude to the necessities of choice, event, and circumstance that the world imposes is quite commonly considered to mark one as being "philosophical" in that widespread use of the term that everyone but philosophers seems to use.

Now although FNW pay no particular attention to cases of acting "philosophically," on their theories the man we have just described clearly counts as acting freely. But despite Frankfurt and Neely's mistaken opinion to the contrary, those theories allow for the possibility of free rational compliance with an (initially) unwelcome threat *only in certain cases,* the very cases about which Spinoza and, I think, we ourselves would be most inclined to say that freedom was exemplified. I would not, however, want to minimize the doubts that can arise about whether freedom really does exist in cases where someone has a "philosophical" attitude in complying with a threat. One might well feel that the king in our earlier example has so effectively intervened in the life of his "philosophical" subject, that the latter's act of visiting the palace is to a significant extent attributable to the king who has changed his options and thus not really, or fully, his own. One may feel, in other words, that however philosophical someone may be, he does not act of his own free will if the acts of another person play such an important role in determining his behavior. (One will presumably still maintain that the "intervention" of natural obstacles does not deprive people of free agency in this way, since, to ordinary ways of thinking, a person may in the course of a journey go around a lake of his own free will, even if the lake has worsened his options and led him to act as he does.)

I can see some force in these claims, but I also think that if one accepts them, one raises problems for oneself that the claims themselves are powerless to deal with (even if one grants the causal distinction between human and nunhuman "interventions" on which they are based). In particular, if we say that a threatener takes away the agency of someone who complies with his threat and that the threatened individual—whatever his inner attitude—does not, in complying, act of his own free will, we will have a problem understanding why highly attractive offers are not usually thought of as depriving us of freedom. For an attractive offer changes our options dramatically, and it seems as reasonable to attribute "ultimate agency" to someone who makes an effective offer as to someone who makes an effective threat. So I think we should be suspicious of the view that effective threats automatically deprive one of free will. What is needed, instead, is a theory of acting freely that can explain why our earlier bank clerk does not hand over the money of his own free will, but also allow for effective offers that do not deprive of freedom. And what is also needed is a theory of free agency that can accommodate our feeling that some offers are so "coercive" and humiliating that if we do take advantage of them, we act no more freely than the bank clerk—a theory, that is, that can explain why some effective offers render us less free as agents than certain others.

I believe that FNW's conception(s) of freedom can achieve these results, once we take into account the sorts of psychological phenomena mentioned earlier and ignored, for the most part, by FNW. Their theory can explain the unfreedom of the original bank clerk in terms of his ambivalence and, ultimately, of the conflict between his effective first-order desire and one of his second-order volitions. And the difference between offers that deprive of free agency and offers that do not can, I believe, be explained in similar terms. If someone offers us an opportunity that offends none of our deeply felt values and that we feel worthy of, then if we take advantage of the opportunity, we presumably do so without ambivalence and (barring other factors that might prejudice the issue) of our own free will. But consider someone who is offered a million dollars if he will lick the offerer's boots. Almost any person who took advantage of such an offer would resent the person who had made such a "coercive" offer and be somewhat ambivalent about taking advantage of it. Most of us have some ideal notion of ourselves as not being the kind of person who can be made to lower and humiliate himself for a price. So even someone who feels that it is rational and worth while for him to lick the boots will also think less of himself for being willing to be rational in this way and wish that he were somehow above this sort of thing; and it is this state of ambivalent conflict that accounts for our intuitive judgment that such a person does not lick the boots of his own free will.

The theories of FNW thus enable us to explain important intuitive distinctions concerning the freedom or lack of freedom involved in typical responses to various sorts of offers and threats. The assumption that an effective threat always deprives of freedom, on the other hand, seems, if anything, to make such distinctions impossible of explanation. Since, moreover, the FNW theories entail that certain people who are philosophical about the threats they comply with act of their own free will, the explanatory and distinction-making power of those theories give us reasons of simplicity and system to deny that effective threats always deprive of free agency. We are, instead, given reason to accept the Spinozistic view that one is free to the extent that one responds calmly and unresentfully to the necessities the world imposes and rationally, without self-recrimination, chooses the good in the light of such necessities.[11]

Of course, there are other reasons already alluded to for thinking that someone who has a philosophical attitude in complying with a threat acts freely. Such a person does, after all, depersonalize things and treat the threat he confronts in the way that most people treat ordinary physical obstacles. Since accommodation to a physical obstacle seems in no way, intuitively, to deprive an agent of his freedom, we have some reason to say the same thing about someone who complies philosophically with a threat. It is important in this connection, however, to avoid overly strong claims about the human capacity for being philosophical, and acting freely, while complying with a threat. Even someone with a capacity for philosophical calm and acceptance may not have the time to cultivate such an attitude if—like our earlier bank clerk or any robbery victim who is told "your money or your life"—he is faced with a threat that requires immediate compliance. The Stoics (and perhaps even Spinoza) seem to have thought both that it was possible to be philosophical and free even in response to such abrupt and immediate threats and that one should cultivate the capacity for such response.[12] But it is at just this point that I find myself in deepest disagreement with the Stoics—and with Spinoza, to the extent that he agrees with them.

Consider the loyal bank clerk of our earlier example. It is a contra-

11. I here follow Spinoza in assuming that there are some occasions when a rational and self-respecting individual will comply with a threat, rather than defy it, without reproaching himself for doing so. (See the *Ethics,* Book 4, props. XX, LXV, and LXIX, proof, corollary, and note.) Frankfurt's clerk may reproach himself for not acting heroically only because he is *not* calm, unangry, and "philosophical" about his situation. Cf. footnote 6, above; and remember, too, that most of us conceive heroism as an ideal to emulate, rather than as a moral obligation.

12. In what follows, I shall play down certain differences between Spinoza and the Stoics, but on the whole the Stoics seem much more committed than Spinoza to the idea that reason can control emotion. In fact, Spinoza explicitly asserts a difference of this kind between his own view and that of the Stoics. (In the *Ethics,* Book 5, preface; but also see Book 5, Proposition X, proof and note; Book 5, Proposition VI; Book 4, Proposition LXXIII.) On the other hand, there are major differences among the Stoics themselves about the extent to which reason can control passion and emotion. The doctrine of total control was advocated by Chrysippus, but Posidonius seems to have held that emotions and passions were in some measure autonomous and not under the direct, immediate control of reason. [On this see F. H. Sandbach, *The Stoics* (London: Chatto & Windus, 1975), pp. 59–67, esp. p. 65.]

diction in terms to suppose that he can have an emotional attitude like loyalty and yet also be able to pick and choose among his emotional *reactions* in such a way as to (decide to) be calm and unresentful at the prospect of handling over the bank's money to an armed intruder. If someone whom we knew to have this sort of loyalty told us that he felt completely detached and emotionless in handing over money to a holdup man, we would very likely conclude that for some reason he was refusing to face his deepest feelings. And all this would also hold, a fortiori, of someone who had to give his own patiently accumulated savings to a holdup man. Faced with threats that require immediate action and that lower our expectations significantly, we cannot be completely philosophical and are incapable of free compliance. It takes time to work through resentment and reluctance, and only if a threat requires action in the relatively distant future will one's capacity for being philosophical have time to take hold. Only with such a temporal breathing space can one work through the inevitable initial reactions and come to accept the necessity of the adverse choice with which one is presented in such a way that, in complying with the threat, one acts of one's own free will.

The Stoic (or Spinoza) will claim that these considerations only show how emotionally attached to worldly things we actually are. If only we cultivated our capacity for emotional detachment, we could learn to respond to immediate threats without ambivalence or emotion and thus to act freely whether we complied with them or not. But I think that what the Stoic says is possible is not really possible, for us. Another, higher sort of being that never went through the dependency of prolonged childhood might never need or want love. But we are not beings of that sort: we seek love from the start and never really outgrow that quest or its urgency. Thus the Stoic or Spinozan ideal of emotional detachment is an illusion for us, an ideal perhaps, but one that we are simply not capable of. And if we make this assumption, then the injunction to cultivate detachment to the greatest extent possible will seem highly problematic, and the Stoic or Spinozan who claims to have achieved emotional detachment will be thought to be papering over his or her own deep (possibly thwarted) yearnings for love.

To the extent, moreover, that we love particular things or persons, we must be capable of resentment, sorrow, and anger. If threats against a loved one really leave one calm and philosophical from the start, the claim actually to love that person may be irretrievably undermined. In the abstract, the capacity to respond to threats philosophically may well be an ideal thing, a perfection. And since love for individuals by its very nature undercuts this capacity, love, as well as the need or desire for love, may constitute human weaknesses. But if these things are weaknesses, they are *basic* human weaknesses. By that I mean that they are weaknesses so endemic to our nature that if one seeks, like the Stoic, to avoid being subject to them, one is likely to get oneself into a worse position than one would have been in if one had simply accepted the weakness in oneself.[13] Love and our tendency to feel sorrow and resentment may be basic human weaknesses in this sense, because if one attempts not to love anyone and not to resent or be sad at anything, no matter how badly one is treated, one may cover up these sorts of feelings, but will also, in doing so, give them all sorts of free rein for subterranean mischief and eventual destructive effect within one's life.

Of course, some of these considerations might incline one to go to the opposite extreme from the Stoics and claim that resentment at the loss of things one loves or values may sink into the depths of our minds, but never completely dissolves. I do not see why we should believe this to be true, but, even if it is, there is no need to modify the conception of free action offered by FNW. It will simply turn out that all cases of complying with an unwelcome threat will qualify as unfree on their own theories, and we will be spared the burden of having to argue for the freedom of those who have a philosophical attitude in complying with threats. On the other hand, if the Stoics are right, and someone really could accommodate himself to all threats immediately and without emotion, there will still be no need to modify the theories of FNW.[14]

III

I would like now to show that the theories of FNW, properly under-stood and supported, have the important consequence that acting of one's own free will—what we shall for brevity sometimes call "free will"—is not necessary to moral responsibility, blameworthiness, and the like. In our earlier example of the reluctant bank clerk, the clerk does not hand over the money of his own free will because he acts from a desire he wishes he could rise above. But nothing in our

13. Cf. Pascal's aphorism: "men are so necessarily mad, that not to be mad would amount to another form of madness," in the *Pensées*, ed. T. S. Eliot (New York: Dutton, 1958), sec. 414, p. 110.

14. I shall not consider whether someone who is philosophical in complying with an effective threat must be thought to act under duress or to have been coerced into doing what he does.

description precludes that he acts thoughtlessly, forgetting that there is an alarm button nearby that he can push to foil the robber. And if that is his situation, then we will feel that he shouldn't hand over the money and is not only morally responsible but blameworthy for doing so.[15]

Frankfurt too believes that his bank clerk can be morally responsible and blameworthy for the way he acts under duress.[16] He also holds that it is one requisite of a good account of free action that moral responsibility should come out entailing freedom, and says that his own theory has that consequence. But it does not have that consequence, if, as we have argued, Frankfurt is mistaken in thinking that his theory commits him to calling his bank clerk a free agent. Even prescinding from Frankfurt's interpretation of his theory for cases of duress, it is not clear that Frankfurt can easily maintain that acting freely is necessary to moral responsibility. For on his account, someone struggling against a strong desire (e.g., an incipient addiction) who in the end gives in to that desire fails to act of his own free will. But nothing in this description forces us to say that the person who succumbs to his desire had to behave as he did, was compulsive rather than morally weak or, more generally, weak-willed. So, once again, Frankfurt will have to allow for cases where his definition of free will is not met but an agent is nonetheless morally responsible and even blameworthy for what he does, unless he takes the risky step of altogether denying the possibility of (blameworthy) moral weakness.

Note further that it sounds jarring and unnatural to say the (reluctant) clerk hands over the money of his own free will quite independently of any assumptions we make about whether he *had* to hand the money over or was *compelled* to do so. But this tends to show how important it is to bring in something like FNW's theories to explain our intuitive judgments about the clerk. For those theories explain why, even if he could have done otherwise, the bank clerk is judged not to act of his own free will. Of course, if the clerk for some reason really cannot do otherwise, then we may say he is not morally responsible for his actions. But as we have just seen, the judgment that

15. We may be tempted to say that he is (fully) responsible or blameworthy not for handing over the money, but only for not pushing the alarm button. However, since we would not naturally say that the clerk omits the button pushing of his own free will (cf. footnote 10, above), we are still left with a case of moral responsibility and culpability for a non-free act (omission). (I am indebted here to Bernard Berofsky.)

For a different attempt to argue for the possibility of being morally responsible for negligence or thoughtlessness in a situation where one does not act freely, see Don Locke, "Three Concepts of Free Action: I," Chapter 3 above, p. 109.

16. Frankfurt, Chapter 4, above, pp. 114–115, and 122.

someone can do otherwise does not entail the judgment that he acts of his own free will.[17] So even if being able to do otherwise is necessary to moral responsibility, that has no tendency to show that we must act of our own free will in order to be responsible for our actions.

Despite what we have said, it might nonetheless be objected at this point that moral responsibility requires freedom in *some* customary (philosophical) sense, even if it does not entail that one act *of one's own free will*. But even if such a sense of 'freedom' exists, why should it be considered immediately relevant to *freedom of will*? Perhaps the free-will problem is simply different from the problem of the conditions of moral responsibility and the contrary opinion only arises from the misconception that the importance of free will depends on its being necessary to moral responsibility.[18] More important still, if such a (further) sense of 'freedom' really were immediately at issue in the free-will question, it would follow that any proof that we sometimes (never) do things of our own free will would by itself be insufficient to show that we had (lacked) free will. And this consequence will surely seem counterintuitive to philosophers in the English-speaking tradition. After all, Paradigm Case "solutions" to the free-will problem are considered objectionable because they are based on the Paradigm Case Argument, not because they assume the special relevance of the notion of acting of one's own free will to the traditional problem of free will. So it cannot perhaps be an objection to the approach of the present paper that it rests on a similar assumption.

## IV

Although I have all along been defending rationality theories, I do not, in the end, think that any of them offers a totally adequate conception of freedom of will. I think they offer us necessary, but not

17. Cf. P. S. Greenspan, "Behavior Control and Freedom of Action," Chapter 9, below, pp. 196–198.

18. In the title essay of *In Defence of Free Will* (London: Allen & Unwin, 1967, p. 36), C. A. Campbell claims that free will is important only if it is necessary to moral responsibility. But the theories of FNW militate against Campbell's conclusion by pointing up how intrinsically undesirable certain sorts of unfreedom can be. If we accept their conception of freedom, then the cases of unwilling addiction and of "philosophical" calm-in-action both illustrate the importance free will has independently of its connection with moral action and moral responsibility.

I am not, however, proposing a complete dissociation of free will and moral responsibility. In the next section, we shall discuss a condition of autonomy in action which is necessary to free will and which seems necessary to moral responsibility as well. This common necessary condition can easily seem incompatible with determinism, and so it is also no part of my intention to deny that determinism poses a threat both to free will and to moral responsibility.

sufficient, conditions of freedom and that the conditions they omit are among the most important for understanding why free will has been such a perennial problem for philosophers.

In "Freedom of the Will and the Concept of a Person," Frankfurt makes clear his commitment to the sufficiency of his conditions for acting freely and claims, in particular, that the existence of free will or agency does not depend on how such freedom comes about.[19] It is precisely here that I (and others)[20] disagree with Frankfurt: certain ways of coming to fulfill Frankfurt's conditions of freedom seem, intuitively, to *deprive* one of free agency. Consider the following example. Robert, who is genuinely undecided between two conflicting first-order desires $X$ and $Y$, is visited by a hypnotist who decides to "solve" his problem by putting him in a trance and inducing in him a second-order volition in favor of $X$; as a result of having this second-order volition, Robert then acts to satisfy $X$, never suspecting that his decisiveness has been induced by the hypnotist. The example may bear the marks of science fiction, but it seems adequate, nonetheless, to point up the conceptual insufficiency of "rationality" conditions of free action. For we would all surely deny that Robert acts of his own free will, when he acts from the second-order volition induced by the hypnotist.

But it is important to consider why we want to say this. We would, after all, describe Robert as having *willingly* satisfied desire $X$; so in denying that he acts *of his own free will*, we must be implicitly assuming that so acting involves something more than willingness taken together with our previous rationality conditions. And I believe that this further condition, in simplest terms, comes down to the requirement that our actions be fully *our own*. The feeling that Robert does not, in satisfying $X$, act of his own free will reflects, I think, our belief that because of the particular way the hypnotist has intervened in his life, his act is not fully his own.[21] And the assumption that acting of one's

19. Chapter 1, p. 80. See also Chapter 4, above, pp. 120ff.
20. See D. Locke, Chapter 3, above, p. 105f.
21. Some kinds of intervention do *not* seem to deprive an agent of his freedom. If, instead of inducing a second-order volition in a given person, someone softens the force of one of his addictions—through a surgical intervention he is unaware of—so that he later finds it easier to resist the addiction, we might not want to deny that the person involved acted of his own free will in successfully resisting the addiction. Note too that the inducing of second-order volitions provides a much better example of an intervention that deprives an agent of freedom by rendering his actions not fully his own, than do the effective threats (or offers) we discussed earlier. I think this has something to do with the fact that someone who complies with a threat (or offer) *knows about the intervention of another person in the situation* and *himself makes a decision to do what*

own free will requires that one's actions be fully one's own also helps us to explain what the words 'one's own' are doing in the phrase 'of one's own free will'[22] and to understand the force of our intuitive distinction, in the above example, between freedom of will and mere willingness.

In order to act of one's *own* free will, then, one's actions must be fully one's own; one must in some sense act autonomously. But these locutions, however intuitive, are extremely vague, and, at this point, there are several problems that must be faced if we are to advance our understanding of free will. We will, to begin with, want to know whether anything more definite can be said about this autonomy that seems necessary to free will but not to be implied by anything in rationality theories. But we must also ask whether such a spelling out of the notion of autonomy can help us to understand the relevance of determinism to freedom of will. FNW's theories make it difficult to see how anyone could think that determinism ever presented a challenge to free will. And it is surely some sort of problem for those theories that they seem to offer no way to make sense of the age-old belief in such a challenge. (After all, for many of us "the problem of free will" is just an ellipsis for "the problem of free will and determinism.") If, however, some sort of autonomy is, as we have claimed, necessary to freedom of will, further specification of that notion may help to explain why determinism makes free will problematic by making it clear why determinism represents a challenge to autonomy thus specified.

Of course, it might turn out that the theories of FNW, even supplemented by an appropriately elaborate conception of autonomy, did not offer sufficient conditions for freedom of will, and that some further condition, e.g., being able to do otherwise, was necessary to freedom and was the aspect of free will on which the relevance of determinism depended.[23] But this suggestion must be treated with caution, since there have long been and even now continue to be important challenges to the notion that the ability to do otherwise is necessary to acting freely. Thus if what I have just been saying is correct, a good part of the free-will problem remains up in the air.

---

*that person wants;* neither of these things seems to be true of the person whose second-order volition is induced in the manner of our example.

22. Cf. W. F. R. Hardie, "My Own Free Will," *Philosophy*, XXXII, 120 (January 1957): 21–23.

23. It also might turn out that they did offer sufficient conditions for freedom of will, that those conditions were also sufficient for being able to do otherwise and that the relevance of determinism depended on this latter fact.

The theories of FNW offer significant necessary conditions of free will, and they have an explanatory power (and important implications) that even their proponents fail to recognize. But they leave other problems untouched; and I only hope that what we have said here may give some indication of the directions we must take in order to make further progress in understanding free will.

# II

## FREEDOM TO DO OTHERWISE AND MORAL RESPONSIBILITY

# 6

# Alternate Possibilities and Moral Responsibility

## HARRY G. FRANKFURT

A dominant role in nearly all recent inquiries into the free-will problem has been played by a principle which I shall call "the principle of alternate possibilities." This principle states that a person is morally responsible for what he has done only if he could have done otherwise. Its exact meaning is a subject of controversy, particularly concerning whether someone who accepts it is thereby committed to believing that moral responsibility and determinism are incompatible. Practically no one, however, seems inclined to deny or even to question that the principle of alternate possibilities (construed in some way or other) is true. It has generally seemed so overwhelmingly plausible that some philosophers have even characterized it as an *a priori* truth. People whose accounts of free will or of moral responsibility are radically at odds evidently find in it a firm and convenient common ground upon which they can profitably take their opposing stands.

But the principle of alternate possibilities is false. A person may well be morally responsible for what he has done even though he could not have done otherwise. The principle's plausibility is an illusion, which can be made to vanish by bringing the relevant moral phenomena into sharper focus.

## I

In seeking illustrations of the principle of alternate possibilities, it is most natural to think of situations in which the same circumstances

"Alternate Possibilities and Moral Responsibility" originally appeared in the *Journal of Philosophy*, 66 (December 1969), 828–39, © 1969 by the *Journal of Philosophy*, and is reprinted here with permission from Harry Frankfurt and from the *Journal of Philosophy*.

both bring it about that a person does something and make it impossible for him to avoid doing it. These include, for example, situations in which a person is coerced into doing something, or in which he is impelled to act by a hypnotic suggestion, or in which some inner compulsion drives him to do what he does. In situations of these kinds there are circumstances that make it impossible for the person to do otherwise, and these very circumstances also serve to bring it about that he does whatever it is that he does.

However, there may be circumstances that constitute sufficient conditions for a certain action to be performed by someone and that therefore make it impossible for the person to do otherwise, but that do not actually impel the person to act or in any way produce his action. A person may do something in circumstances that leave him no alternative to doing it, without these circumstances actually moving him or leading him to do it—without them playing any role, indeed, in bringing it about that he does what he does.

An examination of situations characterized by circumstances of this sort casts doubt, I believe, on the relevance to questions of moral responsibility of the fact that a person who has done something could not have done otherwise. I propose to develop some examples of this kind in the context of a discussion of coercion and to suggest that our moral intuitions concerning these examples tend to disconfirm the principle of alternate possibilities. Then I will discuss the principle in more general terms, explain what I think is wrong with it, and describe briefly and without argument how it might appropriately be revised.

## II

It is generally agreed that a person who has been coerced to do something did not do it freely and is not morally responsible for having done it. Now the doctrine that coercion and moral responsibility are mutually exclusive may appear to be no more than a somewhat particularized version of the principle of alternate possibilities. It is natural enough to say of a person who has been coerced to do something that he could not have done otherwise. And it may easily seem that being coerced deprives a person of freedom and of moral responsibility simply because it is a special case of being unable to do otherwise. The principle of alternate possibilities may in this way derive some credibility from its association with the very plausible proposition that moral responsibility is excluded by coercion.

It is not right, however, that it should do so. The fact that a person was coerced to act as he did may entail both that he could not have done otherwise and that he bears no moral responsibility for his action. But his lack of moral responsibility is not entailed by his having been unable to do otherwise. The doctrine that coercion excludes moral responsibility is not correctly understood, in other words, as a particularized version of the principle of alternate possibilities.

Let us suppose that someone is threatened convincingly with a penalty he finds unacceptable and that he then does what is required of him by the issuer of the threat. We can imagine details that would make it reasonable for us to think that the person was coerced to perform the action in question, that he could not have done otherwise, and that he bears no moral responsibility for having done what he did. But just what is it about situations of this kind that warrants the judgment that the threatened person is not morally responsible for his act?

This question may be approached by considering situations of the following kind. Jones decides for reasons of his own to do something, then someone threatens him with a very harsh penalty (so harsh that any reasonable person would submit to the threat) unless he does precisely that, and Jones does it. Will we hold Jones morally responsible for what he has done? I think this will depend on the roles we think were played, in leading him to act, by his original decision and by the threat.

One possibility is that $Jones_1$ is not a reasonable man: he is, rather, a man who does what he has once decided to do no matter what happens next and no matter what the cost. In that case, the threat actually exerted no effective force upon him. He acted without any regard to it, very much as if he were not aware that it had been made. If this is indeed the way it was, the situation did not involve coercion at all. The threat did not lead $Jones_1$ to do what he did. Nor was it in fact sufficient to have prevented him from doing otherwise: if his earlier decision had been to do something else, the threat would not have deterred him in the slightest. It seems evident that in these circumstances the fact that $Jones_1$ was threatened in no way reduces the moral responsibility he would otherwise bear for his act. This example, however, is not a counterexample either to the doctrine that coercion excuses or to the principle of alternate possibilities. For we have supposed that $Jones_1$ is a man upon whom the threat had no coercive effect and, hence, that it did not actually deprive him of alternatives to doing what he did.

Another possibility is that $Jones_2$ was stampeded by the threat. Given that threat, he would have performed that action regardless of what decision he had already made. The threat upset him so profoundly, moreover, that he completely forgot his own earlier decision and did what was demanded of him entirely because he was terrified of the penalty with which he was threatened. In this case, it is not relevant to his having performed the action that he had already decided on his own to perform it. When the chips were down he thought of nothing but the threat, and fear alone led him to act. The fact that at an earlier time Jones$_2$ had decided for his own reasons to act in just that way may be relevant to an evaluation of his character; he may bear full moral responsibility for having made *that* decision. But he can hardly be said to be morally responsible for his action. For he performed the action simply as a result of the coercion to which he was subjected. His earlier decision played no role in bringing it about that he did what he did, and it would therefore be gratuitous to assign it a role in the moral evaluation of his action.

Now consider a third possibility. Jones$_3$ was neither stampeded by the threat nor indifferent to it. The threat impressed him, as it would impress any reasonable man, and he would have submitted to it wholeheartedly if he had not already made a decision that coincided with the one demanded of him. In fact, however, he performed the action in question on the basis of the decision he had made before the threat was issued. When he acted, he was not actually motivated by the threat but solely by the considerations that had originally commended the action to him. It was not the threat that led him to act, though it would have done so if he had not already provided himself with a sufficient motive for performing the action in question.

No doubt it will be very difficult for anyone to know, in a case like this one, exactly what happened. Did Jones$_3$ perform the action because of the threat, or were his reasons for acting simply those which had already persuaded him to do so? Or did he act on the basis of two motives, each of which was sufficient for his action? It is not impossible, however, that the situation should be clearer than situations of this kind usually are. And suppose it is apparent to us that Jones$_3$ acted on the basis of his own decision and not because of the threat. Then I think we would be justified in regarding his moral responsibility for what he did as unaffected by the threat even though, since he would in any case have submitted to the threat, he could not have avoided doing what he did. It would be entirely reasonable for us to make the same judgment concerning his moral responsibility that we would have made if we had not known of the threat. For the threat did not in fact influence his performance of the action. He did what he did just as if the threat had not been made at all.

III

The case of Jones$_3$ may appear at first glance to combine coercion and moral responsibility, and thus to provide a counterexample to the doctrine that coercion excuses. It is not really so certain that it does so, however, because it is unclear whether the example constitutes a genuine instance of coercion. Can we say of Jones$_3$ that he was coerced to do something, when he had already decided on his own to do it and when he did it entirely on the basis of that decision? Or would it be more correct to say that Jones$_3$ was not coerced to do what he did, even though he himself recognized that there was an irresistible force at work in virtue of which he had to do it? My own linguistic intuitions lead me toward the second alternative, but they are somewhat equivocal. Perhaps we can say either of these things, or perhaps we must add a qualifying explanation to whichever of them we say.

This murkiness, however, does not interfere with our drawing an important moral from an examination of the example. Suppose we decide to say that Jones$_3$ was *not* coerced. Our basis for saying this will clearly be that it is incorrect to regard a man as being coerced to do something unless he does it *because* of the coercive force exerted against him. The fact that an irresistible threat is made will not, then, entail that the person who receives it is coerced to do what he does. It will also be necessary that the threat is what actually accounts for doing it. On the other hand, suppose we decide to say that Jones$_3$ *was* coerced. Then we will be bound to admit that being coerced does not exclude being morally responsible. And we will also surely be led to the view that coercion affects the judgment of a person's moral responsibility only when the person acts as he does because he is coerced to do so—i.e., when the fact that he is coerced is what accounts for his action.

Whichever we decide to say, then, we will recognize that the doctrine that coercion excludes moral responsibility is not a particularized version of the principle of alternate possibilities. Situations in which a person who does something cannot do otherwise because he is subject to coercive power are either not instances of coercion at all, or they are situations in which the person may still be morally responsible for what he does if it is not because of the coercion that he does it. When we excuse a person who has been coerced, we do not excuse him because he was unable to do otherwise. Even though a person is subject to a coercive force that precludes his performing any action but one, he may nonetheless bear full moral responsibility for performing that action.

## IV

To the extent that the principle of alternate possibilities derives its plausibility from association with the doctrine that coercion excludes moral responsibility, a clear understanding of the latter diminishes the appeal of the former. Indeed the case of Jones$_3$ may appear to do more than illuminate the relationship between the two doctrines. It may well seem to provide a decisive counterexample to the principle of alternate possibilities and thus to show that this principle is false. For the irresistibility of the threat to which Jones$_3$ is subjected might well be taken to mean that he cannot but perform the action he performs. And yet the threat, since Jones$_3$ performs the action without regard to it, does not reduce his moral responsibility for what he does.

The following objection will doubtless be raised against the suggestion that the case of Jones$_3$ is a counterexample to the principle of alternate possibilities. There is perhaps a sense in which Jones$_3$ cannot do otherwise than perform the action he performs, since he is a reasonable man and the threat he encounters is sufficient to move any reasonable man. But it is not this sense that is germane to the principle of alternate possibilities. His knowledge that he stands to suffer an intolerably harsh penalty does not mean that Jones$_3$, strictly speaking, *cannot* perform any action but the one he does perform. After all it is still open to him, and this is crucial, to defy the threat if he wishes to do so and to accept the penalty his action would bring down upon him. In the sense in which the principle of alternate possibilities employs the concept of "could have done otherwise," Jones$_3$'s inability to resist the threat does not mean that he cannot do otherwise than perform the action he performs. Hence the case of Jones$_3$ does not constitute an instance contrary to the principle.

I do not propose to consider in what sense the concept of "could have done otherwise" figures in the principle of alternate possibilities, nor will I attempt to measure the force of the objection I have just described.[1] For I believe that whatever force this objection may be thought to have can be deflected by altering the example in the following way.[2] Suppose someone—Black, let us say—wants Jones$_4$ to

1. The two main concepts employed in the principle of alternate possibilities are "morally responsible" and "could have done otherwise." To discuss the principle without analyzing either of these concepts may well seem like an attempt at piracy. The reader should take notice that my Jolly Roger is now unfurled.
2. After thinking up the example that I am about to develop I learned that Robert Nozick, in lectures given several years ago, had formulated an example of the same general type and had proposed it as a counterexample to the principle of alternate possibilities.

perform a certain action. Black is prepared to go to considerable lengths to get his way, but he prefers to avoid showing his hand unnecessarily. So he waits until Jones$_4$ is about to make up his mind what to do, and he does nothing unless it is clear to him (Black is an excellent judge of such things) that Jones$_4$ is going to decide to do something *other* than what he wants him to do. If it does become clear that Jones$_4$ is going to decide to do something else, Black takes effective steps to ensure that Jones$_4$ decides to do, and that he does do, what he wants him to do.[3] Whatever Jones$_4$'s initial preferences and inclinations, then, Black will have his way.

What steps will Black take, if he believes he must take steps, in order to ensure that Jones$_4$ decides and acts as he wishes? Anyone with a theory concerning what "could have done otherwise" means may answer this question for himself by describing whatever measures he would regard as sufficient to guarantee that, in the relevant sense, Jones$_4$ cannot do otherwise. Let Black pronounce a terrible threat, and in this way both force Jones$_4$ to perform the desired action and prevent him from performing a forbidden one. Let Black give Jones$_4$ a potion, or put him under hypnosis, and in some such way as these generate in Jones$_4$ an irresistible inner compulsion to perform the act Black wants performed and to avoid others. Or let Black manipulate the minute processes of Jones$_4$'s brain and nervous system in some more direct way, so that causal forces running in and out of his synapses and along the poor man's nerves determine that he chooses to act and that he does act in the one way and not in any other. Given any conditions under which it will be maintained that Jones$_4$ cannot do otherwise, in other words, let Black bring it about that those conditions prevail. The structure of the example is flexible enough, I think, to find a way around any charge of irrelevance by accommodating the doctrine on which the charge is based.[4]

3. The assumption that Black can predict what Jones$_4$ will decide to do does not beg the question of determinism. We can imagine that Jones$_4$, has often confronted the alternatives—$A$ and $B$—that he now confronts, and that his face has invariably twitched when he was about to decide to do $A$ and never when he was about to decide to do $B$. Knowing this, and observing the twitch, Black would have a basis for prediction. This does, to be sure, suppose that there is some sort of causal relation between Jones$_4$'s state at the time of the twitch and his subsequent states. But any plausible view of decision or of action will allow that reaching a decision and performing an action both involve earlier and later phases, with causal relations between them, and such that the earlier phases are not themselves part of the decision or of the action. The example does not require that these earlier phases be deterministically related to still earlier events.

4. The example is also flexible enough to allow for the elimination of Black altogether. Anyone who thinks that the effectiveness of the example is undermined by its reliance on a human manipulator, who imposes his will on Jones$_4$, can substitute for Black a machine programmed to do what Black does. If this is still not good enough,

Now suppose that Black never has to show his hand because Jones$_4$, for reasons of his own, decides to perform and does perform the very action Black wants him to perform. In that case, it seems clear, Jones$_4$ will bear precisely the same moral responsibility for what he does as he would have borne if Black had not been ready to take steps to ensure that he do it. It would be quite unreasonable to excuse Jones$_4$ for his action, or to withhold the praise to which it would normally entitle him, on the basis of the fact that he could not have done otherwise. This fact played no role at all in leading him to act as he did. He would have acted the same even if it had not been a fact. Indeed, everything happened just as it would have happened without Black's presence in the situation and without his readiness to intrude into it.

In this example there are sufficient conditions for Jones$_4$'s performing the action in question. What action he performs is not up to him. Of course it is in a way up to him whether he acts on his own or as a result of Black's intervention. That depends upon what action he himself is inclined to perform. But whether he finally acts on his own or as a result of Black's intervention, he performs the same action. He has no alternative but to do what Black wants him to do. If he does it on his own, however, his moral responsibility for doing it is not affected by the fact that Black was lurking in the background with sinister intent, since this intent never comes into play.

V

The fact that a person could not have avoided doing something is a sufficient condition of his having done it. But, as some of my examples show, this fact may play no role whatever in the explanation of why he did it. It may not figure at all among the circumstances that actually brought it about that he did what he did, so that his action is to be accounted for on another basis entirely. Even though the person was unable to do otherwise, that is to say, it may not be the case that he acted as he did *because* he could not have done otherwise. Now if someone had no alternative to performing a certain action but did not perform it because he was unable to do otherwise, then he would have performed exactly the same action even if he *could* have done otherwise. The circumstances that made it impossible for him to do otherwise could have been subtracted from the situation without affecting

---

forget both Black and the machine and suppose that their role is played by natural forces involving no will or design at all.

what happened or why it happened in any way. Whatever it was that actually led the person to do what he did, or that made him do it, would have led him to do it or made him do it even if it had been possible for him to do something else instead.

Thus it would have made no difference, so far as concerns his action or how he came to perform it, if the circumstances that made it impossible for him to avoid performing it had not prevailed. The fact that he could not have done otherwise clearly provides no basis for supposing that he *might* have done otherwise if he had been able to do so. When a fact is in this way irrelevant to the problem of accounting for a person's action it seems quite gratuitous to assign it any weight in the assessment of his moral responsibility. Why should the fact be considered in reaching a moral judgment concerning the person when it does not help in any way to understand either what made him act as he did or what, in other circumstances, he might have done?

This, then, is why the principle of alternate possibilities is mistaken. It asserts that a person bears no moral responsibility—that is, he is to be excused—for having performed an action if there were circumstances that made it impossible for him to avoid performing it. But there may be circumstances that make it impossible for a person to avoid performing some action without those circumstances in any way bringing it about that he performs that action. It would surely be no good for the person to refer to circumstances of this sort in an effort to absolve himself of moral responsibility for performing the action in question. For those circumstances, by hypothesis, actually had nothing to do with his having done what he did. He would have done precisely the same thing, and he would have been led or made in precisely the same way to do it, even if they had not prevailed.

We often do, to be sure, excuse people for what they have done when they tell us (and we believe them) that they could not have done otherwise. But this is because we assume that what they tell us serves to explain why they did what they did. We take it for granted that they are not being disingenuous, as a person would be who cited as an excuse the fact that he could not have avoided doing what he did but who knew full well that it was not at all because of this that he did it.

What I have said may suggest that the principle of alternate possibilities should be revised so as to assert that a person is not morally responsible for what he has done if he did it because he could not have done otherwise. It may be noted that this revision of the principle does not seriously affect the arguments of those who have relied on the original principle in their efforts to maintain that moral responsibility and determinism are incompatible. For if it was causally determined that a person perform a certain action, then it will be true that the person performed it because of those causal determinants. And if the fact that it was causally determined that a person perform a certain action means that the person could not have done otherwise, as philosophers who argue for the incompatibility thesis characteristically suppose, then the fact that it was causally determined that a person perform a certain action will mean that the person performed it because he could not have done otherwise. The revised principle of alternate possibilities will entail, on this assumption concerning the meaning of 'could have done otherwise', that a person is not morally responsible for what he has done if it was causally determined that he do it. I do not believe, however, that this revision of the principle is acceptable.

Suppose a person tells us that he did what he did because he was unable to do otherwise; or suppose he makes the similar statement that he did what he did because he had to do it. We do often accept statements like these (if we believe them) as valid excuses, and such statements may well seem at first glance to invoke the revised principle of alternate possibilities. But I think that when we accept such statements as valid excuses it is because we assume that we are being told more than the statements strictly and literally convey. We understand the person who offers the excuse to mean that he did what he did *only because* he was unable to do otherwise, or *only because* he had to do it. And we understand him to mean, more particularly, that when he did what he did it was not because that was what he really wanted to do. The principle of alternate possibilities should thus be replaced, in my opinion, by the following principle: a person is not morally responsible for what he has done if he did it only because he could not have done otherwise. This principle does not appear to conflict with the view that moral responsibility is compatible with determinism.

The following may all be true: there were circumstances that made it impossible for a person to avoid doing something; these circumstances actually played a role in bringing it about that he did it, so that it is correct to say that he did it because he could not have done otherwise; the person really wanted to do what he did; he did it because it was what he really wanted to do, so that it is not correct to say that he did what he did only because he could not have done otherwise. Under these conditions, the person may well be morally responsible for what he has done. On the other hand, he will not be morally responsible for what he has done if he did it only because he could not have done otherwise, even if what he did was something he really wanted to do.

# 7

## Ability and Responsibility

———————

### PETER VAN INWAGEN

I

There was a time when philosophers would debate the relative merits of the doctrines of "liberty" and "necessity," or, as we should say today, debate whether it is more reasonable to believe in free will or in universal causal determinism. As everyone knows, the parties to this debate shared a premise: that free will and universal causal determinism are incompatible. And, as everyone knows, there arose a philosophical tradition—represented by Hobbes, Hume, Jonathan Edwards, Mill, and Moritz Schlick—in which just this premise is denied. Thus the debate between the libertarians and necessitarians was undercut, and most of the debates about free will today are, as they have been for a long time, essentially debates about whether free will and determinism are compatible or incompatible.

But why should anyone care whether we have free will or whether determinism is true? The first part of this question is perhaps easier to answer than the second: we care about free will because we care about moral responsibility, and we are persuaded that we cannot make ascriptions of moral responsibility to agents who lack free will. Recently, however, Harry Frankfurt has denied just this principle, or, at least, a principle that sounds very much like it, which he calls the Principle of Alternate Possibilities.[1] His formulation of the Principle of Alternate Possibilities is

"Ability and Responsibility" originally appeared in the *Philosophical Review*, 87 (April 1978), 201–24, © 1978 by the *Philosophical Review*, and is reprinted here with permission from Peter van Inwagen and from the *Philosophical Review*.
1. "Alternate Possibilities and Moral Responsibility," Chapter 6, above.

PAP A person is morally responsible for what he has done only if he could have done otherwise. (p. 143)

If Frankfurt has made out a good case for the falsity of PAP (and I think he has), then it would seem that he has undercut the debate between the "compatibilists" and the "incompatibilists" (to use the contemporary jargon) in a way very similar to the way in which Hobbes and others undercut the debate between the libertarians and the necessitarians.

Frankfurt supports his contention that PAP is false by means of a certain style of counterexample; I shall call counterexamples in this style, "Frankfurt counterexamples."[2] The following Frankfurt counterexample is due to David Blumenfeld. It is worked out with rather more concrete detail than any of Frankfurt's own counterexamples:

> Suppose that the presence of a certain atmospheric reaction always causes Smith to decide to attack the person nearest to him and to actually do so. Suppose also that he always flushes a deep red when he considers and decides *against* performing an act of violence and that under certain circumstances the atmospheric reaction is triggered by the appearance of just this shade of red. Now imagine that on a day on which circumstances are favorable to the triggering of the reaction, Smith considers whether or not to strike a person with whom he is conversing, decides in favor of it, and forthwith does so.[3]

The general idea behind Frankfurt counterexamples is this. An agent $S$ is in the process of deciding which of $n$ alternative acts $A_i \ldots, A_k \ldots, A_n$ to perform. He believes (correctly) that he cannot avoid performing some one of these acts. He decides to perform, and, acting on this decision, does perform $A_k$. But, unknown to him, there were various factors that *would have* prevented him from performing (and perhaps even from deciding to perform) any of $A_i \ldots, A_n$ *except* $A_k$. These factors would have "come into play" if he had shown any tendency towards performing (perhaps even towards deciding to perform) any of $A_i \ldots, A_n$ except $A_k$. But since he in fact showed no such tendency, these factors remained mere unactualized dispositions of the objects constituting his environment: they played no role whatever in his deciding to perform or in his performing $A_k$.

2. Or perhaps they should be called "Frankfurt-Nozick" counterexamples. See *n*. 2 (p. 148) to Frankfurt's article.

3. David Blumenfeld, "The Principle of Alternate Possibilities," *Journal of Philosophy*, LXVIII (1971), 339–345, *n*. 3 (p. 341).

According to Frankfurt, it is evident that in such cases we should say (*i*) that $S$ had no alternative to performing $A_k$, couldn't have done otherwise than perform $A_k$, and (*ii*) $S$ is nonetheless responsible for having performed $A_k$ (or, at least, if he is *not* responsible for having performed $A_k$, this must be due to some factor other than his inability to perform any act other than $A_k$ for the reason described).

Now if Frankfurt has indeed shown that PAP is false, this may be of no great consequence. For it may well be that some trivial modification of PAP is immune to Frankfurt counterexamples and that this modified version of PAP entails that if universal causal determinism and incompatibilism are both true, then all our ascriptions of moral responsibility are false. Frankfurt argues that this is not the case, however, and that what one might call the "correct version" of PAP (that is, the correct principle governing excuse from responsibility in cases in which alternate possibilities for action are absent) cannot be used to show that determinism and moral responsibility are in conflict.[4] I shall not in this paper try to determine whether Frankfurt's proposed principle is true or false, or discuss whether it in fact plays a role in our deliberations about moral responsibility. I shall instead exhibit three principles, which, if they are not "versions" of PAP, are at least principles very similar to PAP, and which *do* play a role in our deliberations about responsibility. I shall argue that these principles are immune to Frankfurt-style counterexamples. (I shall call counterexamples that are directed against principles similar to but distinct from PAP, and which are as strategically similar to Frankfurt counterexamples as is possible, Frankfurt-*style* counterexamples. I shall reserve the term "Frankfurt counterexample" for counterexamples directed just against PAP itself.)

PAP, as Frankfurt formulates it, is a principle about performed acts (things we have done). In Part II, I shall consider a principle about *unperformed* acts (things we have left undone). In Part III, I shall consider two principles about the *consequences* of what we have done (or left undone). In Part IV, I shall argue that if these three principles are true and if a version of incompatibilism appropriate to each is true, then determinism and moral responsibility are in conflict, even given that PAP is false.

## II

Consider the following principle (the Principle of Possible Action):

4. The "correct version" of PAP is: "A person is not morally responsible for what he has done if he did it only because he could not have done otherwise" (p. 152).

> PPA A person is morally responsible for failing to perform a given act
> only if he could have performed that act.

This principle is intuitively very plausible. But the same might have been said about PAP. Can we show that PPA is false by constructing a counterexample to it that is like Frankfurt's counterexamples to PAP? An adaptation to the case of unperformed acts of Frankfurt's general strategy would, I think, look something like this: an agent is in the process of deciding whether or not to perform a certain act $A$. He decides not to perform $A$, and, owing to this decision, refrains from performing $A$.[5] But, unknown to him, there were various factors that *would have* prevented him from performing (and perhaps even from deciding to perform) $A$. These factors would have come into play if he had shown any tendency towards performing (perhaps even towards deciding to perform) $A$. But since he in fact showed no such tendency, these factors remained mere unactualized dispositions of the objects constituting his environment: they played no role whatever in his deciding not to perform or his failure to perform $A$.

Putative counterexamples to PPA prepared according to this recipe produce, in me at least, no inclination to reject this principle. Let us look at one.

Suppose I look out the window of my house and see a man being robbed and beaten by several powerful-looking assailants. It occurs to me that perhaps I had better call the police. I reach for the telephone and then stop. It crosses my mind that if I do call the police, the robbers might hear of it and wreak their vengeance on me. And, in any case, the police would probably want me to make a statement and perhaps even to go to the police station and identify someone in a lineup or look through endless books of photographs of thugs. And it's after eleven already, and I have to get up early tomorrow. So I decide "not to get involved," return to my chair and put the matter firmly out of my mind. Now suppose also that, quite unknown to me, there has been some sort of disaster at the telephone exchange, and that every telephone in the city is out of order and will be for several hours.

---

5. This schema and the instance of it that follows involve the agent's intentionally refraining from performing a given act. Of course not every case in which we might want to consider holding an agent responsible for failing to perform some act is a case in which the agent intentionally refrains from performing that act: he may never even have considered performing that act. This distinction between two ways of failing to perform a given act is of no importance for our present purposes. The points made in the text would be equally valid if we had chosen to examine a case in which the agent fails even to think of performing the act whose nonperformance we are considering holding him responsible for.

Am I responsible for failing to call the police? Of course not. I couldn't have called them. I may be responsible for failing to *try* to call the police (that much I *could* have done), or for refraining from calling the police, or for having let myself, over the years, become the sort of man who doesn't (try to) call the police under such circumstances. I may be responsible for being selfish and cowardly. But I am simply not responsible for failing to call the police. This "counterexample," therefore, is not a counterexample at all: PPA is unscathed.

It is, of course, proverbially hard to prove a universal negative proposition. Perhaps there are Frankfurt-style counterexamples to PPA. But I don't see how to construct one. I conclude that Frankfurt's style of argument cannot be used to refute PPA.

## III

Both PAP and PPA are principles about acts, performed or unperformed. But, in fact, when we make ascriptions of moral responsibility, we do not normally say things like "You are responsible for killing Jones" or "He is responsible for failing to water the marigolds." We are much more likely to say "You are responsible for Jones's death" or "He is responsible for the shocking state the marigolds are in." That is, we normally hold people responsible not for their acts or failures to act (at least explicitly), but for the results or consequences of these acts and failures. What, ontologically speaking, are results or consequences of action and inaction? What sorts of thing are Jones's death and the shocking state the marigolds are in? The general terms "event" and "state of affairs" seem appropriate ones to apply to these items. But what are events and states of affairs? This question, like all interesting philosophical questions I know of, has no generally accepted answer. Philosophers do not seem even to be able to agree whether events and states of affairs are particulars or universals. In order to avoid taking sides in the debate about this, I shall adopt the following strategy. I shall state a certain principle about excuse from responsibility that seems to me to be a plausible one, provided the events or states of affairs we hold people responsible for are particulars. *And* I shall state a similar principle that seems to me to be plausible, provided the events or states of affairs we hold people responsible for are universals. For each of these principles, I shall argue that it cannot be refuted by Frankfurt-style counterexamples. The first of these principles (which I shall call principles of possible prevention) is:

PPP1 A person is morally responsible for a certain event (particular)
    only if he could have prevented it.

This principle is about events; but if we were to examine a principle, otherwise similar, about "state-of-affairs particulars" (for example, the way secondary education is organized in Switzerland)[6] we could employ arguments that differ from the following arguments only in verbal detail.

What are events if they are particulars? They are items that can be witnessed (at least if they consist in visible changes in visible particulars), remembered, and reported.[7] They are typically denoted by phrases like "the fall of the Alamo," "the death of Caesar," "the death of Caesar in 44 b.c.," and "what Bill saw happen in the garden."[8] How shall we identify and individuate event-particulars (hereinafter, "events")? Individuating particulars, whether events, tables, or human beings is always a tricky business. (Consider the Ship of Theseus.) As Davidson says,

> Before we enthusiastically embrace an ontology of events we will want to think long and hard about the criteria for individuating them. I am inclined to think we can do as well for events generally as we can for physical objects (which is not very well). . . .[9]

In a paper later than the one this quotation is taken from, Davidson tries to "do as well." He tells us that finding a satisfactory criterion of individuation for events will consist in providing "a satisfactory filling for the blank in:

If $x$ and $y$ are events, then $x = y$ if and only if _____"[10]

The "filling" he suggests for this blank is (roughly) "$x$ and $y$ have the same causes and effects." The biconditional so obtained, is, I have no

---

6. Perhaps it is debatable whether this phrase designates a particular.

7. I doubt, however, whether they can be anticipated. The objects of anticipation and other "future-directed" attitudes are, I think, universals.

8. Perhaps the last of these phrases could also be used to name an event-universal. We seem to be using it this way if we say, "What Bill saw happen in the garden happens all too frequently." But, I think, we use it to name a particular when we say, "What Bill saw happen in the garden last night will live in infamy," or "could have been prevented with a little foresight." The phrases "the fall of the Alamo" and "the death of Caesar," however, seem to be suited only for denoting particulars: even if the Alamo had fallen twice, even if Caesar (like Lazarus) had died twice, we could not say, "The fall of the Alamo has happened twice" or "The death of Caesar has happened twice." (This is not due, or not due *solely*, to the presence of the definite article in these phrases, for we can say, "The thing Bill fears most has happened twice.")

9. From Davidson's contribution to a symposium on events and event-descriptions in *Fact and Existence* ed. by J. Margolis (Oxford, 1969), p. 84.

10. "The Individuation of Events," in *Essays in Honor of Carl G. Hempel* ed. by N. Rescher (Dordrecht, 1969), p. 225.

doubt, true. But this biconditional will not be "satisfactory" for our purpose, which is the evaluation of PPP1. What we want to be able to do is to tell whether some event that *would* happen if what we earlier called "unactualized dispositions of the objects constituting the agent's environment" were to come into play, is the same as some event (the event responsibility for which we are enquiring about) that actually *has* happened; that is, we want to know how to tell of some given event whether *it*, that very same event, would (nevertheless) have happened if things had been different in certain specified ways. (For when we ask whether an agent could have *prevented* a certain event *E* by doing, say, *X*, we shall have to be able to answer the question whether *E* would *nonetheless* have happened if the agent had done *X*.)

To see why Davidson's criterion cannot be used to answer our sort of question about event-identity, consider the following formally similar criterion of individuation for persons: "*x* and *y* are the same person if and only if *x* and *y* have the same blood relatives (including siblings)." This criterion, while *true*, does not help us if we are interested in counterfactual questions about persons. For, obviously, any given man might have had different relatives from those he in fact has (he might have had an additional brother, for example). Davidson's proposed criterion is of no help to us for what is essentially the same reason: any given event might have had different effects from the effects it has in fact had. For example, if an historian writes, "Even if the murder of Caesar had not resulted in a civil war, it would nevertheless have led to widespread bloodshed," he does not convict himself of conceptual confusion. But he is certainly presupposing that the very event we call "the murder of Caesar" might have had different effects.

The above considerations are not offered in criticism of Davidson's criterion, which is, after all, *true*, and may be a very useful criterion to employ (say) when we are asking whether a given brain-event and a given mental event are one event or two. But Davidson's criterion is not the *sort* of criterion we need. We need a criterion that stands to Davidson's criterion as "*x* and *y* are the same human being if and only if *x* and *y* have the same causal genesis" stands to the above criterion of personal identity. (I use "causal genesis" with deliberate vagueness. A *necessary* condition for *x* and *y* having the same causal genesis is "their" having developed from the same sperm and egg.[11] But this is not

11. Or so it seems to me. Of course a Cartesian (for example) will have a different view of the matter.

sufficient, or "identical"—monozygotic—twins would be *numerically* identical.) This criterion can be used to make sense of talk about what some particular person would have been like if things had gone very differently for him.[12] Can we devise a criterion for counterfactual talk about events that is at least no *worse* than our criterion for persons? I would suggest that we simply truncate Davidson's criterion: *x* is the same event as *y* if and only if *x* and *y* have the same causes. (Note the similarity of this criterion to the causal-genesis criterion of personal identity.) I do not know how to justify my intuition that this criterion is correct, any more than I know how to justify my belief in the causal-genesis criterion. But, of course, arguments must come to an end somewhere. I can only suggest that since substances (like human beings and tables) should be individuated by their causal origins, and since we are talking about events that, like substances, are particulars, the present proposal is plausible. Moreover, I am aware that this proposed criterion is vague. It is not clear in every case of, say, a story about the events leading up to Caesar's murder, whether it would be correct to say that the murder had "the same causes" in the story that it had in reality. But I think the notion of *same event* is clear just insofar as the notion of *same causes* is clear. And this latter notion is surely not hopelessly unclear: if Cleopatra had poisoned Caesar in 48, then, clearly, there would have happened an event that has not in fact happened, an event that it would have been correct to call "Caesar's death," and which would have had different causes from the event that *is* called "Caesar's death." And, just as clearly, we cannot say of the event we in fact call "Caesar's death," "Suppose *it* had been caused four years earlier by Cleopatra's poisoning Caesar in Alexandria." Moreover, it is hardly to be supposed that we should be able to devise a criterion that will resolve all "puzzle cases," since we are unable to devise such a criterion for people, mountains, or tables.[13]

12. Cf. Saul Kripke, "Naming and Necessity," in *Semantics of Natural Language* ed. by D. Davidson and G. Harman (Dordrecht, 1972), pp. 312–314.

13. A theory of event-particulars that is inconsistent with the view presented in this paper is held by R. M. Martin and Jaegwon Kim. (See Martin's contribution to the symposium referred to in *n.* 9, and, for Kim's latest published views on events, "Causation, Nomic Subsumption, and the Concept of Event," *Journal of Philosophy* LXX (1973), 217–236). If we abstract from the particular twists that each of these authors gives to his own account of events, we may say that, on the "Kim-Martin" theory, the class of events is the class of substance-property-time triples. For example Caesar's death is the triple (Caesar, being dead, 15 March 44 B.C.). (Strictly speaking, the term "15 March 44 B.C." in the preceding sentence should be replaced with a term designating the precise instant at which Caesar died.) A "Kim-Martin" event *happens* just in the case that its first term acquires its second term at its third term. However useful Kim-Martin events may be in certain contexts of discussion, I do not think it is correct to think of them as particulars. They are, rather, highly specified universals, just as the property *being the*

Let us now return to PPP1. Can we devise a Frankfurt-style counterexample to this principle? Let us try.

Gunnar shoots and kills Ridley (intentionally), thereby bringing about Ridley's death, a certain event. But there is some factor, $F$, which (*i*) played no causal role in Ridley's death, and (*ii*) would have caused Ridley's death *if* Gunnar had not shot him (or, since factor $F$ might have caused Ridley's death *by* causing Gunnar to shoot him, perhaps we should say, "if Gunnar had decided not to shoot him"), and (*iii*) is such that Gunnar could not have prevented it from causing Ridley's death except by killing (or by deciding to kill) Ridley himself. So it would seem that Gunnar is responsible for Ridley's death, though he could not have prevented Ridley's death.

It is easy to see that this story is simply inconsistent. What is in fact denoted by "Ridley's death" is not, according to the story, caused by factor $F$. Therefore, if Gunnar had not shot Ridley, and, as a result, factor $F$ had caused Ridley to die, then there *would have been* an event denoted by "Ridley's death" which had factor $F$ as (one of) its cause(s). But then this event would have been an event other than the event *in fact* denoted by "Ridley's death"; the event in fact denoted by "Ridley's death" would not have happened at all. But if this story is inconsistent it is not a counterexample to PPP1. And I am unable to see how to construct a putative Frankfurt-style counterexample to PPP1 that cannot be shown to be inconsistent by an argument of this sort.

Let us now turn to a principle about universals:

PPP2 A person is morally responsible for a certain state of affairs only if (that state of affairs obtains and) he could have prevented it from obtaining.[14]

---

*tallest man* is a highly specified (in fact, "definite") universal (cf. *n.* 20). This property, though only one man can have it, is nonetheless such that it *could have* been possessed by someone other than the man who in fact has it. Similarly, any Kim-Martin event that happens *could have* been caused by quite different antecedent events from those that in fact caused it. To suppose that event-particulars have this feature is to violate my intuitions (at any rate) about particulars. An additional problem: every Kim-Martin event is such that there is some particular moment (its third term) such that the event *must* happen just at that moment if it happens at all. But surely Caesar's death might have happened at least a few moments earlier or later than it in fact did, just as a given man might have been born (or even conceived) at least a few moments earlier or later than he in fact was.

14. Nothing in PPP1 corresponds to the parenthetical qualification "that state of affairs obtains and" in this principle. So far as I can see, to say of a given event-particular that it "happens" is equivalent to saying that it exists. And, of course, there exist no events that do not exist. Thus there exist no events that do not happen. But states of affairs may exist without obtaining, just as propositions may exist without being true or properties without being instantiated.

The states of affairs "quantified over" in this principle are universals in the way propositions are universals. Just as there are many different ways the concrete particulars that make up our surroundings could be arranged that would be sufficient for the truth of a given proposition, so there are many different ways they could be arranged that would be sufficient for the *obtaining* of a given state of affairs. Consider, for example, the state of affairs that consists in Caesar's being murdered. This state of affairs obtains *because* certain conspirators stabbed Caesar at Rome in 44 B.C., but (since it is a universal), *it*, that very same state of affairs, *might have* obtained because (say) Cleopatra had poisoned him at Alexandria in 48. But this is a bit vague. In order the better to talk about "states of affairs," let us introduce "canonical" names for them. Such names will consist in the result of prefixing "its being the case that" (hereinafter, "*C*") to "eternal" sentences.[15] Thus a canonical name for the state of affairs referred to above would be "*C*(Caesar is murdered)." And let us say that the result of flanking the identity-sign with canonical names of states of affairs expresses a truth just in the case that the eternal sentences embedded in these names express equivalent propositions, where propositions are *equivalent* if they are true in just the same possible worlds. (Hereinafter, I shall assume that every proposition is equivalent to and *only* to itself. This assumption could be dispensed with at the cost of complicating the syntax of the sequel.) A state of affairs will be said to *obtain* if the proposition associated with it—that is, the proposition expressed by the sentence embedded in any of its canonical names—is true.[16] Thus *C*(Caesar is murdered), *C*(Caesar is stabbed), and *C*(Caesar is poisoned) are three distinct states of affairs, the first two of which obtain and the last of which does not. To *prevent* a state of affairs from obtaining is to prevent its associated proposition

15. The choice of eternal sentences as the arguments to which the operator "*C*" attaches is made largely for the sake of convenience. If we had chosen in addition to eternal sentences, *non*eternal sentences, sentences that can change their truth-values as time passes, for this purpose, then we should have canonical names for states of affairs that can obtain at one time and fail to obtain at other times. If we were to work out a comprehensive and consistent theory of these entities, we should end up with a theory rather like the theory of "states of affairs" R. M. Chisholm presents in "Events and Propositions," *Noûs*, 4 (1970), pp. 15–24. We might, in fact, say that what *we* are calling "states of affairs" are just that subclass of Chisholm's "states of affairs," that he calls *propositions*. If we were to interpret PPP2 as involving quantification over *all* those things Chisholm calls "states of affairs," then (I claim without argument) we could nevertheless defend it against Frankfurt-style counterexamples by arguments essentially the same as those we shall present in the text, but these arguments would be considerably more complicated. For a discussion of the propriety of applying the term "universal" to "states of affairs," see *n*. 20.

16. On Chisholm's view (see *n*. 15), the proposition "associated with" a given state of affairs just *is* that state of affairs.

from being true (or to *see to it that* or *insure that* that proposition is not true).

Let us now, so armed, return to PPP2. Can we show that PPP2 is false by constructing Frankfurt-style counterexamples to it? What would an attempt at such a counterexample look like? Like this, I think.

Gunnar shoots Ridley (intentionally), an action sufficient for the obtaining of Ridley's being dead, a certain state of affairs. But there is some factor, *F*, which (*i*) played no causal role in Ridley's death, and (*ii*) would have caused Ridley's death *if* Gunnar had not shot him (or had decided not to shoot him), and (*iii*) is such that Gunnar could not have prevented it from causing Ridley's death except by killing (or by deciding to kill) Ridley himself. So it would seem that Gunnar is responsible for Ridley's being dead though he could not have prevented this state of affairs from obtaining.

This case *seems* to show that PPP2 is false. But in fact it does not. Let us remember that if this case is to be a counterexample to PPP2 and not to some other principle, some principle involving particulars, we must take the words "Ridley's being dead" that occur in it as denoting a universal. What universal? Presumably, *C*(Ridley dies). But while it is indeed true that Gunnar could not have prevented *C*(Ridley dies) from obtaining, I do not think it is true that Gunnar is responsible for *C*(Ridley dies). Why should anyone think he is? Well, Gunnar did something (shooting Ridley) that was *sufficient* for *C*(Ridley dies). What is more, he performed this act intentionally, knowing that it was sufficient for this state of affairs. This argument, however, is invalid. For consider the state of affairs *C*(Ridley is mortal). When Gunnar shot Ridley, he performed an act sufficient for (the obtaining of) this state of affairs. But it would be absurd to say that Gunnar is *responsible* for *C*(Ridley is mortal). God, or Adam and Eve jointly, or perhaps no one at all, might be held accountable for Ridley's mortality; certainly not his murderer. (Unless, of course, Ridley would have lived forever if he hadn't been murdered; let's assume that is not the case.)

In fact, it is arguable that *C*(Ridley dies) is the very same state of affairs as *C*(Ridley is mortal). Given our principle of identity for states of affairs, these "two" states of affairs are one if the two eternal sentences "Ridley dies" and "Ridley is mortal" express the same proposition. And what proposition *could* either of them express but the proposition also expressed by "Ridley does not live forever" and "Ridley dies at some time or other"? So, it should seem, Gunnar is not responsible for *C*(Ridley dies), and the attempted counterexample to PPP2 fails.

Nor do matters go differently if (somewhat implausibly) we think of

"Ridley's being dead" as denoting some more "specific" state of affairs, such as $C$(Ridley is killed). If Gunnar is indeed responsible for $C$(Ridley is killed), we shall nevertheless have a counterexample to PPP2 only if Gunnar could not have prevented this state of affairs from obtaining. Let us flesh out "factor F" with some detail to insure that this is the case: suppose there is a third party, Pistol, who would have killed Ridley if Gunnar had not: and suppose Gunnar was able to prevent Pistol's killing Ridley only by killing Ridley himself. By these stipulations, we insure that Gunnar could not have prevented $C$(Ridley is killed). But do we, in making these stipulations, absolve Gunnar from responsibility for this state of affairs, or is his being responsible for it at least consistent with our stipulations?

I think we absolve him, and that we can show this by an argument of the same sort as the one we used in connection with $C$(Ridley dies). Let us first note that we cannot show that Gunnar is responsible for $C$(Ridley is killed) by pointing out that he did something logically or causally sufficient for that state of affairs; for, by the same argument, we could show that he is responsible for $C$(Ridley is mortal). Now consider the state of affairs—call it "$D$"—$C$(either Pistol or Gunnar kills Ridley). Is Gunnar responsible for $D$? Note that $D$ would have obtained no matter what Gunnar had done, just as $C$(Ridley is mortal), $C$(either $2 + 2 = 4$ or Gunnar kills Ridley), and $C$(grass is green or Gunnar kills Ridley) would have. These latter states of affairs are obviously not ones Gunnar is responsible for. Is there some important difference between them and $D$ in virtue of which Gunnar is responsible for $D$? There is only one nontrivial difference I can see: There is *no* possible world in which Gunnar is responsible for $C$(either $2 + 2 = 4$ or Gunnar kills Ridley); and while there are doubtless possible worlds in which Gunnar is responsible for $C$(Ridley is mortal) and others in which he is responsible for $C$(either grass is green or Gunnar kills Ridley), these worlds are exceedingly "remote" from actuality.[17] But some worlds in which Gunnar is responsible for $D$ are much "closer" to actuality than any of these: for example, "close" worlds in which the counterfactual propositions about Pistol that were built into our example are false and Ridley would not have been killed if Gunnar had not shot him. But a miss is as good as a mile; I am arguing only that Gunnar is not *in fact* responsible for $D$.

Now if Gunnar is not responsible for $D$, then he is not responsible for $C$(either Pistol or Gunnar or someone else kills Ridley). And *this*

17. Worlds (say) in which Ridley would have lived forever if Gunnar had not shot him, and worlds in which the color of grass is up to Gunnar.

state of affairs and $C$(Ridley is killed) are one and the same, since the proposition that either Pistol or Gunnar or someone else kills Ridley is equivalent to the proposition that Ridley is killed.[18]

In this example, "factor $F$" involved a second agent who would have shot Ridley if Gunnar had not. But it would have made no real difference if we had imagined factor $F$ being such that it would have caused Ridley's death by "working through" Gunnar. (See Blumenfeld's counterexample to PAP, quoted in Part I.) Suppose, for example, that Gunnar decides to kill Ridley and does so. Suppose that if he had decided *not* to kill Ridley he would have flushed red (which he couldn't help) and that this red flush together with the prevailing atmospheric conditions would have caused him to decide to kill and, as a result of this decision, to kill, Ridley. Suppose the presence of these atmospheric conditions and the effect on him of their copresence with his flushing red are things he has no choice about. It follows from these suppositions that Gunnar could not have prevented $C$(Ridley is killed). But we can show by an argument essentially the same as the argument we employed in the "Pistol" case that Gunnar is not responsible for this state of affairs. We proceed by showing first that Gunnar is not responsible for

> $K$ $C$(Ridley is killed by someone who is caused to kill him by factor $F$ [red flush, atmospheric conditions, and so on] or else Ridley is killed by someone who is not caused to kill him by factor $F$).

18. The editors of *The Philosophical Review* have called my attention to the fact that the validity of this argument appears to depend on the doubtful assumption that "Gunnar is responsible for $x$" is an extensional context. But it need not depend on this assumption. Let us say that in each of the following pairs of sentences the second sentence is a *disjunctive elaboration* of the first.

All grass is green.
All grass in London or elsewhere is green.

Ridley is killed.
Ridley is killed by something or other at some time or other at some place or other.

There is a stack of plates on the table.
There is a stack of plates on the table that contains twelve plates or else some other number of plates.

Then, I think, a defender of the argument presented in the text need appeal to no principle stronger than: From '$S$ is not responsible for $C(p)$', derive '$S$ is not responsible for $C(q)$', provided $p$ is a disjunctive elaboration of $q$. For example, from "Henry is not responsible for $C$(There is a stack of plates on the table that contains twelve plates or else some other number of plates)" we derive "Henry is not responsible for $C$(there is a stack of plates on the table)." This inference seems to me to be plainly valid, even if we suppose Henry to be unable to count beyond three and to be ignorant of the logical principle of Addition.

This state of affairs plays the role played by $C$(either Pistol or Gunnar or someone else kills Ridley) in our demonstration that, in the "Pistol" case, Gunnar is not responsible for $C$(Ridley is killed). We cannot say of $K$ what we said of $D$, and what we could have said of $C$(either Pistol or Gunnar or someone else kills Ridley), that it would have obtained no matter what Gunnar had done, for it would not have obtained if Gunnar had not shot Ridley. But we can say of $K$ that it would have obtained no matter what *choices* or *decisions* Gunnar had made, and this seems to me to entail that Gunnar is not responsible for it. (I owe this point to the editors of *The Philosophical Review*.) The remaining step in the demonstration consists simply in observing that the proposition associated with $K$ is equivalent to the proposition that Ridley is killed and, therefore that $K$ and $C$(Ridley is killed) are one and the same state of affairs, from which fact we infer that Gunnar is not responsible for $C$(Ridley is killed). (Or, if this inference be thought dubious, we can say that the remaining step consists in observing that the sentence embedded in the displayed name of $K$ is a "disjunctive elaboration" of "Ridley is killed," together with an application of the rule stated in footnote 18.)

If we had chosen to examine instead of $C$(Ridley is killed) some even more "specific" state of affairs, such as $C$(Ridley is shot to death at 3:43 P.M., 12 January 1949, in Chicago), this would have made no difference to our argument, which in no way depended on the degree of specificity of $C$(Ridley is killed). An argument of the same sort could be applied to *any* attempt at a Frankfurt-style counterexample to PPP2: the putative counterexample will not be a counterexample *unless* it entails that the agent whose responsibility is in question could not have prevented some given state of affairs; but if the "counterexample" does indeed have this feature, then (I claim) we can always find an argument (sound, I claim), constructed along the lines of the above models, for the conclusion that the agent is not responsible for that state of affairs.

The intuitive plausibility of this conclusion can be shown if we think in terms of the following rather fanciful picture. We are imagining cases in which an agent "gets to" a certain state of affairs by following a particular "causal road," a road intentionally chosen by him in order to "get to" that state of affairs. But, because this state of affairs is a universal, it can be reached by *various* causal roads, some of them differing radically from the road that *is* taken. And, in the cases we imagine, *all* the causal roads that the agent *could* take, all that are *open* to him, lead to this same state of affairs. Perhaps the point of this fanciful talk about "roads" will be clearer if we look at the case of an agent who is unable to prevent a certain state of affairs from obtaining, where this case involves roads in a literal sense. Suppose Ryder's horse, Dobbin, has run away with him. Ryder can't get Dobbin to slow down, but Dobbin will respond to the bridle: whenever Ryder and Dobbin come to a fork in the road or a crossroads, it is up to Ryder which way they go. Ryder and Dobbin are approaching a certain crossroads, and Ryder recognizes one of the roads leading away from it as a road to Rome. Ryder has conceived a dislike for Romans and so (having nothing better to do) he steers Dobbin onto the road he knows leads to Rome, motivated by the hope that the passage of a runaway horse through the streets of Rome will result in the injury of some of her detested citizens. Unknown to Ryder, however, *all* roads lead to Rome: Dobbin's career would have led him and Ryder to Rome by *some* route no matter what Ryder had done. That is, Ryder could not have prevented C(Ryder passes through Rome on a runaway horse). Is Ryder responsible for this state of affairs? It is obvious that he is not. And it seems obvious that he is not responsible for this state of affairs *just because* he could not have prevented it. I conclude that Frankfurt-style counterexamples cannot be used to show that PPP2 is false.

The universals that PPP2 is "about" are states of affairs; but if we had examined a principle, otherwise similar, about "event-universals" (for example, "its coming to pass that Caesar dies") we could have employed arguments that differed from the above arguments only in verbal detail.

It has been suggested to me[19] that these arguments appear less plausible if one reflects on the fact that essentially similar arguments could be used to show, for example, that Gunnar did not *bring about* C(Ridley is killed) or that Gunnar's pulling the trigger did not *cause* this state of affairs. It is certainly true that if the above arguments are sound, then similar arguments can be used to show that Gunnar did not bring about C(Ridley is killed) and that his bodily movements did not cause this state of affairs to obtain. But these conclusions appear to me to be simply *true*. Let us concentrate on

(1) Gunnar did not bring about C(Ridley is killed).

Why should anyone think (1) is false? It would be clearly invalid to argue that (1) is false since Gunnar did something logically or causally sufficient for C(Ridley is killed), for by the same argument we could

19. By the editors of *The Philosophical Review.*

establish the falsity of the (true) proposition that Gunnar did not bring about $C$(Ridley is mortal). Or consider the case of Ryder and Dobbin. In turning down a certain road, Ryder did something causally sufficient for passing through Rome on a runaway horse, but would anyone want to say that Ryder brought about the (for him inevitable) state of affairs $C$(Ryder passes through Rome on a runaway horse)?

The states of affairs we have been considering are *universals*. There are *many* ways the concrete particulars that make up our surroundings could be arranged that would be sufficient for their obtaining. What Gunnar and Ryder can bring about is *which* of these possible arrangements of particulars (which murderer, which road) the universals will be "realized in"; that *some arrangement or other* of the particulars will realize these universals is something totally outside their control; it is not something they bring about. Here is an analogy involving another sort of universal, properties. Chisel is a sculptor and sculpts the heaviest statue that ever was or will be, *The Dying Whale*. Thus Chisel brings it about that a certain particular, *The Dying Whale*, exemplifies the property of being the heaviest statue.[20] But he

---

20. Perhaps some philosophers would be disinclined to call the property of being the heaviest statue there ever was or will be a *universal*, on the ground that a universal must be "sharable," must be capable of being exemplified by more than one object. And, for similar reasons, it might be held that what I have called "states of affairs" are not true universals, since each of them either obtains or fails to obtain without further qualification, whereas a state of affairs that was truly a universal should be capable (say) of obtaining in 1943 but not in 1956 (cf. *n.* 15), or of obtaining in both Britain and the United States but not in France. Well, let us say that our "states of affairs" and properties like being the heaviest statue are, if not "true" universals, at least *cross-world universals*. A property or other abstract object is a cross-world universal if there are worlds $W_1$ and $W_2$ such that $x$ falls under it in $W_1$ and $y$ falls under it in $W_2$ and $x \neq y$. (I use the words "fall under" with deliberate vagueness; what "falls under" a property is whatever has it; what "falls under" a state of affairs is whatever arrangement of particulars realizes it.) If this usage is an extension of traditional philosophical usage, it is a very natural one; I call, e.g., $C$(Gunnar kills Ridley) a "universal" because it is not "tied to" any given arrangement of particulars. I do not pretend that these remarks are very precise. Certainly the notion of an "arrangement of particulars" could do with some clarification. For example, it is not clear what should be said about states of affairs that, unlike those discussed above, involve only a single particular. (Let us say that a state of affairs *involves* a particular if that particular is such that its existence is entailed by the obtaining of that state of affairs.) Consider, for example, $C$(there is such a building as the Taj Mahal). Are there many "arrangements of particulars" in which this state of affairs could be realized? Tentatively, I should say Yes. I should think that "the arrangement of particulars that realizes a given state of affairs" should in general be taken to be an arrangement of a broader class of particulars than those it "involves." For example, $C$(there are humans) does not in the strict sense defined above *involve* you or me (in fact, *no* contingent being is such that this state of affairs involves it), but you and I are, in a very intuitive sense, among those particulars the arrangement of which realizes it. Similarly, though no block of marble is such that $C$(there is such a building as

does not bring it about that this property is exemplified, since, no matter what he had done, this property would "automatically" have been exemplified by something or other: he causes something to exemplify this property, but he does not cause this property to be exemplified.

In affirming (1), I do not mean to affirm the falsehood

(2) Gunnar did not bring about Ridley's death,

where "Ridley's death" denotes an event-*particular* (individuated from other particulars in virtue of having different causal antecedents), one that is also perhaps denoted by "Ridley's death on Thursday," "the only death Gunnar ever caused," and so on. Anyone who feels inclined to reject (1) should make sure that this inclination does not arise from a failure to distinguish between (1) and (2). To revert to the sculpture example, (1) and (2) stand to each other roughly as

Chisel did not cause the property of being the heaviest statue to be exemplified,

and

Chisel did not cause (the particular thing that is) the heaviest statue to exist,

stand to each other. The former is, as I argued above, true, and the latter false.[21]

So, it would seem, we are unable to devise a Frankfurt-style counterexample either to PPP1 or to PPP2. If our attempts at counterexamples looked initially plausible, this, I think, was due to a confusion.

---

the Taj Mahal) involves it—at least on the assumption that mereological essentialism is false—many blocks of marble would seem to be among those particulars the arrangement of which realizes it. Or even if we do not consider *parts* of the Taj Mahal, we must admit that the state of affairs we are considering would obtain if the Taj Mahal were differently placed or differently oriented; and it seems intuitively correct to say that if the place or orientation of the Taj Mahal were different from what it in fact is, then C(there is such a building as the Taj Mahal) would be realized in a different arrangement of particulars.

21. I do not mean to give the impression that one never brings about any state of affairs. For example, (granting the correctness of the Warren Commission Report), Lee Harvey Oswald brought about C(Kennedy dies on 22 November 1963). But it is *not* true that Oswald brought about C(Kennedy dies). That state of affairs was brought about by God or by Adam and Eve or by no one at all. Moreover, it *is* true that Oswald brought about the event-particular, Kennedy's death.

When we hear the Gunnar-Ridley story, it *seems* correct to say that it follows from the story that Gunnar is responsible for Ridley's death *and* that Gunnar could not have prevented Ridley's death. But "Ridley's death" is ambiguous. If we are using this phrase to denote a universal, then we may say that Gunnar could not have prevented Ridley's death, but not that he was responsible for Ridley's death. If we are using this phrase to denote a particular, then we may say that Gunnar was responsible for Ridley's death, but not that he could not have prevented it.

This result might lead us to wonder whether Frankfurt's counterexamples to PAP rest on a similar confusion. Suppose we were to split PAP into two principles, one about "act-particulars" (event-particulars that are voluntary movements of human bodies) and one about "act-universals" (that is, things that could be done by distinct agents, such as murder, prayer, or killing Jones at noon on Christmas Day, 1953): should we then see that Frankfurt's alleged counterexamples to PAP depend for their plausibility on treating one and the same act as a particular at one point in the argument, and a universal at another?

I do not think that Frankfurt is guilty of any such confusion. The "acts" that figure in his counterexamples seem to me to be treated consistently as universals. If this is the case, it raises two questions. Let us split PAP into two principles as was suggested in the preceding paragraph: PAP1 (about particulars) and PAP2 (about universals). The first question: If indeed Frankfurt's "acts" are universals, he is arguing against PAP2; can his argument be met by considerations like those we raised in defense of PPP2? The answer seems to me to be No, but I am not at all sure about this. The considerations raised in defense of PPP2 depended on our having at our disposal a fairly precise notion of "state-of-affairs universal," and I am not at present able to devise an equally precise notion of "act-universal" that I find satisfactory.[22] The second question: what about PAP1? I do not find

---

22. An adequate construction of such a notion would require the introduction of a canonical language for act-universals. I am unable to devise a language for this purpose that comes close to satisfying me. Even without having such a language at my disposal, however, I think I see a serious obstacle to any attempt to refute Frankfurt's arguments against PAP2 by raising considerations like those used to defend PPP2 in the text. Let us suppose that "the act of killing Ridley" denotes a certain act-universal, an act such that *it*, that very act, could be the act of any among a number of agents and be performed under a great variety of conditions. Consider the following Frankfurt counterexample to PAP2: Gunnar performs the act of killing Ridley; moreover, if he had decided not to perform it, some third party, Cosser, would have caused him to perform it. If we were to try to refute this counterexample by arguments parallel to those we

this question interesting, since I do not think that "event-particulars that are voluntary movements of human bodies" are what we hold people responsible for. I shall not, however, defend this view here. An adequate defense of it would be fairly complex, and I do not think my reasons for thinking what I do on this matter are worth developing merely to establish a negative conclusion.

## IV

We have shown that three principles relating ability and responsibility cannot be refuted by Frankfurt-style counterexamples:

PPA   A person is morally responsible for failing to perform a given act only if he could have performed that act.

PPP1  A person is morally responsible for a certain event only if he could have prevented it.

PPP2  A person is morally responsible for a certain state of affairs only if (that state of affairs obtains and) he could have prevented it from obtaining.

Now consider three versions of incompatibilism:

If determinism is true, then if a given person failed to perform a given act, that person could not have performed that act.

If determinism is true, then no event is such that anyone could have prevented it.

---

used in defense of PPP2, we should have to find an act-denoting phrase that stands to "the act of killing Ridley" roughly as "C(either Pistol or Gunnar or someone else kills Ridley)" stands to "C(Ridley is killed)." I am not sure what such a phrase would look like, but I think something like this:

The act of killing Ridley, either without having been caused to kill Ridley by anyone, or as a result of having been caused to kill Ridley by Cosser or someone else.

I am very doubtful whether this phrase makes any sense. To take a simpler case, given that there is such an act as eating forbidden fruit, an act one might perform as a result of one's having been given bad advice, is there such an act as the act of eating forbidden fruit as a result of having been given bad advice? I find the notion of such an act difficult to grasp. But if no coherent act-universal-name can be found to play the formal role played by "C(either Pistol or Gunnar or someone else kills Ridley)" in our defense of PPP2, then no parallel argument in defense of PAP2 can be constructed. These considerations, of course, do not show that Frankfurt's attack on PAP is successful. They do, however, raise serious doubts about the possibility of defending PAP against this attack by constructing an argument formally parallel to our argument in defense of PPP2.

If determinism is true, then if a given state of affairs obtains, then no one could have prevented that state of affairs from obtaining.[23]

Obviously, if these three theses are true, then (since PPA, PPP1, and PPP2 are true) it follows that determinism entails that no one has ever been or could ever be responsible for any event, state of affairs, or unperformed act. Moreover if the following schema

R    If S is responsible for Φing, then there is some event or state of affairs for which S is responsible,

(here "Φing" is to be replaced by any grammatically appropriate action phrase) is valid, then determinism is (assuming incompatibilism) incompatible not only with our being responsible for the consequences of our acts but for our acts themselves. And this schema is extremely plausible. I cannot myself conceive of a case in which an agent is responsible for having performed some act but is responsible for *none* of the results or consequences (either universal or particular) of this act.[24]

Thus, if all three versions of incompatibilism are true, and if deter-

---

23. I think I am justified in calling these three theses "versions" of a single doctrine, since, *if* there were a good argument for any of them, then, I should think, it could be easily modified to yield a good argument for either of the others. I have presented arguments for what is essentially the first of these three versions of incompatibilism in "A Formal Approach to the Problem of Free Will and Determinism," *Theoria* XL (1974) Part 1, pp. 9–22, and "The Incompatibility of Free Will and Determinism," *Philosophical Studies* 27 (1975) pp. 185–199.

24. An obvious argument for the validity of R is this: If someone Φs and is responsible for so acting, then, whatever other events or states of affairs he may be responsible for, he is at least responsible for its being the case that he Φs. But this argument is unsound. Consider the case (p. 215 above) involving the counterfactual propensities of atmospheric conditions to cause Gunnar to decide to kill, and to kill, Ridley. I argued that in that case Gunnar is not responsible for C (Ridley is killed). A similar argument could be used to show that in that case Gunnar is not responsible for C (Gunnar kills Ridley). But it does not follow that Gunnar is not responsible for killing Ridley. For Gunnar might have freely decided to kill Ridley and have killed him as a result of this free decision (and thus be responsible for killing Ridley); nevertheless, *if* he had (freely) decided *not* to kill Ridley, external factors outside his control would *then* have "come into play" and caused him (unfreely, of course) to kill Ridley. Therefore, while Gunnar is responsible for killing Ridley, he is not responsible for C (Gunnar kills Ridley freely or Gunnar kills Ridley unfreely) and hence is not responsible for C (Gunnar kills Ridley). Thus our "obvious" argument for the validity of R is fallacious. Nonetheless, R seems to me to be valid. Certainly the case we have just considered is not a counterexample to its validity. For, in this case, while Gunnar is not responsible for C (Gunnar kills Ridley), he *is* responsible for C (Gunnar kills Ridley without having been caused to do so by atmospheric conditions). Moreover, he is responsible for the event-particular, Ridley's death.

minism is true, then there is simply no such thing as moral responsibility. There is such a thing as moral responsibility only if someone is responsible for something he has done, or for something he has left undone, or for the results or consequences of what he has done or left undone. And the principles for which I have argued (PPA, PPP1, PPP2, and the validity of schema $R$) entail that if incompatibilism is true, then determinism is incompatible with anyone's being responsible for anything whatever.

Therefore, even if PAP is false,[25] and even if Frankfurt's "correct version" of PAP (see footnote 4) cannot be used to show that determinism and moral responsibility are incompatible, it is *nonetheless* true that unless free will and determinism are compatible, determinism and moral responsibility are incompatible. Thus, Frankfurt's arguments do not, even if they are sound, rob the compatibilist-incompatibilist debate of its central place in the old controversy about determinism and moral responsibility.[26]

25. Of course, if the above arguments are correct, and if determinism and incompatibilism are both true, then PAP *is* true: it is vacuously true because no one, in that case, is responsible for anything he does. Frankfurt, of course, does not mean to deny that PAP might be, as a matter of contingent fact, vacuously true.

26. I should like to thank the editors of *The Philosophical Review* for their careful comments on earlier versions of this paper, which have led to many improvements. I am especially grateful to them for pointing out to me that an argument I employed was invalid.

# 8

# Responsibility and Control

───────────

## JOHN MARTIN FISCHER

Most philosophers have held that a person is morally responsible for what he has done only if he could have done otherwise. If responsibility requires freedom to do otherwise and this freedom is incompatible with causal determinism, then responsibility is incompatible with determinism.

Harry Frankfurt has contended recently that freedom to do otherwise is *not* necessary for responsibility:[1] Frankfurt thus attempts to show that the question of the consistency of determinism with responsibility can be separated from that of the consistency of determinism with freedom to do otherwise. I shall discuss two ways of responding to Frankfurt's examples. The first response claims that Frankfurt has *not* successfully dissociated responsibility from "control" (that is, freedom to do otherwise), in which case the compatibility of determinism with responsibility continues to depend on the compatibility of determinism with freedom to do otherwise. The second response concedes that Frankfurt *has* successfully pried apart responsibility and control, but it claims that he has not thereby established the consistency of responsibility with determinism. Though it is usually thought that determinism threatens responsibility because it erodes control, I show how an incompatibilist about determinism and responsibility can agree with Frankfurt that responsibility need not require control.

I am indebted to Carl Ginet, T. H. Irwin, and especially John G. Bennett for useful comments. I benefited from reading this paper at colloquia at Cornell, Stanford, and Dartmouth. "Responsibility and Control" originally appeared in the *Journal of Philosophy*, 89 (January 1982), 24–40, © 1982 by the *Journal of Philosophy* and is reprinted here with permission from the *Journal of Philosophy*.
1. "Alternate Possibilities and Moral Responsibility," Chapter 6 above in this volume.

*I. Frankfurt's Examples*

Let me start by reviewing some of the larger issues into which the topic of this paper fits. An incompatibilist about responsibility and determinism might make an argument against compatibilism by appealing to what Frankfurt calls the "principle of alternate possibilities." This principle says that

> A person is morally responsible for what he has done only if he could have done otherwise.

The incompatibilist argues that if universal causal determinism is true, then no one could ever have done other than he actually did. Consequently, by the principle of alternate possibilities, no one is ever morally responsible for what he has done, if causal determinism is true.

In understanding this argument it is important to see that something like the principle of alternate possibilities is usually accepted by *both* compatibilists and incompatibilists. This is why the incompatibilist's argument is powerful. Usually both camps associate responsibility with control, but, whereas the incompatibilist holds that determinism rules out control, the compatibilist argues that one might have been able to do otherwise, in the relevant sense, even though one's action was in fact causally determined by antecedent events over which one had no control.

Harry Frankfurt has suggested a new attack on the incompatibilist's argument. Instead of disputing the incompatibility of determinism with control, he attacks the principle of alternate possibilities itself— that is, the claim that responsibility requires control.

Frankfurt's examples have the following general form:[2] A person is in the process of deciding which of $n$ alternative acts $A_i, \ldots, A_k, \ldots,$ $A_n$ to perform. He believes (correctly) that he cannot avoid performing some one of the acts, although there is no one act of which he believes that he can't avoid performing it. He decides to perform and, acting on this decision, does perform $A_k$. But, unknown to him, there were various factors that *would have* prevented him from performing (and also from deciding to perform) any of $A_i, \ldots, A_n$ except $A_k$. These factors would have come into play if he had shown any tenden-

---

2. In summarizing the form of Frankfurt's examples, I closely follow Peter van Inwagen, "Ability and Responsibility," Chapter 7 above, especially p. 154.

cy toward performing (or deciding to perform) any of the alternatives except $A_k$. But, since he in fact showed no such tendency, these factors played no role whatever in his actually deciding to perform and in his performing $A_k$.

I want to describe a case of the Frankfurt sort in some detail; this is a somewhat extreme case, but it poses all the problems in an especially pressing way. Black is a nefarious neurosurgeon. In performing an operation on Jones to remove a brain tumor, Black inserts a mechanism into Jones's brain which enables Black to monitor and control Jones's activities. Jones, meanwhile, knows nothing of this. Black exercises this control through a computer which he has programmed so that, among other things, it monitors Jones's voting behavior. If Jones shows an inclination to decide to vote for Carter, then the computer, through the mechanism in Jones's brain, intervenes to assure that he actually decides to vote for Reagan and does so vote. But if Jones decides on his own to vote for Reagan, the computer does nothing but continue to monitor—without affecting—the goings-on in Jones's head.

Suppose Jones decides to vote for Reagan on his own, just as he would have if Black had *not* inserted the mechanism into his head. Then Frankfurt claims that Jones is responsible for voting for Reagan, regardless of the fact that he could not have done otherwise. His voting for Reagan is something we can charge to his credit or discredit; it expresses something about Jones's character. But the principle of alternate possibilities does not seem to be satisfied; there is no way that Jones could have avoided voting for Reagan—if he had been on the verge of doing so, the computer would have intervened and ensured that he vote for Reagan. If the computer *had* intervened, then I think it is obvious that Jones would not have been responsible. But since the computer did *not* intervene, it is plausible to think, along with Frankfurt, that Jones is responsible.

Frankfurt endorses a revision of the principle of alternate possibilities, one which, he claims, does not conflict with the view that moral responsibility is compatible with determinism:

> A person is not morally responsible for what he has done if he did it *only* because he could not have done otherwise (Chapter 6, p. 152).

On this revision, if a person "really wanted" to do what he did and did it because he really wanted to do so, then he can be morally responsible for his act, even if his act was causally determined. In a later article, Frankfurt sets up the apparatus of higher-order desires to explain what it is for an agent to act because he really wants to.[3]

In order better to understand Frankfurt's account of responsibility, we should consider one of Don Locke's criticisms of Frankfurt.[4] Locke asks us to compare a willing and an unwilling drug addict; both, we suppose, act on irresistible desires to take a drug, but whereas the unwilling addict struggles against this desire, the willing addict embraces it. Locke claims, essentially, that a contented slave is still a slave. Both addicts, insofar as they are addicts and thus act on irresistible desires, act unfreely. He claims that the willing and unwilling addicts are both not responsible for taking the drug, even though it seems that Frankfurt must say that the willing addict is responsible, but the unwilling addict is not.

Although Frankfurt himself is not explicit about this, it is useful, on Frankfurt's theory, to distinguish between two "willing" addicts. The first is actually motivated to take the drug by the thought that, were he to try to abstain, he would experience an irresistible desire for the drug; the irresistibility of the desire (or his belief in its irresistibility) is his sole reason for action. Yet, were he to consider the issue of whether it is good that he has an irresistible desire for the drug, he would be pleased; he doesn't mind being that sort of person. The second willing addict is actually motivated by his desire for the drug; the irresistibility of this desire plays no role in explaining his behavior—he may be quite unaware of its irresistibility. Frankfurt should say of the second but not of the first willing addict that he (like the nonaddict) is responsible for taking the drug.

This follows from two components of Frankfurt's theory:

(1) What explains the second willing addict's taking the drug may be exactly the same as what explains the taking of the drug by a nonaddict who takes it simply because he likes taking it,[5]

and thus

(2) What the second willing addict's action reveals about him is the same as what is revealed by the nonaddict. It is not the same as what the action of the unwilling addict reveals (*loc. cit.*).

3. "Freedom of the Will and the Concept of a Person," Chapter 1 above.
4. "Three Concepts of Free Action: I," Chapter 3 above, p. 101.
5. "Three Concepts of Free Action: II," Chapter 4 above, pp. 117–118.

If one associates responsibility ascriptions with acts that reveal features of an agent's character, then Frankfurt can be defended against Locke's criticism.[6] On Frankfurt's account of responsibility, if the fact that a desire is irresistible plays a certain role in an agent's deliberation, the agent is not responsible. That is, if an agent believes that a desire is irresistible and if this belief is a part of his reason for acting on the desire, then the agent is not responsible for so acting. But, if the fact that the agent couldn't have done otherwise plays no role in the agent's deliberation, then the agent may be responsible for what he did; this explains why the second sort of willing addict, but not the unwilling addict, may be responsible for taking the drug, and it explains why responsibility is compatible with determinism. Responsibility is compatible with determinism, on this theory, since an agent may not know that determinism is true (if it is), or, even if he does know the truth of determinism, he need not know *which* act (among his alternatives) is determined; the lack of an open alternative need not play a role in the agent's deliberations even if determinism is true (and he knows this) (Cummins, pp. 412–413).

Frankfurt's theory of responsibility poses a formidable challenge to the incompatibilist about determinism and responsibility. I shall now discuss two approaches to meeting this challenge. The first strategy claims that Frankfurt has *not* dissociated responsibility from control.

*II. The First Criticism of Frankfurt*

There is considerable disagreement about what sorts of things we hold persons responsible for. Some philosophers believe that we hold agents responsible only for their choices, and not for their acts (if these are different from their choices); some believe that we hold agents responsible for their acts, but not for the consequences of these acts, whereas others insist that we hold agents responsible for the consequences of their acts (as well as the choices and acts themselves). Among philosophers who believe that we hold agents responsible for events of certain sorts, there is disagreement as to the ontological status of these events: are they to be construed as particulars or universals? For the purposes of this discussion, I shall attempt to steer clear of such disagreements, as much as possible. I shall assume that we might hold persons responsible for events construed as particulars or universals and that these events might be acts, the consequences of

6. This association is emphasized in Robert Cummins, "Could Have Done Otherwise," *The Personalist*, LX, 4 (October 1979): 411–414.

these acts, or events related to these acts by relations such as Alvin Goldman's "level-generation" (or some similar relation). I want to be very liberal about the metaphysics of responsibility.

Consider again Jones and the "counterfactual intervener," Black. Black wants Jones to vote for Ronald Reagan and would bring it about (through the computer) that Jones decides to vote for Reagan and then does so, should Jones show an inclination to decide to vote for Carter. But Jones decides on his own to vote for Reagan and does so. Is this a counterexample to the principle of alternate possibilities? Is Jones responsible for voting for Reagan, even though he couldn't have done otherwise?

A version of the first approach to denying that Frankfurt's examples undermine the principle of alternate possibilities is developed by Peter van Inwagen (Chapter 7). I call this the *associationist strategy*—the strategy that insists on the *association* of responsibility with control. The associationist divides the principle of alternate possibilities into one principle applicable to particulars and one applicable to universals:

(PAP1) A person is morally responsible for a particular event only if he could have prevented it.

(PAP2) A person is morally responsible for the obtaining of a state of affairs only if he could have prevented the obtaining of that state of affairs.

Consider first the principle applicable to event particulars. Is Jones responsible for the particular event of his voting for Reagan? The associationist adopts the following principle of event individuation:

(E) $x$ is the same particular event as $y$ if and only if $x$ and $y$ have the same causes.

I shall call this the *essentialist principle,* since it asserts the essentiality of the causal genesis of an event. This principle is supposed to license certain counterfactual inferences; it is supposed to provide a way of identifying events across possible worlds. That is, event $a$ in world $\alpha$ is the same particular event as event $b$ in world $\beta$ just in case $a$ and $b$ have the same causal antecedents. Donald Davidson argues that events $x$ and $y$ which occur in the actual world are numerically the same just in case they have the same causes and effects; the criterion accepted by van Inwagen applies the Davidsonian intuition to counterfactual talk about events; it provides a way of answering the question, "Under certain circumstances which didn't actually obtain, would $y$ have been the same event as the actual event, $x$?"

If we accept the essentialist principle, then we can see that the story of Jones and Black might not undermine the principle of alternate possibilities. If we accept this approach we can say that Jones is responsible for the particular act of voting for Reagan because *it* was avoidable; if he had shown signs of deciding otherwise he would have voted for Reagan surely enough, but that would have been a *different* act of voting for Reagan from the actual act, because it would have had different causes. So the particular act of voting for Reagan need not have occurred; it was avoidable.

Now the associationist considers whether Jones is responsible for the fact that Jones votes for Reagan. Is Jones responsible for the obtaining of a certain state of affairs which *could* have been instantiated in various different ways? The associationist (again, following van Inwagen) claims that Jones is *not* responsible for its being the case that he votes for Reagan, and he argues as follows. Jones is *not* responsible for its being the case that either he votes for Reagan on his own or he is caused by Black's computer to vote for Reagan. If he were responsible for this state of affairs, then why not also for something for which he is obviously *not* responsible: its being the case that either he votes for Reagan on his own or $2 + 2 = 4$? But if he is not responsible for its being the case that either he votes for Reagan on his own or he is caused by Black's computer to vote for Reagan, Jones is not responsible for its being the case that he votes for Reagan.

The associationist then responds to Frankfurt as follows: Jones is responsible for the particular voting for Reagan, but *this* was avoidable; Jones is *not* responsible for the fact that he votes for Reagan, and he couldn't have avoided that. Thus the association of responsibility with control is preserved. Further, there is a universal for the obtaining of which Jones is responsible: this universal is "Jones voting for Reagan on his own" (or perhaps, "Jones voting for Reagan in the normal way"). But Jones *could* have prevented the obtaining of this state of affairs; again the association of responsibility with control is maintained.

I find the associationist's approach unconvincing. First, this approach to blocking Frankfurt's claim depends on the essentialist principle for event individuation, but this principle might be challenged.[7] Consider, for instance, a complex event such as Japan's attack on Pearl Harbor in 1941. Suppose the Emperor of Japan actually initi-

7. W. R. Carter, "On Transworld Event Identity," *Philosophical Review*, LXXXVIII, 3 (July 1979): 443–452.

ated the attack by saying, "Commence the attack." If instead he had initiated the attack by saying, "Destroy Pearl Harbor now," it may seem implausible to conclude that that would have been a different attack on Pearl Harbor from the actual attack. It is hard to see how to resolve the question of the adequacy of the essentialist principle of event individuation, but I contend that one need *not* accept this principle in order to deny that Frankfurt's examples undermine incompatibilism about determinism and responsibility; though van Inwagen's criticism of Frankfurt depends on the essentialist principle, I shall present a criticism of Frankfurt that does not depend on any such controversial principle of event individuation.

But there is a second problem with the associationist approach. Consider again whether Jones is responsible for the particular event that is his voting for Reagan. Even if we accept the essentialist principle of event individuation, in what sense could Jones have done otherwise? When we associate responsibility with control, we normally mean that a person is responsible for a particular event only if there is some alternate sequence open to the agent in which he performs a different act (or brings about a different event by performing some act that issues in the event). But if Black's computer were to intervene, it is not clear that Jones would be acting (in the relevant sense) at all. Were Black's computer to intervene and directly manipulate Jones's brain state, we might say that Jones's bodily movements would not in the appropriate sense be *his* actions (or actions at all).

But, even if one insists that there is a sense in which Jones acts in the alternate sequence, we can see that there is a problem for the associationist. When we demand that an agent have control, we mean that there must exist an alternate sequence in which the agent chooses and acts as a result of his character or practical reasoning; but, in Jones's case, in the alternate sequence Jones is caused by an external agent to choose and to act, and the external agent produces a choice and an act *unrelated* to the intention Jones begins to manifest.

For the agent to have control, in the relevant sense, there must be an alternate sequence in which the agent does otherwise as a result of *an appropriate sort* of chain of events. In Jones's case, if his practical reasoning inclines him to vote for Carter, he'll nevertheless be made to choose to vote for Reagan and to vote for Reagan, and his practical reasoning will be superseded. For the agent to have *deliberate control* (in the sense required for responsibility), there must be an alternate sequence in which there is an action rationalized by his practical reasoning; but in Jones's case, in the alternate sequence his choice and act do not flow from his practical reasoning in the appropriate way.

If we grant to van Inwagen the essentialist principle, then he may have established that a different event would have occurred in the alternate sequence, but he hasn't shown that Jones was capable of exercising deliberate control; van Inwagen thus confuses the ability deliberately to do otherwise with the possibility of something different occurring. Van Inwagen's mistake is to assume that the *only* way in which Frankfurt's example could threaten the principle of alternate possibilities would be by presenting an alternate sequence in which the same event particular (as the actual event) occurs; I have argued that this is false.[8] The rather attenuated alternate possibility preserved by the associationist doesn't look to me very much like the possibility of deliberately doing otherwise—it doesn't preserve Jones's *control* over the outcome.

One who agrees with the position I have been developing will insist on the following revision of the principle of alternate possibilities applicable to particulars:

(PAP1*) $S$ is responsible for event $e$ only if there exists some property $F$ such that $F(e)$ and an alternate sequence open to $S$ in which $S$ brings about $\sim F(e')[(e \neq e')]$ as a result of an intention to do so.

On (PAP1*), Jones is not responsible for voting for Reagan, since he is incapable of exercising deliberate control. Let 'F' name the property, "not being caused to vote for Reagan by the computer." If $e$ is Jones's actual act of voting for Reagan and $e'$ is the act in the alternate sequence, $e$ has $F$ and $e'$ lacks $F$ but in the alternate sequence $S$ does *not* bring it about that $e'$ lacks $F$ as a result of an intention that $e'$ lack $F$. Adoption of (PAP1*) shows how van Inwagen's criticisms can be attacked *without* rejecting the essentialist principle of event individuation. An associationist should adopt (PAP1*), but Frankfurt's examples undermine (PAP1*).

In light of these worries about the associationist strategy, it will be prudent for the incompatibilist to develop another response to Frankfurt's examples. This second strategy, which dissociates responsibility from control, is a radical departure from the conventional incompatibilist approach; but I shall argue that it is an appealing position.

*IV. The Second Criticism of Frankfurt*

The first sort of critic of Frankfurt insists that Frankfurt has not separated responsibility from control, and thus Frankfurt hasn't

8. Van Inwagen's assumption plays a crucial role at van Inwagen, Chapter 7, p. 161.

shown responsibility to be compatible with determinism. Underlying this sort of criticism is the traditional view that, if determinism threatens responsibility, it does so in virtue of undermining control. But I shall argue that an incompatibilist about determinism and responsibility can agree with Frankfurt that an agent might be morally responsible for doing something that he is *not* free to avoid doing. For the incompatibilist, the reason why determinism threatens responsibility *need not* be that it undermines control.

To see this, we should consider again the example of Jones and the "counterfactual intervener," Black. Suppose that the world actually proceeds via a sequence that is *not* causally deterministic; that is, though there are some causal laws, not all events are causally determined. Suppose further that the world proceeds in just the sort of way in which a libertarian says it must, if agents are to be morally responsible for what they do. Although an agent's desires and purposes explain his choices and acts, they do not causally necessitate them; the agent freely "identifies" with some of his desires, where this identification is not causally necessitated. Perhaps the identification is explained in terms of agent causality, although this notion need not play a role. In this sort of world, one in which human choices and actions are not causally necessitated, the libertarian can certainly say that Jones is morally responsible for voting for Reagan, even if Black *would have* brought it about that Jones vote for Reagan, if Jones had shown signs of deciding to vote for Carter. That is, nothing about Frankfurt's example *requires* the actual sequence issuing in the decision and action to proceed in a deterministic way; if it proceeds in a nondeterministic way that satisfies the libertarian, then Jones can be held responsible, even though he could not have done otherwise.

The kernel of truth in Frankfurt's example is that responsibility attributions are based on what happens in the actual sequence; an incompatibilist about responsibility and determinism can agree with this and thus admit that, if determinism is false, an agent who couldn't have done otherwise might be responsible for his action. But of course this doesn't show that *determinism* is compatible with moral responsibility; determinism is a doctrine about what happens in the actual sequence. The point could be put as follows: there are two ways in which it might be true that one couldn't have done otherwise. In the first way, the actual sequence compels the agent to do what he does, so he couldn't have initiated an alternate sequence; in the second way, there is no actual-sequence compulsion, but the alternate sequence would prevent the agent from doing other than he actually does. Frankfurt's examples involve alternate-sequence compulsion;

the incompatibilist about determinism and responsibility can agree with Frankfurt that in such cases an agent can be responsible even while lacking control, but he will insist that, since determinism involves *actual-sequence* compulsion, Frankfurt's examples do not establish that responsibility is compatible with determinism.

So whereas van Inwagen's criticism of Frankfurt contends that he has not dissociated responsibility from control, the approach I am developing concedes this dissociation, but argues that the transition from this dissociation to the compatibility of determinism with responsibility is a spurious transition. This is because the reason why determinism threatens responsibility is not *that* it undermines control, but because of the way in which it undermines control; determinism involves actual-sequence compulsion, and such compulsion might be incompatible with moral responsibility. Thus it is open to an incompatibilist about responsibility and determinism to accept the kernel of truth in Frankfurt's examples without swallowing the compatibility contention, and to defend his position without relying on a controversial principle of event individuation.

The account of responsibility which I have suggested that the incompatibilist might adopt is, like Frankfurt's account, an "actual-sequence" approach; such an approach might take the following general form:

> An act (or decision) is unfree (compelled) if and only if (a) it is causally determined, or (b) it is not in an appropriate sense the agent's act (or decision), or (c) it issues from a desire of an intensity $i$, and (i) the desire's having intensity $i$ explains why the act occurs, and (ii) any desire with intensity $i$ is irresistible.

This is a plausible libertarian actual-sequence approach to responsibility, which will be elaborated on below; it entails that Jones is morally responsible for voting for Reagan (in the world in which determinism is false), even though Jones couldn't have done otherwise. Although some philosophers have argued that the causal determination of an event need not entail the possibility, in principle, of predicting its occurrence, this example shows that the possibility in principle of predicting the occurrence of an event need not entail its causal determination.

Of course, what is predictable in advance is that Jones will vote for Reagan, though we can't predict which sequence will actually take place. When we predict that an event will occur, we predict that some event of a certain kind will occur. The example shows that the possibility, in principle, of predicting that Jones will vote for Reagan doesn't entail that Jones's particular act of voting for Reagan is causally determined. Although one might worry about determinism because one worries about predictability, a wedge can be driven between determination and predictability; and when the two pull apart, the incompatibilist's fundamental concern is with determination.

### V. A Possible Objection

I wish now to consider a possible objection to the approach I have developed. Someone might say that even in the libertarian world I sketched above in which Jones votes for Reagan on his own and Black does not play any causal role—nevertheless Jones's voting for Reagan is causally determined. This is because, given the setup of the actual sequence including the dispositional properties of agents such as Black, it is true that antecedent states of the world plus the causal laws entail that Jones will vote for Reagan.

Call the actual sequence "A," and the counterfactual sequence, in which Black intervenes, "C." Say that the obtaining of a state of affairs $P$ (construed broadly to include the occurrence of an event or sequence of events) at a time $T$ (a point or interval) is nomologically inevitable (at $T$) just in case some state of affairs which obtains prior to $T$, together with the laws of nature, entails that $P$ obtains at $T$.

In the example discussed above, neither $A$ (the actual sequence) nor, of course, $C$ (the counterfactual sequence) is nomologically inevitable (at the relevant time), although Jones's voting for Reagan *is* nomologically inevitable. Hence it might be claimed that Jones's voting for Reagan is (in the relevant sense) causally determined, and I have not presented an example of an uncompelled (i.e., non-causally-determined) act to which there was no alternate possibility.

But this objection is not cogent. If the doctrine of causal determinism is true, then each state of affairs that actually obtains at each time is nomologically inevitable. Hence, a causally determined act (in the sense that follows from the truth of causal determinism) is and must be a part of a sequence of states of affairs all of which are nomologically inevitable. But the actual sequence $A$ (in the example discussed above) is *not* such a sequence; for instance, the state of affairs "Black's not intervening in Jones's decision" is a non-nomologically-inevitable component of the actual sequence (as is the state of affairs "Jones's deciding on his own to vote for Reagan"). So even if one thinks that the nomological inevitability of Jones's voting for Reagan is compatible with his moral responsibility for it, it doesn't follow that Jones's responsibility for voting for Reagan is compatible with its being causally determined.

The objection might rest on a confusion between events construed as particulars and as universals. Inevitability is most naturally applied to event universals. (I'm not sure that it is coherent to talk of the inevitability of an event particular.) If it is inevitable that Jones will vote for Reagan, then perhaps it is causally determined that Jones will perform *some* act that is a voting for Reagan; but this leaves it open whether Jones's particular act issues from a sequence that is not causally deterministic. Inevitability, which is a property of event universals, need not entail the causal determination of the particular events that instantiate the universals.[9]

The approach I suggest to responsibility is strongly *path-dependent.* That is, where there are various alternate paths to an event of a certain sort, one focuses on the path that actually leads to the event. There may be no deterministic process on this path, though the event is inevitable. The control model of responsibility is path-independent in the sense that the fact of lack of control is consistent with various paths with radically different properties leading to the event.

The example discussed above also illustrates clause (b) of the account of responsibility. A libertarian will want to say that, since sequence *A* issues in Jones's voting for Reagan, Jones is responsible for so acting, but, if sequence *C* had occurred, then he would *not* have been responsible. But in *C* Jones's voting for Reagan does not issue from a causally deterministic sequence (in the sense sketched above); there are states of affairs (such as "Jones's showing signs of voting for Carter") which are non-nomologically-necessitated components of *C*. But, because of the direct intervention of Black, there is a clear sense in which the decision to vote for Reagan is not (in an appropriate sense) *Jones's* own decision.

Consider the frequently discussed case of the demonic neurologist who directly manipulates a person's brain to induce all his desires, beliefs, and decisions. Now contrast this case with a counterfactually intervening demonic neurologist (similar to Black), a neurologist who does not actually intervene, but would do so if the person showed any

9. The account I have given above of nomological inevitability is a standard account of causal determination. The example shows that this account does *not* adequately capture the notion of causal determination as applied to event particulars. Elsewhere I discuss an example which points to the inadequacy of the "standard" sort of account of causal determinism (the doctrine that all events are causally determined)—Lehrer's "duplicate universe" example; see my "Lehrer's New Move: *'Can' in Theory and Practice,*" *Theoria,* XLV, 2 (1979): 49–62.

sign of deciding otherwise than he actually decides. Neither the person subject to the actual intervener nor the person subject to the counterfactual intervener *controls* his decisions and actions; but, although both lack control, the second person's acts are *his* in a way in which the first person's are not. An act can be yours without its being up to you; you can be in charge without being in control. Although both lack control, the first person (subject to the actual intervener) is a marionette manipulated by someone else, but the second is not (though he *would* be under other circumstances). A theory of responsibility should reflect this difference; a path-dependent theory (but not a control model) can capture this intuition.

## VI. Actual-Sequence Theories of Responsibility

On some theories, responsibility is associated with control (freedom to do otherwise); but we have seen that, on these theories, persons might not be held responsible for all the acts for which we believe they are culpable. On the other theories, responsibility is associated with willing action (or acting freely); this is Frankfurt's theory, a modified version of which is accepted by Gary Watson.[10] I have suggested a different theory—an actual-sequence approach—which associates responsibility neither with freedom to do otherwise nor with acting freely, but with free, or uncompelled action.

Patricia Greenspan has argued that acts can be unfree even though the agent was free to do otherwise.[11] I have argued that acts can be free though the agent was *not* free to do otherwise. Also, an agent can act freely (in the Frankfurt-Watson sense) though the act is unfree (in my sense); that is, one can "identify with" an act that is compelled. (I thus preserve Locke's intuition about the happy slave.) Whereas some philosophers (including G. E. M. Anscombe, and most recently, Richard Sorabji)[12] argue that responsibility is associated with acts that are *caused* but not rendered inevitable by those causes, I have suggested that one might allow that responsible acts are sometimes inevitable but uncaused (or not causally determined) events.

The traditional account of responsibility claims that what is wrong with determinism is that it erodes control; the account I offer claims that what is wrong with lack of control is that it usually (but not

10. "Free Agency," Chapter 2, above.
11. "Behavior Control and Freedom of Action," Chapter 9, below.
12. *Necessity, Cause and Blame* (Ithaca: Cornell University Press, 1980).

always) indicates actual-sequence compulsion. Thus the reason why lack of control normally rules out responsibility is that it normally points to actual-sequence compulsion. But when lack of control is not accompanied by actual-sequence compulsion, we need not rule out responsibility.

The actual-sequence approach to responsibility which I have sketched solves a problem faced by Frankfurt's theory. Consider Frankfurt's statement in Chapter 6.

> Now if someone had no alternative to performing a certain action [and did indeed perform it] but did not perform it because he could not have done otherwise, then he would have performed exactly the same action even if he *could* have done otherwise . . . Whatever it was that actually led the person to do what he did, or that made him do it, would have led him to do it or made him do it even if it had been possible for him to do something else instead.
>
> Thus it would have made no difference, so far as concerns his action or how he came to perform it, if the circumstances that made it impossible for him to avoid performing it had not prevailed . . . . When a fact is in this way irrelevant to the problem of accounting for a person's action it seems quite gratuitous to assign it any weight in the assessment of his moral responsibility. (pp. 150–151)

But, if Frankfurt is right, then it seems as though an agent will be responsible for too many things. This criticism, including the following example, was presented to me by Carl Ginet. Suppose someone had no alternative to failing to stop the rain but it is not the case that he failed to stop it *because* he could not have done otherwise; he thought (incorrectly, of course) that he could stop it any time he wanted to by uttering a certain prayer. It follows that he would have failed to stop the rain even if he could have done otherwise. Whatever it was that actually led him to fail to stop the rain would have led him to do so even if it had been possible for him to stop it. Thus it would have made no difference, so far as concerns his failing to stop the rain or how he came to do so, if the circumstances that made it impossible for him to avoid failing to stop the rain had not prevailed. If Frankfurt is right, then when a fact is in this way irrelevant to the problem of accounting for someone's failing to stop the rain, it seems quite gratuitous to assign it any weight in the assessment of his moral responsibility.

So it seems that Frankfurt will need to say that this agent is morally responsible for failing to stop the rain; other persons might be morally responsible for failing to stop the Earth's rotation, etc. But a theory of moral responsibility which has this sort of result is inconsistent with our intuitions about moral responsibility.

On the actual-sequence account of responsibility I sketched above, we can explain why the agent is not morally responsible for failing to stop the rain. Even in a libertarian world (in which human choices or actions are not causally necessitated), there are certain causal laws governing natural phenomena which (given present technology) entail that no agent can stop the rain by uttering a prayer. Thus the actual sequence of events proceeds in such a way that the agent's not stopping the rain is causally necessitated. Similarly, the physical laws that obtain (even in a libertarian world) are such that (given present technology) it is causally necessitated that no person can stop the Earth's rotation. If we accept the claim that actual-sequence causal necessitation is incompatible with responsibility, we can explain why no agent is morally responsible for failing to stop the rain. An actual-sequence model, but *not* of the Frankfurt-Watson sort, can explain why agents are not responsible for (say) failing to stop the rain.

## VII. Conclusion

It might be objected against the approach I have sketched that causal determination needn't constitute *compulsion;* after all, it is consistent with Frankfurt's presentation of his example that Jones's voting for Reagan is actually causally determined. Hence it might seem that responsibility is obviously compatible with determinism. Though this may be so, it is crucial to see that the battleground has now shifted; the question now is whether causal necessitation in the actual sequence constitutes compulsion, that is, whether causally deterministic actual sequences lack components required for moral responsibility. The compatibilist about responsibility and determinism will say no, but the incompatibilist will say yes; they will both point to features of causally deterministic sequences in order to establish their positions, but Frankfurt-style examples concerning what would happen in alternate sequences will not support either position. Frankfurt-style examples will be irrelevant to resolving *this* dispute.

In summary, Frankfurt's examples seem to separate responsibility from control and hence to show responsibility compatible with determinism even if determinism is inconsistent with control. One strategy of response is to challenge the divorce of responsibility from control. I discussed two problems with this strategy: the tenuousness of the essentialist principle of event individuation and the fact that alternate-sequence interventions of the Frankfurt sort do not establish that the agent has the deliberate control required for responsibility. I developed a second strategy of response: this strategy concedes the dissociation of responsibility from control but argues that this dissociation needn't entail the consistency of determinism with responsibility.

I have not argued *for* incompatibilism about determinism and responsibility; I have had the more modest project of showing how the incompatibilist is not forced into inconsistency by Frankfurt's examples. Both the compatibilist and the incompatibilist alike can unite in conceding that enough information is encoded in the actual sequence to ground our responsibility attributions; as philosophers we need to decode this information and see whether it is consistent with deterministic causation.

# 9

# Behavior Control and Freedom of Action

I would like to begin to understand the notion of psychological compulsion—what it is to *have* to do something, and hence to do it unfreely, on psychological grounds. I am interested in a wide range of problematic cases from the psychological literature, such as conditioning, drug addiction, brainwashing, and posthypnotic suggestion, which involve unfreedom in *some* form or forms and might be thought to involve psychological compulsion. But where I can find mention of such cases in the philosophical literature, they often seem to be entangled in the free-will question, as if it were natural to treat them as cases of determination by psychological causes. I want to see whether I can detach a few of them, and the explanation of their unfreedom, from all the main views on the traditional free-will question—the question of freedom versus *determination*—even views on the *compatibility* of freedom and determination.[1] Here I shall suggest a

"Behavior Control and Freedom of Action" originally appeared in the *Philosophical Review*, 87 (April 1978), 225–40, © 1978 by the *Philosophical Review*, and is reprinted here with permission from P. S. Greenspan and from the *Philosophical Review*.

An earlier version of this paper, written while I was a Mellon Postdoctoral Fellow at the University of Pittsburgh during 1975–1976, was read at the December, 1976, meetings of the American Philosophical Association, Eastern Division. I owe thanks to Alvin Goldman for perceptive comments.

1. For readers unfamiliar with the literature: the traditional freewill question really amounts to a conjunction of two questions, the question of determinism and the question of compatibilism. The main views on it might be graphed as follows:

|  | *the question of determinism* | |
|---|---|---|
|  | determinism | indeterminism |
| compatibilism<br>*the question of*<br>*compatibilism* | SOFT DETERMINISM | [NO NAME] |
| incompatibilism | HARD DETERMINISM | LIBERTARIANISM |

simple (and rough) explanation of unfreedom which makes no reference to determination by psychological causes, but which seems to
account for at least some cases of psychological compulsion, of the
sort that Skinner has in mind (and takes to go "beyond freedom") in
*Beyond Freedom and Dignity*.[2]

These are the cases at issue in the recent popular debate over the
unfreedom entailed by behavior control, or the practical upshot of
the theory of reinforcement and conditioning, the Skinnerian behaviorist's science; and I shall focus particularly on one of the most extreme, the fictional (and somewhat fanciful) case of the reconditioned
criminal Alex in *A Clockwork Orange*.[3] The behavior control debate
itself sometimes strays onto the free-will question; but I shall use
Alex's case to support a general position in the debate which bypasses
the free-will question entirely. My suggestions will actually have some
bearing on our treatment of the free-will question; but in this paper I
shall just say enough to introduce them (Section I) and to exhibit their
most important consequences (II), in answer to a fairly narrow question about the relationship between behavior control and freedom of
action.[4] Can we explain how Alex, first of all, is *compelled* to act as he
does, without deciding whether his behavior may be determined? I
shall argue that we can—and that we can then see why less extreme
cases of conditioning need *not* involve unfreedom—if we treat psychological compulsion as rationally motivated, on the model of
coercion.

I

By repeatedly viewing violent films under the influence of an emetic, or a nausea-inducing drug, Alex is conditioned to experience such

---

In "detaching" some cases of unfreedom from these views, I mean just to argue that the
cases have no *special* relevance to the freewill question. Of course they might share some
feature with a larger class of cases—e.g., actions generally—which bears on the question; but I shall ignore such broader issues here.

2. B. F. Skinner, *Beyond Freedom and Dignity* (New York: Bantam/Vintage, 1972).

3. Anthony Burgess, *A Clockwork Orange* (New York: Ballantine, 1962). For evidence
that the case is not *completely* fanciful, see the report of the California prison experiment
in (e.g.) Philip J. Hilts, *Behavior Mod* (New York: Harper's Magazine, 1974), pp. 128–
131.

4. I extend my suggestions to another sort of case and show how they bear on our
treatment of the free-will question in "Unfreedom and Indeterminism" (unpublished).
[1986 note: for a successor to this paper, with some qualifications and additions to the
view of freedom suggested here, see "Unfreedom and Responsibility," in F. Schoeman,
ed., *New Directions in Responsibility* (Cambridge: Cambridge University Press, forthcoming).] In this paper, to keep my main argument brief and perspicuous, I shall make
copious use of footnotes explaining details, problems, and qualifications.

intense discomfort at images of violence that he henceforth "has no choice" but to refrain from violence himself.[5] This is enough, I take it, to make Alex unfree; and I shall ignore any further elements of the story, facts incidental to the conditioning process itself, which may compound his unfreedom. For instance, Alex is also unable to bear listening to music, after his reconditioning; and it is unclear whether he undergoes the process freely, since he is never fully informed of its details, and consents to it, in any case, with long imprisonment as his only alternative.[6] These facts and others bear importantly on the question of the dangers of behavior control in particular practical cases; and by ignoring them I shall be cutting off my discussion from much of the popular debate. But I want to concentrate on the process and results of Alex's reconditioning, as central to the question of how behavior control itself may interfere with freedom of action. In Alex's case (though not in some others I shall introduce later), conditioning does seem to give rise to unfreedom—indeed, to a variety of psychological compulsion—quite apart from any problems about side-effects and free consent. Once conditioned, Alex *has* to refrain from violence; and I want to see what this means.

A behaviorist would describe Alex's case as a two-stage process of aversive conditioning, in which a kind of punishment of certain responses with aversive stimuli conditioned to follow them in turn conditions incompatible responses, which escape the punishment and are said to be "negatively reinforced."[7] In the novel, the punished re-

5. See Burgess, op. cit., pp. 101–105, pp. 111–112. Throughout my argument, I shall take the appropriateness of expressions like "has no choice" and "has to" (cf., e.g., p. 96) as a sign of compulsion, and hence of unfreedom (a broader notion, as I shall suggest below). What I shall try to explain, in explaining Alex's unfreedom, is the sense in which he *has* to do what he does. I shall make no attempt to offer necessary and sufficient conditions of compulsion or unfreedom, since I think that our intuitions in this area are too messy to support that attempt. (For instance, to be compelled is not necessarily to have *a* compulsion, as we commonly speak; and an action may be unfree even where we would not say that the agent performs it unfree*ly*. See nn. 8 and 14.)

6. See Burgess, op. cit., pp. 114–116, p. 95.

7. For a standard account of the two-stage process, see e.g., David C. Rimm and John C. Masters, *Behavior Therapy: Techniques and Empirical Findings* (New York: Academic, 1974), pp. 355–356, pp. 369–372. From the point of view of the first stage, the images of violence are stimuli, and the feelings of discomfort responses; but this is reversed in the second stage, and hence in my attempt to sum up the two-stage process. Just below, I shall describe the process in commonsense terms; but here is how a fuller technical description of it would run: in the first stage, an unconditioned stimulus (the emetic) is repeatedly paired with a conditioned stimulus (violent images) to produce a conditioned response (nausea); in the second stage, this conditioned response acts as an aversive stimulus, and a new conditioned response (avoiding violent images) is produced by repeated pairings with a negative reinforcer (relief of nausea), which amounts to an escape from the aversive stimulus. My parenthetical explanations would not

sponses would seem to be images (or the contemplation of images) of violence, and the aversive stimuli feelings of discomfort. A strict behaviorist, of course, would insist on translating such mentalistic talk into talk of observable events; but I shall follow the novel (as well as texts on the methods of behavior control) and ignore these complications too. In common-sense terms, then, Alex's reconditioning divides into two stages: first, a stage of classical or Pavlovian conditioning, in which images of violence, repeatedly paired with the effects of the emetic, come to be followed by feelings of discomfort; next, a stage of operant or Skinnerian conditioning, in which images of violence, repeatedly followed by feelings of discomfort, come to be avoided. The question for us is: what is it about this two-stage process that makes Alex unfree?

Someone might suggest that the process makes Alex unfree because it brings his behavior under the control of certain causes, the stimuli which give rise to conditioned responses. After the process is complete, images of violence produce in him feelings of discomfort which, in combination with his history of reinforcement for avoiding such images, *cause* him to avoid them; and so he has no choice but to refrain from violence. He *has* to refrain because his behavior is causally determined, or necessitated by prior events. However, while this sort of causal explanation seems plausible enough, in application to the data of conditioning, it is not the only plausible explanation of those data. (It is a presupposition, not a consequence, of the Skinnerian behaviorist's science that talk of purposes, like mentalistic talk, plays no role in that explanation.) The first stage of conditioning, or what we might call the stage of *reaction*, whereby feelings of discomfort come to follow images of violence, can best be explained causally, perhaps; but the second stage, or the stage of *action*, whereby images of violence come to be avoided, also allows for a kind of rational explanation in terms of purposes.[8] Alex avoids images of violence,

---

satisfy a strict behaviorist, as I go on to say; but they should give the reader some idea of the workings of the two-stage process.

8. I take it that purposive explanation *need* not be causal, even if it *may* be, and hence that behavior may be explained as nonrandom without being explained as necessitated by prior causes, or causally determined. Though I call it a kind of rational explanation, I shall go on to show how it allows for some elements of *ir*rationality—just enough, I think, to support our intuitive view that the subject of psychological compulsion is *neither* fully rational nor totally insane. (See nn. 9, 11, 12.) To explain how he is compelled or unfree, though, it is not enough to point to the irrational features of his act—even to the fact (which Bernard Gert has pointed out) that it would persist in *situations* where it is irrational. This may or may not be enough to pick out what we call "a" compulsion, but it would certainly not be enough to *explain the phenomenon* of compulsion—the sense in which the agent *has* to perform the compelled act. At most,

once the conditioning process is complete, *in order to* avoid reacting to them with feelings of discomfort. Such action—to avoid immediate discomfort—seems perfectly reasonable, even in cases where some incompatible action might be *more* reasonable. If he still prefers to engage in violence, for example, Alex might be best advised to submit to some immediate discomfort in the hopes of eventually extinguishing his conditioned response, now that the emetic is no longer being administered.[9] But as long as the first stage of the conditioning process is in effect, and Alex does react to images of violence with feelings of discomfort, it will also be reasonable for him to avoid images of violence; and the second stage of the conditioning process can be explained noncausally.

That is, it can be explained noncausally as well as *any* behavior can; and this means that the explanation of Alex's behavior as conditioned cannot show that it is *specially* unfree—unfree in some way in which a normal decision to refrain from violence is not. There is no reason to suppose that Alex's behavior must be caused—or caused in some way that is abnormal. A number of philosophers hold that normal behavior is caused (that actions, for example, are caused by wants and beliefs); but in any case, a libertarian interpretation of our common-sense view of behavior seems quite compatible with the data of conditioning.[10] About the second stage of Alex's conditioning process, or the stage of action, all the data really entitle one to say is that the likelihood of his avoiding images of violence is increased, not that he is caused to avoid such images, any more than we normally are. And at the first stage, the stage of reaction, although Alex's reactions to

---

the act's irrationality would serve as evidence for the claim that he has to do it; but I want to see what that claim means, since it is that claim that suggests, I think, that cases of psychological compulsion involve determination, and hence that their unfreedom has something to do with the traditional free-will question.

9. At the end of the novel, Alex is simply subjected to the extinction process, and its details are not made clear; see Burgess, op. cit., pp. 169–172. If he had the knowledge and ability to bring about extinction himself, however, but failed to do so, Alex might seem to be *weak-willed,* and hence in one way not fully rational. If he refrained from violence, he might be acting against his real values to avoid immediate discomfort. (Some authors seem to think this sort of conflict is essential to unfreedom; but I shall take issue with them below.)

10. See Alvin I. Goldman, *A Theory of Human Action* (Englewood Cliffs, N.J.: Prentice-Hall, 1970), pp. 146–157, for a use of the causal theory of action to support a general argument that the data of conditioning may be given a purposive explanation. Since my more limited argument is independent of the causal theory (which is generally tied to determinism), I see no problem about combining it with libertarianism. (I think it could be rephrased, moreover, to satisfy those philosophers who object to talk of causes, but still see actions as determined by natural law. For simplicity's sake, however, I shall think of determinism as the view that every event is necessitated by prior causes.)

images of violence do seem to be caused, so do normal reactions to such images, and other states (like emotions and wants) which normally influence rational behavior, whether or not they cause it in turn. A determinist, of course, might insist that both stages are best explained causally; but he would need to say something further to explain Alex's unfreedom, on our intuitive view that Alex's unfreedom is abnormal.

If normal reactions are caused, and normal actions are rationally influenced by them, then the causes of Alex's behavior would not seem to differ in *kind* from the causes of a normal decision to refrain from violence. What is abnormal, in Alex's case, would seem to be the *intensity* of his reactions to violence. Most of us, presumably, are somewhat repelled by images of violence, at least in real life; but after his reconditioning, Alex cannot bear them. His reactions impose special constraints on his actions—put special pressure on him to refrain from violence—because they are so extreme; and this, I would suggest, is what makes Alex specially unfree. He has no choice but to refrain from violence *if* he wants (as all of us must) to avoid unreasonable discomfort. He *has* to refrain *or* suffer the consequences—consequences which make it unreasonably hard for him to do otherwise. He is unfree, in short, because he is faced with a kind of threat, like a robbery victim coerced at gunpoint, with intense discomfort as his only option to compliance. This means that the action he is compelled to take will be reasonable—reasonable in light of an *un*reasonable threat—and hence that this case of psychological compulsion can be given a kind of rational explanation. Though the agent's reactions are deranged, in a way, his actions are rationally influenced by them; so we need not refer to any nonrational principles of motivation to explain his compulsion to act. If the behaviorists are right, in fact, all or most cases of psychological compulsion (phobias, for example) can be given a similar rational explanation, with anxiety generally playing the role that nausea plays for Alex.[11] But I shall concentrate, for the moment, on Alex's case. Is its explanation complete?

Certainly more could be said about what amounts to "unreasonable" discomfort—enough of a threat to make an agent unfree. I see no hope of formulating a precise criterion, though, since I suspect that freedom shades into unfreedom by degrees. Here, at any rate, I am interested only in arguing that, whether or not it can be made

11. See, e.g., the view of deviant behavior in general which is assumed in Albert Bandura, *Principles of Behavior Modification* (New York: Holt, Rinehart, and Winston, 1969), esp. pp. 2–5, pp. 19–20. Even if compulsion is rationally explainable, the compelled agent would not be fully rational, on this view, since he would presumably experience irrational anxiety.

precise, the criterion will not commit us to a particular position on the freewill question. Someone might suggest that Alex is unfree just because his reaction to images of violence makes it *impossible* for him to engage in violence; he is threatened with incapacitating discomfort if he tries to. In fact, the novel does suggest this point; but in any case, I think we would still call Alex unfree if his intense discomfort simply interfered with acts of violence, without strictly preventing them. If the discomfort he faced were sufficiently intense, then whether or not he was capable of violence, we would still say that Alex was compelled to refrain from it—as we would say that a robbery victim, facing a similar threat, is compelled to hand over his money. He need not be *unable* to resist the threat, or completely incapacitated by fear, though I think it may be crucial that he does *fear* the threatened consequence, rather than calmly preferring to avoid it, and hence that his ability to resist is somehow limited.[12] We say he has no choice because he has

12. See Harry G. Frankfurt, "Coercion and Moral Responsibility," in T. Honderich, ed., *Essays on Freedom of Action* (London: Routledge & Kegan Paul, 1973), esp. p. 77, for a view of coercion as involving an *irresistible* threat. The weaker view which Frankfurt means to improve upon may be found in Robert Nozick, "Coercion," in S. Morgenbesser et al., eds., *Philosophy, Science, and Method: Essays in Honor of Ernest Nagel* (New York: St. Martin's, 1969), esp. p. 442, where a threat seems to count as coercive just as long as it makes some option substantially worse. The intermediate possibility I suggest here allows for the importance of the agent's fear without insisting that he be incapacitated by it. Since fear disrupts deliberation, it can be seen as pressuring or driving the agent to comply with the threat, and thus as supporting another sense in which an agent subjected to a coercive threat would not be fully rational. Also, by bringing in fear, I hope to suggest a way around some possible problems with the "no real option" account of unfreedom. For instance, what if an agent merely *thinks*—mistakenly, as it happens—that he has no real option to some act? I would be inclined to say that he then merely thinks—mistakenly, once again—that he is compelled to perform that act, were it not for the fact that fear is itself aversive. As long as his alternative to performing the act is viewed with sufficient fear—or some similar emotion like anxiety—I think we would grant that he really is unfree; and I suspect that it is the intensity of his emotion, rather than the intensity of the further discomfort he faces, which directly determines his degree of unfreedom in cases where the emotion is *not* based on a mistake. This holds for ordinary cases of coercion, as well as the cases of psychological compulsion which I want to explain on the model of coercion.

Moreover, by focusing on the unfree agent's emotional state, I think we can avoid some further problems by insisting that the agent is involved in a kind of escape situation. In Alex's original case, he responds to violent images with nausea more or less immediately; but what if he eventually adjusted to his situation, and came to avoid violent images automatically, without even anticipatory thoughts of nausea? I think we would still consider him unfree, as long as he acted out of (conscious or unconscious) *fear* of his reactions to violence. But we would not say, on the other hand, that an agent is compelled not to break his own nose (an example I owe to Alvin Goldman), or to refrain from doing all the things that he *would* fear if it ever occurred to him to do them. Compulsion seems to be limited to choices an agent actually *faces*, so that his fear actually operates as a motive. (If he fears *both* alternatives—because he is threatened no matter which way he turns—I think we would say that he is compelled to choose the alternative he fears *less*, as in ordinary cases of coercion.)

no *real* choice—no real or reasonable option to turn to instead—and not because there is literally only one thing he can do. So on one very simple model, at least, unfreedom need not involve the inability to do otherwise.

Perhaps an act is unfree if it would be unreasonable to *expect* the agent to do otherwise, even where he has good reason to—so that unreasonable discomfort, the amount sufficient for unfreedom, is discomfort too intense to expect the agent to bear, relative to some presumed or standard set of circumstances. I suspect that something roughly like this is correct—something with normative (exculpatory) force—but if so, incompatibilists could argue that a causally impossible act would be unreasonable to expect of an agent even if it were not too *hard* to expect of him. This point has some plausibility; but philosophers who challenge it—most notably those who accept the hypothetical analysis of "can" and hold that an agent might be *able* to do what is causally impossible—could accept compatibilism.[13] The important point for us, though, is that we need not reach a decision on the question of compatibilism to handle Alex's case. Whether or not it is causally possible for him to do otherwise—indeed, whether or not he is *able* to do otherwise—Alex would still seem to be unfree. The discomfort he faces if he engages in violence is intense enough to rule out that option as unreasonable to expect of him, even if it is perfectly possible for him—and even if he still has an urge to choose it. As far as I can see, our inclination to insist that Alex must be unable to do otherwise if he really is compelled or unfree is just a product of our tendency to interpret freedom of action in terms of the traditional freewill question.

If we resist that tendency, I think we can account for many of our intuitions on unfreedom by applying the explanation I have suggested to possible variants of Alex's case. For instance, Alex would still seem to be unfree—to have no choice but to refrain from violence—even if he did *not* still want to engage in violence when the conditioning process was complete. His unfreedom does not seem to depend, that is, on his experiencing some sort of conflict about violence, as a number of recent authors on unfreedom apparently would maintain.[14] In fact, there is some evidence to suggest that Alex's recondi-

13. For a version of the hypothetical analysis of "can," combined with a causal theory of action, see Goldman, op. cit., esp. 204–205. For some problems with the hypothetical analysis, see my "Wiggins on Historical Inevitability and Incompatibilism," *Philosophical Studies*, XXIX, 4 (April 1976), 235–247.

14. See especially Gary Watson, "Free Agency," Chapter 2, above, esp. pp. 91–92; also, Frankfurt, "Freedom of the Will and the Concept of a Person," Chapter 1, above, esp. pp. 72–75. Perhaps we would say that Alex refrains from violence free*ly*, where he

tioning would not be effective unless he really wanted it to succeed, and hence identified with a higher-order desire not to be motivated by the desire for violence.[15] But at any rate, even supposing that he has no conflicting urges at all, the conditioning process would still seem to leave Alex in a state where he is compelled to refrain from violence, since he has no reasonable option to refraining—like a philanthropic robbery victim, coerced into doing what he wants to do anyway. Perhaps his unfreedom would be less morally disturbing in such a case (another complication I shall ignore); but he *would* still seem to be unfree. I shall now turn to some further variant cases which would *not* seem to involve unfreedom, at least in the form where it resembles coercion, and thus counts as psychological compulsion, on the model I have sketched.

## II

My explanation of Alex's unfreedom applies only to extreme cases of aversive conditioning; so if it is correct, less extreme cases need not involve unfreedom. If Alex's conditioning were accomplished simply by punishing images of violence with disapproval (supposing, rather absurdly, that this would work), we would then be able to count his behavior as free, even if *less* free than before his reconditioning. He might still have a reasonable option to refraining from violence, if his images of violence were accompanied only by mild anxiety, or the like, once the conditioning process was complete; for his behavior, however unreflective and habitual, would then be no different from a normal decision to refrain from violence, which may also be a result of prior conditioning.[16] The same holds, moreover, for even extreme

---

welcomes the results of the conditioning process; but he would still not seem to be free, as long as those results are in force.

15. See Bandura, "The Ethics and Social Purposes of Behavior Modification," in C. M. Fronks and G. T. Wilson, eds., *Annual Review of Behavior Therapy*, Vol. III (New York: Brunner/Mozel, 1975). My talk of higher-order desires follows Frankfurt, Chapter 1, esp. p. 70.

16. Although some habits (e.g. smoking) may be particularly hard to break for special reasons (e.g. because the agent has come to rely on them to discharge tension, or the like), I take it that habitual behavior *need* not be unfree, however predictable. Consider, for instance, someone's habit of washing his face *before* brushing his teeth in the morning; I see no reason to think that there must be limits on his ability to do otherwise. Similarly, our normal habit of refraining from violence can be broken easily enough, supposing that it is conditioned to mild anxiety. The same holds, moreover, even for *extreme* cases of aversive conditioning whose *results* are not so extreme—where the eventual effect of the intense discomfort produced by some drug, say, is simply to neutralize the agent's original positive reaction to violence, leaving him with the same mild anxiety as the rest of us, or even with no particular reaction (and no mistaken fear

cases of conditioning accomplished by reward rather than punishment, or what behaviorists call "positive control," if writers on coercion are right in insisting on a sharp distinction between offers and threats.[17] If an offer, no matter how tempting, cannot be said to coerce, then only cases involving some sort of aversive control can fit my suggested model of unfreedom. My model, then, differs importantly from the causal model I have rejected above; for with unfree behavior explained as behavior which is *caused* (necessitated by prior events, so that alternatives to it are causally impossible), all cases of conditioning would seem to involve the same degree of unfreedom, even if some are especially disturbing because they also involve the infliction of extreme pain. In the behavior control debate, in fact, aversive control is treated as somehow worse than positive control but is not distinguished from it in point of freedom; and I suspect that some sort of causal model is taken for granted.

But what if Alex could be conditioned to refrain from violence simply by instituting a system of rewards within the prison, so that good behavior earned him points towards various privileges he wanted, like access to the prison stereo or a private room?[18] Again, we must ignore possible complications and suppose, for example, that Alex's original life in prison is decent enough to leave him with a reasonable option if he refuses to participate in the system.[19] But if

---

of one), but just a habit of refraining from violence. In such a case, on my view, the agent would not be unfree once the conditioning process was complete—though he would have passed through a temporary stage of unfreedom to get to that point. This is surely *less* morally disturbing than Alex's case; and I suspect that it comes closer to what goes on in real life cases of aversive conditioning.

17. See e.g., Nozick, op. cit. pp. 447–453, pp. 458–465. Since compulsion seems to be a broader notion than coercion (only the latter requires the direct intervention of another agent, as author of the threat), Nozick's explanation of the distinction, in terms of subjection to another agent's will, needs to be broadened to allow for this extension. For some further important differences between compulsion and coercion, see n. 19.

18. The institution of such a "token system" is a common method of behavior control; for a brief, nontechnical account, see Perry London, *Behavior Control* (New York: Harper & Row, 1969), p. 94.

19. If it does not, then any reward the system gives him may equally be described as an escape from punishment, and the case as a case of aversive control. This is one way in which an agent can be compelled to accept an offer—because his alternative to accepting it is sufficiently bad to count as a kind of threat, even if it is not a consequence of the offer (or even, in some cases, of any intervention by an agent), so that the offer itself cannot be said to coerce. In fact, perhaps an agent might sometimes be compelled to accept an offer where his alternative to accepting it involves extreme disappointment, frustration, etc., partly because the offer is extremely large. So the limitation of my argument to "pure" cases of positive control is a very important one. Apart from this qualification, however, I would deny that a large offer could compel an agent to act. It would not be unreasonable to expect him to do otherwise *if he had good reason to;* but we would not say the same, e.g., if a gun were pointed at his head—if he were faced with an option he intensely *feared,* that is.

we do treat this as a *pure* case of positive control, unmixed with any aversive elements, we ought to be able to count Alex's behavior as free. That seems to be our intuitive view; for otherwise a normal decision to get something by modifying one's behavior—the response to a normal offer—would also seem to be unfree, since it is equally susceptible to causal explanation. We do not think that instituting a system of monetary rewards for behavior in the world outside the prison interferes with freedom just because it increases the likelihood of certain responses. Granting that the agent does have a reasonable option to them, responses repeatedly followed by satisfaction of his desires need not be specially unfree, even if they are conditioned; so if conditioning is interpreted as a causal process, the causal model of unfreedom seems either wrong or incomplete. Positive control need not involve unfreedom (or unfreedom beyond what a hard determinist would take to be normal), despite the suggestions of Skinner and other behaviorists.

That is, positive control need not involve unfreedom in the form appropriate to psychological compulsion; but perhaps it may sometimes involve it in a different form—one tied to problems about the agent's knowledge of his motivation, rather than limitations on his ability to modify his behavior. What if Alex's non-aversive reconditioning could somehow be accomplished without his awareness, by offering him some subtler kind of reward, like approval, which behavior may be aimed at unconsciously? If he did not realize that he was being weaned away from violence, Alex might seem to be unfree because he was manipulated, or unwittingly influenced by others. But even granting that manipulation should be taken as a form of unfreedom (and I think our intuitions are unclear on this point), the manipulated agent *has a choice* about what he does; his freedom is only limited by the fact that he does not see *why* he does what he does. Consider the parallel case of the behaviorist professor whose class gradually conditioned him to move away from his preferred corner of the room.[20] The class conspiracy—to shape the teacher's behavior by selectively reinforcing it with signs of attention and interest—might seem to interfere with the teacher's freedom, in a way, by bringing his behavior under external control. His behavior—the series of moves he made in front of the class—would still seem to be purposive, though, despite his unawareness of its purposes. He was perfectly able to modify it, but lacked control over it only because he lacked

20. This case is part of the behaviorist folklore, but I cannot find a written reference to it. For similar cases, see Hilts, op. cit., pp. 55–57, and J. R. Millenson, *Principles of Behavioral Analysis* (New York: Macmillan, 1967), pp. 81–82.

knowledge of its real motivation. If he understood why he was moving away from his preferred corner—to get a better response from the class—I think we would count him as perfectly free. So it is the fact that he is unaware of external control, and not the external control itself, which might seem to make him unfree—in the sense of *manipulated*, not *compelled*.

In fact, it might be only in this sense that some of the standard cases of unfreedom really involve it. We can see how the model of coercion might be applied to cases of drug addiction, for example, where the agent faces withdrawal symptoms if he goes too long without his drug; and similarly for at least *some* cases of brainwashing, those which rely on methods of aversive control. But brainwashing *purely* by positive control (*if* that is possible) and posthypnotic suggestion—as well as some further problematic cases, like subliminal advertising—might seem to be cases of manipulation rather than compulsion. In posthypnotic suggestion, for instance, the subject apparently does what he does (opens the window, say) only because he wants to (he suddenly feels too warm); and is he any less able than we normally are to resist his wants and do otherwise? There is at least room for doubt (amid the various different interpretations of the phenomenon of hypnosis) about whether the subject in any sense *has* to act on the hypnotist's suggestion. But in any case, he might still seem to be unfree where he is not aware of the external source of his wants, and thus may be said to be manipulated by the hypnotist who implants them in him. This has nothing to do with psychological compulsion, though—with doing something (on my account) because you have no reasonable option to doing it. Nor does it appear to have anything to do with the freewill question, since our wants would normally seem to be caused in *some* way or other (to be *re*actions rather than actions), and the subject of hypnosis might not be unfree if he knew which of his wants was caused in a *special* way, by the mediation of the hypnotist while he was in a suggestible state. I take it, then, that variants of Alex's case in which he lacks knowledge will not undercut my claims about psychological compulsion and the freewill question. In fact, they may suggest that the real threat of behavior control to human freedom is something quite different from psychological compulsion, something to do with unconscious motivation, without even apparent bearing on the freewill question.

What I have in mind is this: If we stick to our common sense interpretation of the data of conditioning, and allow talk of purposes, the data indicate that we sometimes act on purposes we are unaware of. Conditioning itself need not pose any threat to human freedom, if

I am right; there is nothing particularly disturbing (or surprising) about the fact that the probability of behavior increases when it is repeatedly followed by reward or escape from punishment. But if this can happen without the agent's awareness, then he can be manipulated by others, even in a case of positive control. There may be no limitations on his *ability* to do otherwise; but he will still lack full control over his behavior, since he does not understand its motivation, and thus is deprived of possible *reasons* for doing otherwise.[21] Once the conditioning process is complete, then, it may be wrong to say that the agent has no choice; but since the choices he does make are not fully conscious, perhaps we ought to count him (or them) as unfree. If so, there may be cases of positive control which do involve unfreedom. But the point is that there would then seem to be different *forms* of unfreedom, which are commonly lumped together in the behavior control debate; and some of them have nothing to do with the issues that concern me here. Positive control may involve manipulation; but it does not seem to involve compulsion, or anything that even *appears* to link it to the free-will question. On the model I have sketched, psychological compulsion as a result of conditioning would seem to be rather rare; but manipulation may be much more pervasive, if an agent can be conditioned without his knowledge.

This means that no behavior controller should conclude from my argument that there is nothing morally disturbing about positive control, or even that it never involves unfreedom. My argument has focused on metaphysical issues surrounding one important form of unfreedom, the one that often seems to be entangled in the free-will question; and I have not attempted to draw any moral conclusions. (Indeed, I have not even said enough to show that behavior control *is* morally disturbing where it *does* involve psychological compulsion. In Alex's original case, for instance, someone might suggest that interference with his freedom is amply justified by the crimes he has committed.) To evaluate particular practical cases of behavior control,

---

21. I take it that the fact that one's motivation seems to be out of one's control may count as good reason for resisting it; and that if an agent is unaware of the reasons for choosing some option, it would be unreasonable to expect him to choose it. On the explanation of unfreedom I suggest above, then, manipulation *might* seem to make an agent unfree. I leave open many further questions about manipulation, though, since it is enough, for my purposes here, just to argue that it does not even appear to bear on the freewill question, since it does not involve *having* to do some act. For instance, is it his unawareness specifically of external control, or just his unawareness of his motivation generally, which makes the manipulated agent unfree? I have hinted at my suspicion that the latter is sufficient (in which case theories like behaviorism—and for that matter, psychoanalysis—would pose a threat to human freedom even apart from the possibility of manipulation); but my point here does not depend on this view.

one would need to bring in complications like those about side-effects and free consent which I have ignored from the start; and these would introduce still other possible forms of unfreedom. But I hope I have made some headway on the initial theoretical questions which seem to cause confusion in the behavior control debate and elsewhere. Unfreedom, in the form where it amounts to psychological compulsion, appears to be limited to extreme cases of aversive conditioning; and those cases can be explained as rationally motivated, on the model of coercion, without taking a particular position on the free-will question.

# 10

## Free Will as the Ability to Will

---

BERNARD GERT AND TIMOTHY J. DUGGAN

The opposite of Determinism is Indeterminism, but what is the opposite of Free Will?[1] Is it most fruitful to regard the denial that someone has Free Will as the claim that his actions are coerced, or more generally, a claim about the circumstances that the man finds himself in; or, on the other hand, as a claim about the man himself, about his lacking some power or ability? In his chapter on Free Will in *Ethics*, G. E. Moore makes the following remark.

> The statement that we have Free Will is certainly ordinarily understood to imply that we really sometimes have the power of acting differently from the way in which we actually act; and hence, if anybody tells us that we have Free Will, while at the same time he means to deny that we ever have such power, he is simply misleading us. ([20]: 126)

However, Moore never reaches a firm conclusion as to what kind of power we must have if we are properly to be said to have Free Will. It is our contention in this paper that a person has Free Will in so far as he has what we call the "ability to will" or "volitional ability." We are thus in agreement with Moore that the question whether man has Free Will is best viewed as a question about whether he has a certain power (we prefer to talk of ability) not as a question about whether

"Free Will as the Ability to Will" originally appeared in *Noûs*, 13 (May 1979), 197–217, © 1979 by Indiana University, and is reprinted here by permission of the authors and the editor of *Noûs*.

1. This paper is a development and application of concepts first analyzed in [10]. However, the analyses have been modified and there have been some terminological changes. In this paper we show how the concept of the ability to will can and, indeed, must be employed in the solution of the problem of Free Will. (We use "the ability to will" and "volitional ability" interchangeably.)

what a man willed to do was the result of coercion. Consequently, we regard analyses of sentences like "He did it of his own free will" to be somewhat misleading in a discussion of the problem of Free Will. For admittedly, to assert that a man did something of his own free will generally means more than that he did it voluntarily, i.e., he did it intentionally and he had the ability to will to do it; it also means that he did it freely, i.e., no one forced him to do it.[2]

Often the "Problem of Free Will" has been conceived of in all or nothing fashion: does man have Free Will or not? We think it is more fruitful to ask: does a particular person have Free Will with respect to a particular kind of action? For example, does a person have Free Will with respect to entering small, confined places, or, as we prefer to put it, does he have the ability to will to enter such places? One obvious advantage of this approach is that it permits us to speak, as psychiatrists and others do, of persons having or lacking Free Will with respect to certain kinds of actions. Also, in taking Free Will as the ability to will, we can provide a positive characterization of Free Will without mentioning determinism. As far as we can see, man's having Free Will is related to the truth or falsity of determinism in the same way as a thing's being red is related to its being a certain size or shape. Thus our account certainly seems as if it allows for the compatibility of Free Will with both determinism and indeterminism.[3]

In this paper we do two things. First, we provide an account of the ability to will (volitional ability), voluntary action and related concepts. Second, we show that much of the traditional discussion of the problem of Free Will can be best understood if Free Will is taken as the ability to will, and thereby show how this problem relates to some issues concerning excusing conditions and mental illness. Though in this paper we are primarily concerned with the ability to will (volitional ability), such an ability is of little value without some associated mental or physical ability. Thus we think that it is worthwhile to make

2. In ordinary discourse the term "voluntary" as applied to actions has a number of senses which though related are, nonetheless, distinct. Of these, three are central: (1) a voluntary act is simply an intentional (as opposed to an accidental) act; (2) a voluntary act is a free (as opposed to a constrained) act; (3) a voluntary act is an intentional act done by an agent who has what we have described as the ability to will (volitional ability) to do that kind of action.

3. Isaiah Berlin, a critic of compatabilism, asks if determinism is true: ". . . what reasons can you, in principle, adduce for attributing responsibility or applying moral rules to (people) which you would not think it reasonable to apply in the case of compulsive choosers—kleptomaniacs, dipsomaniacs, and the like?" ([4]: 20–21.) Our account of the ability to will provides the reasons for not attributing responsibility and not applying moral rules to kleptomaniacs, dipsomaniacs and the like, and in addition, it permits us to specify what Berlin expresses by the phrase "and the like."

clear that we regard the more important concept to be that of "voluntary ability." (See [10].) A voluntary ability consists of a volitional ability plus a related mental or physical ability.

Voluntary abilities, as well as volitional abilities and mental or physical abilities, are related to *kinds* of actions, unspecified with regard to a particular time or agent. Thus, when we say that $A$ has the voluntary ability to do $X$, $X$ stands for this kind of action. We can make no clear sense of the remark "$A$ has the ability to do $X$ at noon today." We can, of course, say "$A$ *had* the ability to do $X$ at noon yesterday" or "$A$ will have the ability to do $X$ at noon tomorrow." But these remarks do not conflict with the claim that $X$ stands for a kind of action which is not specified with regard to a particular time. For they have to be interpreted as follows: At noon yesterday, $A$ had the ability to do $X$: at noon tomorrow $A$ will have the ability to do $X$. They are not to be interpreted as: $A$ has a very *special* ability, viz., the ability to do $X$ at noon yesterday; the ability to do $X$ at noon tomorrow. We can, of course, say "At noon today $A$ had the ability to do $X$" or even "$A$ has the ability to do $X$ now," but these sentences like the preceding sentences are clearly about a kind of action unspecified with regard to a particular time.

One reason it is important to realize that all abilities are related to kinds of actions unspecified with regard to a particular time is that usually abilities are relatively enduring properties of persons. Mental and physical abilities are the kinds of properties we are interested in when, for example, we hire a person to perform some work. If we hire an accountant we want to know if he has the ability to work with numbers in the appropriate ways. When we hire a secretary we want to know if he has the ability to type and take shorthand. But in maintaining that abilities are directly related to kinds of actions unspecified with regard to a particular time, we do not deny that one may have an ability to do something at one time and not at another. Indeed, we regard it as obviously true that people gain and lose abilities. Athletes generally begin to lose some of their abilities after forty, and many abilities, e.g., playing a musical instrument, require constant practice in order to be maintained.

Having shown that abilities are related to kinds of actions unspecified with regard to a particular time, it is now important to show that they are related to kinds of actions unspecified with regard to a particular agent. That is, when we say that $A$ has the ability to do $X$, $X$ stands for a kind of action, such as, sinking a 10 foot putt, not $A$'s sinking a 10 foot putt. This is required by the fact that we often compare the abilities of two different people to do the *same* kind of action. Thus we say that though both $A$ and $B$ have the ability to sink 10 foot putts, $A$ has a greater ability than $B$. Were the kind of action that abilities are related to specified with regard to particular agents, it would be impossible for $A$ to have greater ability than $B$ to do the very same kind of action, for $A$ would have the ability to perform $A$'s sinking of 10 foot putts, and $B$ would have the ability to perform $B$'s sinking of 10 foot putts. Thus, $A$ and $B$ would have the abilities to do two different kinds of actions. Hence it would make no sense to say that $A$ had a greater ability than $B$ to do the same kind of action, for neither one could have the ability to perform the same kind of action as the other. We now consider it established that abilities are related to kinds of actions unspecified with regard to a particular time or agent.[4] When an action is specified with regard to a particular time and agent, we call it a particular act. Actions that are actually performed, can be regarded as either particular acts, or as kinds of actions, either specified with regard to a particular time, or specified with regard to a particular agent, or unspecified by either. When we talk of kinds of actions we shall always mean the latter.

In order to judge accurately a person's abilities, we usually have to watch him perform several times. Of course, there are so many different kinds of abilities and they are related to one another in so many different ways that we may be convinced that a person has the ability to do $X$ simply by watching him perform once, and even by watching him perform some particular act of kind $Y$. However, it is completely implausible to maintain, as some have, that trying and succeeding when one has a reasonable opportunity logically entails that one has the related ability. (See [15] and [16].) To hold this view would result in someone's doing a particular act of kind $X$ by luck entailing his having the ability to do that kind of action. We also see no merit in the view that failure to do something when one has a reasonable opportunity and tries, logically entails that one does not have the related ability. These views would require us to say that abilities come and go with every success and failure and would result in abilities not being the kinds of relatively enduring properties of persons that are important in everyday life, but rather the kind of useless properties that only philosophers care about. We suspect it is misplaced zeal for precision that has led some philosophers into holding that abilities are related to particular acts and not to kinds of actions. Perhaps there

4. While abilities are always related to kinds of actions, intentions are often related to particular acts, as indicated by the following sentence, "I did exactly what I intended to do, I raised my flag precisely at noon on July 4, 1976." For a further discussion of the relation between intentions and actions, see [6]: 149–154.

are also ontological considerations at work, for if we can talk of abilities only if we are willing to talk of kinds of actions, those who refuse to talk of kinds will have to cease talking about abilities. There might be involved here as well the mistaken view that since we can give a clear sense to, "A *can* do X at noon today," "A *has the ability to* do X at noon today" can also be given a clear sense. But clearly one cannot always substitute "has the ability to" for "can." (See [19].)

We define "A has a physical or mental ability to do X" as follows: For a reasonable number of times if A were to will to do a particular act of kind X, then simply given reasonable opportunity, A would do that particular act of kind X; and willing to do a particular act of kind X is not a logically necessary condition for doing that particular act of kind X.[5]

We present this definition because Moore sometimes talks as if the only power that is needed in order to have Free Will, closely resembles what we have called mental or physical ability. He says,

> There is, therefore, much reason to think that when we say that we *could* have done a thing which we did not do, we often mean merely that we *should* have done it *if* we had chosen. . . . And for my part I must confess that I cannot feel certain that this may not be all that we usually mean and understand by the assertion that we have Free Will. ([20]: 134)

But Moore is aware that there is a problem here; he is aware that some people maintain that "it is not true that we have Free Will unless it is also often true that we could have chosen differently." ([20]: 135.) However, Moore then tries to analyze the power to choose (the ability to will) in a way parallel to the way that he analyzed the power to act (mental or physical ability).

> If by saying that we *could* have done what we did not do, we often mean merely that we *should* have done it, *if* we had chosen to do it, then obviously, by saying that we *could* have *chosen* to do it, we may merely mean that we *should* have so chosen *if* we had chosen to make the choice." ([20]: 135)

---

5. This last clause is not meant to deny that one may have the physical or mental ability to do something that may constitute that for which willing is a logically necessary condition, e.g., as swallowing pills may be to committing suicide, or making false statements may be to perjury; it simply means that we do not regard abilities to do these kinds of actions, e.g., committing suicide or perjury, for which willing is logically necessary as physical or mental abilities, but rather as *voluntary* abilities. Although we do not provide an analysis of *willing*, we define "willing" as doing intentionally or trying to do. (See [10]: 206.) For a fuller account of *willing*, see [6].

Moore then says, "this is a very important sense in which it is often in our power to make a choice" ([20]: 135).

We do not deny that this is *an* important sense (we do not affirm it either), but we doubt that it is *the* important sense in discussing the problem of Free Will. For one thing, such an analysis of the power to choose seems immediately open to the objection that what is then needed for Free Will is the power to choose to make the choice. Moore provided the analysis of the power to choose that he did because he thought that only such an analysis would be compatible with determinism. Moore wanted an analysis which made Free Will logically compatible with determinism for he thought it clearly true that man had Free Will. Thus if determinism turned out to be true this fact would not count against man having Free Will. We are of two minds whether determinism could turn out to be true and non-vacuous, but we agree with Moore that the power that he called Free Will should be defined in a way that, at least, makes no explicit reference to determinism. This does not, however, require an analysis of the ability to will which is parallel to the analysis of mental or physical ability.

Our analysis of the ability to will is as follows: $S$ has the ability to will to do $X$, if and only if,

(1) $S$ has the ability to believe that there are many and varied coercive incentives for doing any particular act of kind $X$, and almost always, if $S$ believed that any of these coercive incentives were present he would will to do that particular act of kind $X$.

(2) $S$ has the ability to believe that there are many and varied non-coercive incentives for doing any particular act of kind $X$, and for each of several of these incentives, if $S$ believed that it was present he would, at least sometimes, will to do that particular act of kind $X$.

(3) $S$ has the ability to believe that there are many and varied coercive incentives for *not* doing any particular act of kind $X$, and almost always, if $S$ believed that any of these coercive incentives were present he would will *not* to do that particular act of kind $X$.

(4) $S$ has the ability to believe that there are many and varied non-coercive incentives for *not* doing any particular act of kind $X$, and for each of several of these incentives, if $S$ believed that it was present he would, at least sometimes, will *not* to do that particular act of kind $X$.[6]

$S$ has the ability to believe that $P$, if and only if, if $S$ were presented with overwhelming evidence that $P$, then $S$ would believe that $P$. And

6. This analysis of the ability to will differs somewhat from the original analysis presented in [10]. The modifications were required in order to meet objections raised by Don Locke and an anonymous referee for *Noûs*.

if $S$ were presented with overwhelming evidence that not-$P$, then $S$ would believe that not-$P$.

A coercive incentive is one which it would be unreasonable to expect *any* rational person not to act on. A non-coercive incentive is an incentive which is not coercive. There are many different kinds of incentive; moral, prudential, patriotic, etc. Moreover, while money can serve as in incentive, one sum of money, e.g., $100.00, is a different incentive from another sum of money, e.g., $5,000.00.[7]

This analysis is considerably more complex than the analysis of a mental or physical ability. First, and perhaps most obvious, having the ability to will to do $X$ entails that circumstances might arise in which one would will *not* to do a particular act of kind $X$. Thus one cannot conclude that $A$ has the ability to will to do $X$ simply by observing that he, in fact, wills to do a particular act of kind $X$, not even if he does so very often. Whereas a mental or physical ability is normally demonstrated by a number of performances of particular acts of the same kind, the ability to will normally requires only one performance of a particular act of that kind in appropriate circumstances, but in addition at least one non-performance if appropriate circumstances arise. A person does not demonstrate his ability to will to carry books with him whenever he leaves his house if he never wills not to carry books with him.

It is important to note that for $A$ to have the ability to will to do $X$, he must have two distinguishable characteristics, viz., (1) he must have the ability to believe that there are coercive and non-coercive incentives both for doing $X$ and for *not* doing $X;$ and (2) his beliefs about these coercive incentives must almost always have the effect that he acts in accordance with them, and his beliefs about these non-coercive incentives must, at least sometimes, have the effect that he acts in accordance with them.[8] The lack of either of these characteristics entails the lack of the ability to will. In a fairly rough sense we might say that those who lack the ability to believe are in that respect like delusional psychotics, and those who believe but are not appropriately affected by those beliefs are in that respect like compulsive or phobic neurotics.[9]

---

7. For a fuller account of incentives, see [13]: 30–48. For the account of *rational person* see [14]: 20–43.

8. We do not discuss the way in which wants and beliefs affect actions. Our analysis of the ability to will is compatible with all of the various causal theories of action with which we are acquainted, including those which rely on the concept of agent causality. For various accounts of these theories see [6], [7], [8], and [17].

9. There is an important difference between compulsives and those suffering from

An example of someone who lacks the first feature is a person who believes that his not going to visit the grave of his mother every Sunday will have bad consequences, and it is impossible to get him to believe that there is any set of circumstances such that there are coercive incentives for not doing so, nor even any significant non-coercive incentives. That is, it is impossible to convince him of the existence of any state of affairs such that he should not visit her grave. Since he lacks the ability to believe that there are coercive or non-coercive incentives for not visiting her grave, he does not have the ability to will not to visit the grave. Nor does he have the ability to will to visit the grave, although he does, in fact, will to do so; for the ability to will to do $X$, requires the ability to believe there are coercive and non-coercive incentives for *not* doing any particular act of kind $X$. Such a person lacks the ability to will as completely and probably less modifiably than someone who realizes that there are coercive incentives for not visiting the grave, but goes nonetheless.

An example of someone who lacks the second characteristic would be the compulsive hand-washer who not only has the ability to believe that there are both coercive and non-coercive incentives for not washing his hands once every waking hour, but actually knows that he has such incentives for refraining from washing his hands, and yet does not act in accordance with these incentives, and indeed laments his failure to act in accordance with them. Such a person lacks the ability to will to wash his hands once every waking hour, even though he does intentionally wash his hands. Compulsive action of this kind provides the clearest example of someone who acts intentionally yet not voluntarily. As we explain more fully in the next section of this paper, we can account for this category of action by noting that such a person wills to do a particular act of kind $X$ which he does not have the ability to will to do, because having the ability to will to do $X$ requires willing to refrain from doing particular acts of kind $X$ when there are appropriate incentives for so willing. It should also be noted that on our analysis of the ability to will, someone who was never affected by any incentives, coercive or otherwise, would not be freer than other persons, as seems to be suggested by Stoicism; rather, such

---

phobias. The latter, in normal circumstances, always avoid that which they are phobic about. Compulsives, however, often refrain from doing what they do compulsively, e.g., a compulsive hand washer often refrains from washing his hands. What he cannot do is refrain from washing his hands, for, say, six waking hours or for one hour after eating. This shows that the description of what a person lacks the ability to will to do may sometimes be quite complex. Alcoholism, in its strict sense, may involve the lack of the ability to will to take a second drink. That is, an alcoholic may have the ability to take or refuse to take the first drink, but not have the ability to refuse a second. These observations were promoted by discussions with Dr. Charles Culver, a psychiatrist.

·

a person would lack the ability to will to do anything and hence would be completely without Free Will.

We do not make any claims about what is responsible for one's lacking a particular volitional ability. What we say is compatible with the claims of both psycho-analysis and behaviorism. Concerning the son who visits his mother's grave every Sunday, we can say that guilt feelings due to real or imagined mistreatment of his mother, create such anxiety that he does not have the ability to believe he should not visit her grave, or if he can come to believe this, it does not affect his actions. Or we can say that he was conditioned to behave with such a schedule of reinforcement that he either cannot conceive of acting in any other way, or if he can conceive of it, is unable to carry out any attempt to do so. Our account is even compatible with some causal explanation in terms of physiology or neurology. We are simply offering an account of a concept and are making no scientific claims at all about it. Of course we are interested in this concept because we believe that, as a matter of empirical fact, there are people who have the ability to will to do different kinds of actions. Moreover, insofar as someone lacks what we call volitional ability they lack what many philosophers have called Free Will, and insofar as they have this ability they have what is appropriately called Free Will. On our account it is quite clear that most of us have the ability to will to do most, if not all, of the kinds of actions, particular acts of which we will to do. However, some lack the ability to will to do some kinds of actions even though they will to do particular acts of those kinds.

Further, our account of the ability to will makes clear the close relationship between Free Will and Moral Responsibility that has given the problem of Free Will its particular prominence. If one does an action intentionally, and is not subject to coercive incentives, then whether or not one is to be held morally responsible for that action is determined by whether or not one had the ability to will to do that kind of action. Intentional actions which are done by someone who does not have the ability to will to do that kind of action are not voluntary actions but are, e.g., compulsive actions. Indeed, we think that it is most appropriate to define voluntary actions as intentional actions done by someone with the ability to will to do that kind of action.[10] Thus for us it is often possible to determine whether an

10. We do not provide an analysis of intentional action; this is done by those who offer the various causal theories of action referred to in footnote 8. Nor do we discuss the question of the causes of intentional action, in particular what properties must a mental event have if it is to be the proximate cause of intentional action. Myles Brand in [5] addresses himself to these issues. Our contention is that regardless of which of these accounts is accepted, our concept of the ability to will is needed in order to distinguish

intentional action is voluntary or not, for often we can test whether or not the person has the ability to will to do that kind of action. And this test will also be relevant to determining whether the person should be held responsible for his action. Taking Free Will as the ability to will, therefore, allows us to show the close connection between the philosophical discussion of Free Will and the practical questions concerning responsibility. (See [11].)

## II

In this section, we provide a general schema for classifying human behavior and, more particularly, excusing conditions. On our schema all excuses can be put into four broad categories, each of these categories can be further divided into various subcategories, but we shall not, for the most part, in this paper concern ourselves with the various subcategories.[11] Excuses as we are concerned with them are invoked in order to lessen or eliminate responsibility for doing something wrong or for the bad consequences of something one has done. What counts as an acceptable excuse depends upon the standards that are employed in assessing responsibility. (See [14]: 183–5.) Often what will count as excusable ignorance in a minor matter will not be accepted when the situation is regarded as a more serious one. Generally speaking, in offering excuses, we try to show that our relationship to the bad consequences for which we are being held responsible differs in a significant way from a case in which we must accept full responsibility, viz., one in which (1) we acted intentionally in order to bring about those bad consequences; (2) we did not, at the time, suffer from any relevant disability of the will, and (3) our intentional action was not due to our being subject to coercive incentives. In other words, the paradigm case of someone who is held fully responsible for bringing about bad consequences is a person who acted intentionally, voluntarily and freely. We call such actions free actions (A). Thus in offering excuses one move is to try to show that what was done was not done freely, i.e., that it was done as the result of coercive incentives. We call such actions unfree actions (B). Another move is to show

---

intentional action from voluntary action. The authors in [6] and [17] fail to make this crucial distinction. On [6]: 282, Castañeda says, ". . . let us examine a case of voluntary action . . . ," the case he examines is one of intentional action. Similarly Goldman fails to distinguish the intentional and the voluntary. See his discussion of voluntary acts, pp. 192–4, especially note his remark "I have shown that there are causally compossible worlds in which voluntary acts—*i.e.,* acts which one *chooses* or decides to do—are scientifically predicted," p. 192. The *"i.e."* is important. See footnote 16.

11. J. L. Austin is almost completely concerned with the various subcategories of our category (D) ([3]: 123–53).

that the action was not done voluntarily, i.e., to claim that what was done was due to some disability of the will (volitional disability). We call such actions *unvoluntary* actions (C).[12] A third move is to deny that we intended to bring about the consequences that we are being held responsible for. This is the most discussed kind of excuse, and includes the various subcategories that Austin discusses, e.g., accident and mistake. We call such actions non-intentional (D). A fourth move is to claim that though the consequence is caused by some movement (or lack of movement) of our body, that movement is not properly described as an action of ours at all. We call such movement (or lack of movements) non-actions (E). The following diagram shows how these various categories are related to each other.

Bodily Movements (or lack of bodily movements)

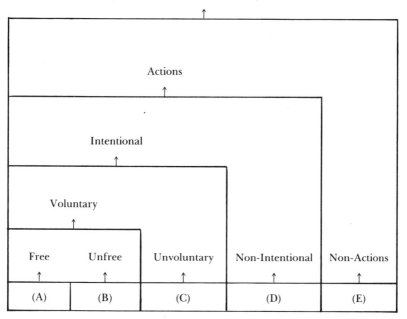

12. We coin the rather ugly term "unvoluntary" to denote this crucially important category of actions. The term "involuntary" would have been inappropriate since typically "involuntary" is understood to mean bodily movements that are not subject to the will as, for example, a reflexive knee jerk or blinking of the eyes. These we call non-actions (E). We avoid using "non-voluntary" because of its confused Aristotelian associations. There is also, as luck would have it, a parallelism between the terms, "unvoluntary" and "unfree."

We do not claim that it is always possible to state clearly what category a given excuse fits into. But often absolutely no distinction is made between category (E) and category (D); both are simply lumped together as non-intentional actions. However, though there are significant borderline cases, there are also clear examples of each category. If A is pushed by B into C, then when C complains to A about being bumped into, A can truthfully say, "I didn't do anything, I was pushed by B." This kind of case is the clearest example of non-action. But there are other cases which also seem to be non-actions, such as movements of a person in an epileptic seizure, reflexive behavior, such as knee jerks, eye blinks and all movements of a new born infant. Less clear cases would be complex movements made during sleep, as in somnambulism. We think that allowing for a distinct category of non-actions allows one to use the term "action" in a philosophically more fruitful fashion.

The clearest cases of actions fitting in category (D) are cases of accident, e.g., in reaching for the salt, I knock over your glass of water, or mistake, e.g., I put a teaspoon of salt into my tea instead of sugar. All of the clear cases of actions that fit into (D) involve a person who is intentionally doing something, but not intentionally doing the action (bringing about the consequences) at issue. Thus if we take as an example of a non-intentional action a hunter who in shooting at a bird wounds the picnicker behind the bush, then that involves the intentional action of shooting at the bird in the bush. Category (D), therefore, unlike category (E) typically involves some intentional action on the part of the agent. However, there are some unclear cases, e.g., actions done unthinkingly or *out of habit*. Suppose an habitual smoker lights up a cigarette in a hospital room where a patient is receiving oxygen. Suppose further that this action is done *out of habit*, that is, the person is at the time not even consciously aware that he is lighting his cigarette. We would like to include such behavior in category (D), even though it does not involve any intentional action.[13] We wish to do so not merely because such behavior is acquired, but also because it involves the exercise of what we call physical abilities, and is the kind of behavior that is usually done only when one wills to do it. Thus we do not limit actions to behavior which is at least partly intentional (though these will constitute the largest part). We also include as actions behavior which is done out of habit. But since one can do

13. Many would not want to call actions done out of habit, unintentional actions, reserving this term for mistakes, and accidents, *i.e.*, actions in which something is done intentionally. Thus we use "non-intentional" for category (D), so as to include in it actions done out of habit, as well as unintentional action.

something out of habit only if one formerly did that kind of action intentionally, the relationship between actions and doing something intentionally is never completely severed.

Whether the claim that an action was not done intentionally serves as an excuse will depend upon many factors. In the case of mistakes, an important factor will be the degree of carefulness that we think appropriate. This in turn will depend largely on the seriousness of the consequences which ensue. Similar considerations will apply in the case of accidents. One of the more interesting issues is the degree to which the fact that one did not intend the consequence in question counts as an excuse, even though one foresaw that consequence. But although there are many important and interesting topics in this area, they are not our concern in this paper.

It is category (C), unvoluntary action, that we are primarily concerned with in this section, but before we discuss it, some discussion of categories (A), free action, and (B), unfree action, is in order. An act done freely, or a free action (A), is one that is also intentional and voluntary, i.e., it is willed by a person who has the ability to will to do that kind of action, and what makes it free is that there were no coercive incentives that were successful in leading the person to do it. Normally an unfree action is also one that is willed by someone with the ability to will to do that kind of action. It is unfree because there were coercive incentives which *were* successful in leading the person to do it. A classical example of such an unfree though voluntary act is Aristotle's case of the sea captain who, in order to save his ship and crew, jettisons his cargo in a storm. But there may be extraordinary cases where an act is unfree even though the person who wills to do it did not have the ability to will to do that kind of action. For example, an extreme claustrophobiac may not have the ability to will to go into a small enclosed place but does so intentionally after being threatened with death or other coercive incentives if he does not. We would call such an action unfree even though the person performing it lacked the ability to will to do the act in question. However, the overwhelming number of cases of acts done because of coercive incentives are those which are both intentional and voluntary, so that we think it appropriate to consider free and unfree actions as subclasses of voluntary actions.

As far as we know, no one has proposed as a separate kind of excuse the lack of the ability to will—what we call unvoluntary actions (C).[14] At least since Aristotle there has been a very strong tendency to

14. The distinctions which our category of unvoluntary actions allows us to make

try to fit all excuses into only two categories, compulsion and igno-rance. Often what we list as categories (D) and (E) are lumped to-gether and regarded as examples of action done through ignorance. Our categories (B) and (C) are also often lumped together and re-garded as examples of actions done because of compulsion. We have already given our reason for distinguishing categories (D) and (E); now we wish to explain why we think it important to distinguish between (B) and (C), i.e., to distinguish between unfree actions and unvoluntary ones. Briefly, we regard unfree actions as those that are caused by something external to the agent, something about the situa-tion he finds himself in, viz., being subject to coercive incentives. Were these coercive incentives removed, the person would be free to refrain from doing the contemplated action. However, we regard unvoluntary actions as those caused by something within the agent, viz., a specific volitional disability or disability of the will. We hold that in no normal situation would the person be able to act differently than he did in fact act. The typical use of the term "compulsion" to cover both categories (B) and (C) is unfortunate, for it leads very naturally to talk of "inner compulsion" which is thought to resemble external compulsion, e.g., coercion, in all respects except that it comes from within the person rather than from without. But talk like this ob-scures the fact that "external compulsion," e.g., coercion, typically affects the doing of particular actions—your money (here and now) or your life—whereas "inner compulsion," i.e., disability of the will, always affects the doing or the refraining from doing of kinds of actions.[15]

Undoubtedly one of the reasons that disability of the will has been so completely ignored in contemporary philosophical discussion of excuses is that the major philosophers of the past seem to have ig-nored it. Aristotle in his discussion of compulsion makes it quite clear that for him an act done under compulsion is always the result of some external cause. Further, as the following quotation makes clear, Aristotle thought that insofar as the agent was in any way the cause of

---

have been aimed at by several philosophers. Watson in [22] tries to distinguish between desiring and valuing. He speaks of the conflict between valuing and desiring, and of persons motivated "in spite of themselves." We are of the opinion that the distinction Watson is trying to make cannot be made without employing the concept of unvolun-tary action. Similar remarks would apply to the distinction that Frankfurt tries to make between higher-order volitions and first-order desires. (See [12].)

15. Though it is usually the case, one *could* be coerced into doing or refraining from doing a kind of action. However, disabilities of the will can *never* be concerned with particular acts, though the kind of act may be so highly specified that an instance of that kind occurs only once.

his action, then he could no longer be said to be acting under compulsion.

> Actions are commonly regarded as involuntary when they are performed (A) under compulsion, or (B) as the result of ignorance. An act, it is thought, is done under compulsion when it originates in some external cause of such a nature that the agent or person subject to the compulsion contributes nothing to it. Such a situation is created, for example, when a sea captain is carried out of his course by a contrary wind or by men who have got him in their power. But the case is not always so clear. One might have to consider an action performed for some fine end or through fear of something worse to follow. For example, a tyrant who had a man's parents or children in his power might order him to do something dishonorable on condition that, if the man did it, their lives would be spared; otherwise not. In such cases it might be hard to say whether the actions are voluntary or not. A similar difficulty is created by the jettison of cargo in a storm. When the situation has no complications you never get a man voluntarily throwing away his property. But if it is to save the life of himself and his mates, any sensible person will do it. *Such actions partake of both qualities*, though they look more like voluntary acts. For at the time they are performed, they are the result of a deliberate choice between alternatives . . . ([1]: 77–8. Our emphasis.)

Aristotle's indecisiveness here is understandable. The actions in question are undoubtedly intentional or willed, and since in these cases, there is no suspicion of a disability of the will, they are properly regarded as being voluntary. At the same time, the agents are presented with coercive incentives for doing what they do, and this argues against classification as free acts. However, Aristotle did not have available to him the category of voluntary but unfree actions into which such cases would comfortably fit. Thus, though he recognizes that they "partake of both qualities," he is forced by his lack of the appropriate category to classify these acts simply as voluntary, the deciding consideration being: "their origin is in the agent." The fact that they "are deliberately chosen at a given time and in a given circumstances in preference to a given alternative" ([1]: 79) is allowed to override the presence of coercive incentives. This is because Aristotle lacked a classificatory scheme which would have permitted him to take adequate account of both facts.

It is clear from this quotation that Aristotle would label those actions that are due to a disability of the will as completely voluntary actions since there are no external forces acting on the agent. Indeed, for Aristotle all intentional actions (deliberately chosen actions) are regarded as voluntary ones, because "their origin is in the agent" ([1]:

79). Since Aristotle does not make any distinction between unfree and unvoluntary actions, it is evident that there is more than a mere verbal difference between our view and Aristotle's. Admittedly, he regards coercive incentives as presenting a problem as to whether or not an action is voluntary whereas we would prefer to say that it is a problem as to whether the action is free or unfree, and this perhaps *is* merely a verbal matter. But it is not merely a verbal matter that on his view coercive incentives are not sufficient to make an action involuntary, whereas we do regard them as sufficient to make an action unfree. Nor, more importantly, is it merely a verbal matter that on his account an action due to a disability of the will is voluntary and hence not excusable whereas we would regard it as unvoluntary and hence excusable.

Aristotle's simplistic criteria for deciding whether or not an action is voluntary, viz., whether its origin is in the agent or not, i.e., whether it is willed or not, has had an extraordinary impact on succeeding philosophers. Many of them have simply equated intentional action with voluntary action. Thus our category of intentional unvoluntary action has been completely overlooked by philosophers and jurisprudents. The long tradition of identifying the voluntary with what is willed is seen also in Hobbes, who writes

> In deliberation the last appetite or aversion immediately adhering to the action, or to the omission thereof, is what we call the *will;* the act, not the faculty of willing . . . *a voluntary act* is that which proceedeth from the *will,* and no other. ([18]: 38)

John Austin is another influential writer who identifies the voluntary with what is willed. He writes, "A voluntary movement of my body *or* a movement which follows a volition (i.e., a movement which is willed) is an *act* . . ." ([2]: 98. Our emphasis on "or").[16] H. L. A. Hart follows this quotation with the gloss

> Conduct is 'voluntary' *or* the 'expression of an act of will' if the muscular contraction which, on the physical side, is the initiating element in what are loosely thought of as simple actions, is caused by a desire for those same contractions. ([2]: 99. Our emphasis.)

That Hart himself is tempted to identify the voluntary with what is

---

16. The use of "or" in this quotation which implies that it is a matter of indifference which expression we use, "a voluntary movement" or "a movement which follows a volition," is an instance of what we call "The Fallacy of Assumed Equivalence."

willed is suggested by an earlier passage where in commenting on such cases as drunken stupor, sleepwalking, epilepsy, etc., he asks

> But what precisely is wrong in these cases? What common feature have they leading to their classification as cases where there is no 'act of will' *or* no 'expression of the will' *or* no 'voluntary conduct'? Or to put the same point in a different way, what is it that is present in normal action which makes it a satisfactory example of 'voluntary conduct' *or* '*willing*' . . . ([2]: 97. Our emphasis.)[17]

Thus, in Aristotle, Hobbes, Austin and perhaps Hart we see operating the assumption that if an act is willed (follows a volition, etc.) it is thereby a voluntary act. This is a serious mistake which has as a consequence ignoring a category of actions the recognition of which is the key to the understanding of Free Will, voluntary action, and some forms of mental illness. The category, of course, is that of the intentional, i.e., willed, but unvoluntary actions performed by agents who lack the volitional ability to do the acts they do intentionally. This is a paradoxical sounding but by now, we trust, perfectly intelligible category of actions.

The category of unvoluntary acts has a special relationship to mental illness. Indeed, to suffer a disability of the will is to suffer one form of mental illness, as is evident from considering those who suffer from phobias or compulsions. The concept of the ability to will, and the related category of unvoluntary, as distinguished from unfree, actions, provide a simple answer to the question why mental illness is more closely connected to questions of responsibility than physical illness. The answer is that some mental illness involves a disability of the will, and when the action that is performed is due to this disability of the will, then it is an unvoluntary action and hence one for which the person is not responsible, or not fully responsible. Indeed the discussion of mental illness even provides some linguistic support of the view put forward in the title of this paper, that Free Will is the ability to will, for most are prepared to say of those mentally ill persons whose actions are due to lack of the relevant ability to will or volitional ability, that they did not act of their own free will.

*Appendix*

Our account of Free Will as the ability to will falls completely within what Sellars calls the "manifest image" of man; it does not involve in

---

17. Notice the continual use of "or." It is the fallacy of assumed equivalence again.

any way what he calls the "scientific image" of man. It is because of this that we say that our account *seems* perfectly compatible with determinism and indeterminism, for we have provided an account of Free Will such that very often it can be decided by ordinary observation whether or not a given person has Free Will with respect to a certain kind of action. And this is independent of any advances in scientific discovery. Further, we have shown that Free Will, on our account does in fact play a *practical* role in determining responsibility. Thus we think that our account satisfies all of the reasonable demands of those who have wanted an account of Free Will. We even allow that in exactly the same circumstances a person might sometimes act on a given non-coercive incentive and sometimes not so act. What we do not provide in our account of Free Will, that has sometimes been demanded, is that it must always be the case that if a person has Free Will it must be possible that in exactly the same circumstances he sometimes acts in different ways. We think that such a demand is unreasonable. For it seems totally wrong-headed to hold that a person who prefers football to opera, is not acting of his own Free Will if he always watches a football game rather than an opera when there are no other incentives involved, even if it is possible to predict on the basis of his preferences that in exactly the same circumstances he will always watch the football game.

As far as we know, our account of Free Will as the ability to will is the only account which satisfactorily provides all of the features an account of Free Will should provide. However, it has been claimed that our account cannot adequately deal with the following case:

An evil genius causes Duggan to will to kill Gert. Suppose further that the way in which the evil genius causes Duggan to will to kill Gert is by direct stimulation of Duggan's brain and not by offering him riches if he kills Gert or threatening him with death if he does not kill Gert. And suppose Duggan is unable to prevent the evil genius from causing him to will to kill Gert. Further, there are no coercive or non-coercive incentives which would lead Duggan to will not to kill Gert.[18]

For some reason, it is thought that because the control of the evil genius is of a very short duration, our analysis entails that Duggan has the ability to will to kill Gert, whereas it is clearly true that Duggan does not have Free Will in this case. But our account of the ability to will does not require that one suffer from a chronic disability of the will rather than a brief or acute one. Volitional abilities like physical and mental abilities usually endure for a considerable period of time,

18. This example is due to an anonymous referee for *Noûs*.

but there is nothing in our analysis that requires this to be so.[19] Hypnotism can create temporary disabilities of the will. Strong emotions can also result in temporary loss of volitional ability, and the person may then be regarded as suffering from temporary insanity. But that one suffers from these temporary disabilities of the will entails that during that temporary period, non-coercive and perhaps even coercive incentives would have had no effect. We cannot always test for disability of the will when the time period is very short, but that is an epistemological problem and does not present any difficulties for our analysis.

Though, on our analysis of Free Will, it cannot *always* be determined whether or not a person has Free Will with regard to a particular kind of action, we often have overwhelming evidence that determines whether he has it or not. On the analysis offered by Sellars, not only is there no clear connection between his account of Free Will and questions of responsibility, but further (and this may account for the complete lack of any practical application of Sellars' account), there is no way to determine whether any person ever has Free Will with regard to any kind of action. ([21])

Alan Donagan notes in his discussion of Sellars' article, "Sellars' treatment of the ability to will is very compressed" ([9]: 68). We hold that Sellars does not even come close to providing an analysis of the ability to will, but is at most concerned with providing an analysis of what it is for someone *to be able to will* to do some particular act. Neither Sellars nor Donagan seems to be aware of the difference between having *the ability to do* a kind of act, and *being able to do* a particular act. This is shown by the fact that both go from "being able" to "ability" with no indication that any move has been made at all. Thus we find that Sellars, after saying, "We can introduce this broader sense of 'able' for which we are looking," provides a definition and follows it with this remark: "As before, ability *at a time* is derivative from ability *over a period*" ([21]: 173). Donagan uncritically follows Sellars in giving what he thinks should be Sellars' definition of "being able to will," and then follows it with the question, "Given Sellars' analysis, is determinism compatible with ability to will otherwise than one wills?" ([9]: 68). As these quotations show, both Sellars and Donagan move from talk about "being able," to talk about "ability" without realizing that this move has significance. It is therefore our view upon reading Sellars' article and Donagan's discussion of it that nei-

19. However, we agree with Sellars ([21]) that ability over a period is more basic than ability at a time.

ther Sellars nor Donagan has provided a serious alternative to our account of the ability to will.[20]

*References*

[1] Aristotle, *Nichomachean Ethics,* trans. J. A. K. Thompson (Penguin, 1955).

[2] John Austin, *Lectures on Jurisprudence,* 1932, Lecture XVIII, quoted by H. L. A. Hart, *Punishment and Responsibility* (Oxford, 1968).

[3] J. L. Austin, "A Plea for Excuses," in *Philosophical Papers* (Oxford, 1961): 123–53.

[4] Isaiah Berlin, *Four Essays on Liberty* (Oxford, 1969).

[5] Myles Brand, "The Fundamental Question in Action Theory," in *Time and Cause: Essays Presented to Richard Taylor,* ed. Peter van Inwagen (Dordrecht: D. Reidel, 1980).

[6] Hector-Neri Castañeda, *Thinking and Doing* (Dordrecht: D. Reidel, 1975).

[7] Roderick M. Chisholm, "Freedom and Action," in Keith Lehrer (ed.), *Freedom and Determinism* (Random House, 1966).

[8] ____, "Reflections on Human Agency," *Idealistic Studies* 1 (1971).

[9] Alan Donagan, "Determinism and Freedom: Sellars and the Reconciliationist Thesis," in Hector-Neri Castañeda (ed.), *Action, Knowledge and Reality, Studies in Honor of Wilfrid Sellars* (Bobbs-Merrill Co., 1975).

[10] Timothy J. Duggan and Bernard Gert, "Voluntary Abilities," *American Philosophical Quarterly,* IV (1967): 127–35. Reprinted in Myles Brand, ed., *The Nature of Human Action* (Scott Foresman and Co., 1970): 204–16. Subsequent references will be to this work.

[11] Herbert Fingarette, "Disabilities of Mind and Criminal Responsibility— A Unitary Doctrine," *Columbia Law Review* 76 (1976).

[12] Harry Frankfurt, "Freedom of the Will and the Concept of a Person" (Chapter 1 of the present volume).

[13] Bernard Gert, "Coercion and Freedom," *Nomos* XIV (Aldine Atherton, Inc., 1972).

[14] ____, *The Moral Rules,* 2nd ed. (Harper & Row, 1975).

[15] ____ and James Martin, "What a Man Does He Can Do," *Analysis* (1973).

[16] ____ and ____, "Outcomes and Abilities," *Analysis* (1973).

[17] Alvin Goldman, *A Theory of Human Action* (Prentice-Hall, Inc., 1970).

[18] Thomas Hobbes, *Leviathan,* ed., M. Oakeshott (Basil Blackwell, 1957).

[19] Don Locke, "The 'Can' of Being Able," *Philosophia* (1976): 1–20.

[20] G. E. Moore, *Ethics* (Oxford, 1912).

[21] Wilfrid Sellars, "Fatalism and Determinism," *Freedom and Determinism,* ed. Keith Lehrer (Random House, 1966).

[22] Gary Watson, "Free Agency" (Chapter 2 of the present volume).

20. We wish to thank the editor of *Noûs* for his encouragement and many helpful suggestions.

# 11

## Asymmetrical Freedom

SUSAN WOLF

In order for a person to be morally responsible, two conditions must be satisfied. First, he must be a free agent—an agent, that is, whose actions are under his own control. For if the actions he performs are not up to him to decide, he deserves no credit or discredit for doing what he does. Second, he must be a moral agent—an agent, that is, to whom moral claims apply. For if the actions he performs can be neither right nor wrong, then there is nothing to credit or discredit him with. I shall call the first condition, *the condition of freedom,* and the second, *the condition of value.* Those who fear that the first condition can never be met worry about the problem of free will. Those who fear that the second condition can never be met worry about the problem of moral skepticism. Many people believe that the condition of value is dependent on the condition of freedom—that moral prescriptions make sense only if the concept of free will is coherent. In what follows, I shall argue that the converse is true—that the condition of freedom depends on the condition of value. Our doubts about the existence of true moral values, however, will have to be left aside.

I shall say that an agent's action is *psychologically determined* if his action is determined by his interests—that is, his values or desires—and his interests are determined by his heredity or environment. If all our actions are so determined, then the thesis of psychological determinism is true. This description is admittedly crude and simplistic. A

"Asymmetrical Freedom" originally appeared in the *Journal of Philosophy,* 77 (March 1980), 151–66, © 1980 by the *Journal of Philosophy,* and is reprinted here with permission from Susan Wolf and from the *Journal of Philosophy.*

I am greatly indebted to Douglas MacLean, Thomas Nagel, and Milton Wachsberg for conversations that led up to this paper, as well as for comments on an earlier draft.

more plausible description of psychological determination will include among possible determining factors a wider range of psychological states. There are, for example, some beliefs and emotions which cannot be analyzed as values or desires and which clearly play a role in the psychological explanations of why we act as we do. For my purposes, however, it will be easier to leave the description of psychological determinism uncluttered. The context should be sufficient to make the intended application understood.

Many people believe that if psychological determinism is true, the condition of freedom can never be satisfied. For if an agent's interests are determined by heredity and environment, they claim, it is not up to the agent to have the interests he has. And if his actions are determined by his interests as well, then he cannot but perform the actions he performs. In order for an agent to satisfy the condition of freedom, then, his actions must not be psychologically determined. Either his actions must not be determined by his interests, or his interests must not be determined by anything external to himself. They therefore conclude that the condition of freedom requires the absence of psychological determinism. And they think this is what we mean to express when we state the condition of freedom in terms of the requirement that the agent "could have done otherwise."

Let us imagine, however, what an agent who satisfied this condition would have to be like. Consider first what it would mean for the agent's actions not to be determined by his interests—for the agent, in other words, to have the ability to act despite his interests. This would mean, I think, that the agent has the ability to act against everything he believes in and everything he cares about. It would mean, for example, that if the agent's son were inside a burning building, the agent could just stand there and watch the house go up in flames. Or that the agent, though he thinks his neighbor a fine and agreeable fellow, could just get up one day, ring the doorbell, and punch him in the nose. One might think such pieces of behavior should not be classified as actions at all—that they are rather more like spasms that the agent cannot control. If they are actions, at least, they are very bizarre, and an agent who performed them would have to be insane. Indeed, one might think he would have to be insane if he had even the ability to perform them. For the rationality of an agent who could perform such irrational actions as these must hang by a dangerously thin thread.

So let us assume instead that his actions are determined by his interests, but that his interests are not determined by anything external to himself. Then of any of the interests he happens to have, it must be the case that he does not have to have them. Though perhaps he loves his wife, it must be possible for him not to love her. Though perhaps he cares about people in general, it must be possible for him not to care. This agent, moreover, could not have reasons for his interests—at least no reasons of the sort we normally have. He cannot love his wife, for example, because of the way his wife is—for the way his wife is is not up to him to decide. Such an agent, presumably, could not be much committed to anything; his interests must be something like a matter of whim. Such an agent must be able not to care about the lives of others, and, I suppose, he must be able not to care about his own life as well. An agent who didn't care about these things, one might think, would have to be crazy. And again, one might think he would have to be crazy if he had even the ability not to care.

In any case, it seems, if we require an agent to be psychologically undetermined, we cannot expect him to be a moral agent. For if we require that his actions not be determined by his interests, then *a fortiori* they cannot be determined by his moral interests. And if we require that his interests not be determined by anything else, then *a fortiori* they cannot be determined by his moral reasons.

When we imagine an agent who performs right actions, it seems, we imagine an agent who is rightly determined: whose actions, that is, are determined by the right sorts of interests, and whose interests are determined by the right sorts of reasons. But an agent who is not psychologically determined cannot perform actions that are right in this way. And if his actions can never be appropriately right, then in not performing right actions, he can never be wrong. The problem seems to be that the undetermined agent is so free as to be free *from moral reasons*. So the satisfaction of the condition of freedom seems to rule out the satisfaction of the condition of value.

This suggests that the condition of freedom was previously stated too strongly. When we require that a responsible agent "could have done otherwise" we cannot mean that it was not determined that he did what he did. It has been proposed that 'he could have done otherwise' should be analyzed as a conditional instead. For example, we might say that 'he could have done otherwise' means that he would have done otherwise, if he had tried. Thus the bank robber is responsible for robbing the bank, since he would have restrained himself if he had tried. But the man he locked up is not responsible for letting him escape, since he couldn't have stopped him even if he had tried.

Incompatibilists, however, will quickly point out that such an analysis is insufficient. For an agent who would have done otherwise if he had tried cannot be blamed for his action if he could not have tried. The compatibilist might try to answer this objection with a new conditional analysis of 'he could have tried.' He might say, for example, that 'he could have tried to do otherwise' be interpreted to mean he would have tried to do otherwise, if he had chosen. But the incompatibilist now has a new objection to make: namely, what if the agent could not have chosen?

It should be obvious that this debate might be carried on indefinitely with a proliferation of conditionals and a proliferation of objections. But if an agent is determined, no conditions one suggests will be conditions that an agent could have satisfied.

Thus, any conditional analysis of 'he could have done otherwise' seems too weak to satisfy the condition of freedom. Yet if 'he could have done otherwise' is not a conditional, it seems too strong to allow the satisfaction of the condition of value. We seem to think of ourselves one way when we are thinking about freedom, and to think of ourselves another way when we are thinking about morality. When we are thinking about the condition of freedom, our intuitions suggest that the incompatibilists are right. For they claim that an agent can be free only insofar as his actions are not psychologically determined. But when we are thinking about the condition of value, our intuitions suggest that the compatibilists are right. For they claim that an agent can be moral only insofar as his actions are psychologically determined. If our intuitions require that both these claims are right, then the concept of moral responsibility must be incoherent. For then a free agent can never be moral, and a moral agent can never be free.

In fact, however, I believe that philosophers have generally got our intuitions wrong. There is an asymmetry in our intuitions about freedom which has generally been overlooked. As a result, it has seemed that the answer to the problem of free will can lie in only one of two alternatives: Either the fact that an agent's action was determined is always compatible with his being responsible for it, or the fact that the agent's action was determined will always rule his responsibility out. I shall suggest that the solution lies elsewhere—that both compatibilists and incompatibilists are wrong. What we need in order to be responsible beings, I shall argue, is a suitable combination of determination and indetermination.

When we try to call up our intuitions about freedom, a few stock cases come readily to mind. We think of the heroin addict and the kleptomaniac, of the victim of hypnosis, and the victim of a deprived childhood. These cases, I think, provide forceful support for our incompatibilist intuitions. For of the kleptomaniac it may well be true that he would have done otherwise if he had tried. The kleptomaniac is not responsible because he could not have tried. Of the victim of hypnosis it may well be true that he would have done otherwise if he had chosen. The victim of hypnosis is not responsible because he could not have chosen.

The victim of the deprived childhood who, say, embezzles some money, provides the most poignant example of all. For this agent is not coerced nor overcome by an irresistible impulse. He is in complete possession of normal adult faculties of reason and observation. He seems, indeed, to have as much control over his behavior as we have of ours. He acts on the basis of his choice, and he chooses on the basis of his reasons. If there is any explanation of why this agent is not responsible, it would seem that it must consist simply in the fact that his reasons are determined.

These examples are all peculiar, however, in that they are examples of people doing bad things. If the agents in these cases were responsible for their actions, this would justify the claim that they deserve to be blamed. We seldom look, on the other hand, at examples of agents whose actions are morally good. We rarely ask whether an agent is truly responsible if his being responsible would make him worthy of praise.

There are a few reasons why this might be so which go some way in accounting for the philosophers' neglect. First, acts of moral blame are more connected with punishment than acts of moral praise are connected with reward. So acts of moral blame are likely to be more public, and examples will be readier to hand. Second, and more important, I think, we have stronger reasons for wanting acts of blame to be justified. If we blame someone or punish him, we are likely to be causing him some pain. But if we praise someone or reward him, we will probably only add to his pleasures. To blame someone undeservedly is, in any case, to do him an injustice. Whereas to praise someone undeservedly is apt to be just a harmless mistake. For this reason, I think, our intuitions about praise are weaker and less developed than our intuitions about blame. Still, we do have some intuitions about cases of praise, and it would be a mistake to ignore them entirely.

When we ask whether an agent's action is deserving of praise, it seems we do not require that he could have done otherwise. If an agent does the right thing for just the right reasons, it seems absurd to ask whether he could have done the wrong. "I cannot tell a lie," "He couldn't hurt a fly" are not exemptions from praiseworthiness but testimonies to it. If a friend presents you with a gift and says "I couldn't resist," this suggests the strength of his friendship and not the weakness of his will. If one feels one "has no choice" but to speak out against injustice, one ought not to be upset about the depth of one's commitment. And it seems I should be grateful for the fact that if I were in trouble, my family "could not help" but come to my aid.

Of course, these phrases must be given an appropriate interpretation if they are to indicate that the agent is deserving of praise. "He couldn't hurt a fly" must allude to someone's gentleness—it would be perverse to say this of someone who was in an iron lung. It is not admirable in George Washington that he cannot tell a lie, if it is because he has a tendency to stutter that inhibits his attempts. 'He could not have done otherwise' as it is used in the context of praise, then, must be taken to imply something like 'because he was too good'. An action is praiseworthy only if it is done for the right reasons. So it must be only in light of and because of these reasons that the praiseworthy agent "could not help" but do the right thing.

But when an agent does the right thing for the right reasons, the fact that, having the right reasons, he *must* do the right should surely not lessen the credit he deserves. For presumably the reason he cannot do otherwise is that his virtue is so sure or his moral commitment so strong.

One might fear that if the agent really couldn't have acted differently, his virtue must be *too* sure or his commitment *too* strong. One might think, for example, that if someone literally couldn't resist buying a gift for a friend, his generosity would not be a virtue—it would be an obsession. For one can imagine situations in which it would be better if the agent did resist—if, for example, the money that was spent on the gift was desperately needed for some other purpose. Presumably, in the original case, though, the money was not desperately needed—we praise the agent for buying a gift for his friend rather than, say, a gift for himself. But from the fact that the man could not resist in this situation it doesn't follow that he couldn't resist in another. For part of the explanation of why he couldn't resist in this situation is that in this situation he has no reason to try to resist. This man, we assume, has a generous nature—a disposition, that is, to perform generous acts. But, then, if he is in a situation that presents a golden opportunity, and has no conflicting motive, how could he act otherwise?

One might still be concerned that if his motives are determined, the man cannot be truly deserving of praise. If he cannot help but have a generous character, then the fact that he is generous is not up to him. If a man's motives are determined, one might think, then *he* cannot control them, so it cannot be to his credit if his motives turn out to be good. But whether a man is in control of his motives cannot be decided so simply. We must know not only whether his motives are determined, but how they are determined as well.

We can imagine, for example, a man with a generous mother who becomes generous as a means of securing her love. He would not have been generous had his mother been different. Had she not admired generosity, he would not have developed this trait. We can imagine further that once this man's character had been developed, he would never subject it to question or change. His character would remain unthinkingly rigid, carried over from a childhood over which he had no control. As he developed a tendency to be generous, let us say, he developed other tendencies—a tendency to brush his teeth twice a day, a tendency to avoid the company of Jews. The explanation for why he developed any one of these traits is more or less the same as the explanation for why he has developed any other. And the explanation for why he has retained any one of these tendencies is more or less the same as the explanation for why he has retained any other. These tendencies are all, for him, merely habits which he has never thought about breaking. Indeed, they are habits which, by hypothesis, it was determined he would never think about breaking. Such a man, perhaps, would not deserve credit for his generosity, for his generosity might be thought to be senseless and blind. But we can imagine a different picture in which no such claim is true, in which a generous character might be determined and yet under the agent's control.

We might start again with a man with a generous mother who starts to develop his generosity out of a desire for her love. But his reasons for developing a generous nature need not be his reasons for retaining it when he grows more mature. He may notice, for example, that his generous acts provide an independent pleasure, connected to the pleasure he gives the person on whom his generosity is bestowed. He may find that being generous promotes a positive fellow feeling and makes it easier for him to make friends than it would otherwise be. Moreover, he appreciates being the object of the generous acts of others, and he is hurt when others go to ungenerous extremes. All in all, his generosity seems to cohere with his other values. It fits in well with his ideals of how one ought to live.

Such a picture, I think, might be as determined as the former one. But it is compatible with the exercise of good sense and an open frame of mind. It is determined, because the agent does not create his new reasons for generosity any more than he created his old ones. He does not *decide* to feel an independent pleasure in performing acts of generosity, or decide that such acts will make it easier for him to make friends. He discovers that these are consequences of a generous nature—and if he is observant and perceptive, he cannot help but discover this. He does not choose to be the object of the generous acts of others, or to be the victim of less generous acts of less virtuous persons. Nor does he choose to be grateful to the one and hurt by the other. He cannot help but have these experiences—they are beyond his control. So it seems that what reasons he *has* for being generous depends on what reasons there *are*.

If the man's character is determined in this way, however, it seems absurd to say that it is not under his control. His character is determined on the basis of his reasons, and his reasons are determined by what reasons there are. What is not under his control, then, is that generosity be a virtue, and it is only because he realizes this that he remains a generous man. But one cannot say for *this* reason that his generosity is not praiseworthy. This is the best reason for being generous that a person could have.

So it seems that an agent can be morally praiseworthy even though he is determined to perform the action he performs. But we have already seen that an agent cannot be morally blameworthy if he is determined to perform the action he performs. Determination, then, is compatible with an agent's responsibility for a good action, but incompatible with an agent's responsiblity for a bad action. The metaphysical conditions required for an agent's responsibility will vary according to the value of the action he performs.

The condition of freedom, as it is expressed by the requirement that an agent could have done otherwise, thus appears to demand a conditional analysis after all. But the condition must be one that separates the good actions from the bad—the condition, that is, must be essentially value-laden. An analysis of the condition of freedom that might do the trick is:

> He could have done otherwise if there had been good and sufficient reason.

where the 'could have done otherwise' in the analysans is not a conditional at all. For presumably an action is morally praiseworthy only if there are no good and sufficient reasons to do something else. And an action is morally blameworthy only if there are good and sufficient reasons to do something else. Thus, when an agent performs a good action, the condition of freedom is a counterfactual: though it is required that the agent would have been able to do otherwise *had there been* good and sufficient reason to do so, the situation in which the good-acting agent actually found himself is a situation in which there was no such reason. Thus, it is compatible with the satisfaction of the condition of freedom that the agent in this case could not actually have done other than what he actually did. When an agent performs a bad action, however, the condition of freedom is not a counterfactual. The bad-acting agent does what he does in the face of good and sufficient reasons to do otherwise. Thus the condition of freedom requires that the agent in this case could have done otherwise in just the situation in which he was actually placed. An agent, then, can be determined to perform a good action and still be morally praiseworthy. But if an agent is to be blameworthy, he must unconditionally have been able to do something else.

It may be easier to see how this analysis works, and how it differs from conditional analyses that were suggested before, if we turn back to the case in which these previous analyses failed—namely, the case of the victim of a deprived childhood.

We imagined a case, in particular, of a man who embezzled some money, fully aware of what he was doing. He was neither coerced nor overcome by an irresistible impulse, and he was in complete possession of normal adult faculties of reason and observation. Yet it seems he ought not to be blamed for committing his crime, for, from his point of view, one cannot reasonably expect him to see anything wrong with his action. We may suppose that in his childhood he was given no love—he was beaten by his father, neglected by his mother. And that the people to whom he was exposed when he was growing up gave him examples only of evil and selfishness. From his point of view, it is natural to conclude that respecting other people's property would be foolish. For presumably no one had ever respected his. And it is natural for him to feel that he should treat other people as adversaries.

In light of this, it seems that this man shouldn't be blamed for an action we know to be wrong. For if we had had his childhood, we wouldn't have known it either. Yet this agent seems to have as much control over his life as we are apt to have over ours: he would have done otherwise, if he had tried. He would have tried to do otherwise, if he had chosen. And he would have chosen to do otherwise, if he had had reason. It is because he couldn't have had reason that this agent should not be blamed.

Though this agent's childhood was different from ours, it would seem to be neither more nor less binding. The good fortune of our childhood is no more to our credit than the misfortune of his is to his blame. So if he is not free because of the childhood he had, then it would appear that we are not free either. Thus it seems no conditional analysis of freedom will do—for there is nothing internal to the agent which distinguishes him from us.

My analysis, however, proposes a condition that is not internal to the agent. And it allows us to state the relevant difference: namely that, whereas our childhoods fell within a range of normal decency, his was severely deprived. The consequence this has is that he, unlike us, could not have had reasons even though there were reasons around. The problem is not that his reason was functioning improperly, but that his data were unfortuitously selective. Since the world for him was not suitably cooperating, his reason cannot attain its appropriate goal.

The goal, to put it bluntly, is the True and the Good. The freedom we want is the freedom to find it. But such a freedom requires not only that we, as agents, have the right sorts of abilities—the abilities, that is, to direct and govern our actions by our most fundamental selves. It requires as well that the world cooperate in such a way that our most fundamental selves have the opportunity to develop into the selves they ought to be.

If the freedom necessary for moral responsibility is the freedom to be determined by the True and the Good, then obviously we cannot know whether we have such a freedom unless we know, on the one hand, that there *is* a True and a Good and, on the other, that there *are* capacities for finding them. As a consequence of this, the condition of freedom cannot be stated in purely metaphysical terms. For we cannot know which capacities and circumstances are necessary for freedom unless we know which capacities and circumstances will enable us to form the *right* values and perform the *right* actions. Strictly speaking, I take it, the capacity to reason is not enough—we need a kind of sensibility and perception as well. But these are capacities, I assume, that most of us have. So when the world cooperates, we are morally responsible.

I have already said that the condition of freedom cannot be stated in purely metaphysical terms. More specifically, the condition of freedom cannot be stated in terms that are value-free. Thus, the problem of free will has been misrepresented insofar as it has been thought to be a purely metaphysical problem. And, perhaps, this is why the problem of free will has seemed for so long to be hopeless.

That the problem should have seemed to be a purely metaphysical problem is not, however, unnatural or surprising. For being determined by the True and the Good is very different from being determined by one's garden variety of causes, and I think it not unnatural to feel as if one rules out the other. For to be determined by the Good is not to be determined by the Past. And to do something because it is the right thing to do is not to do it because one has been taught to do it. One might think, then, that one can be determined only by one thing or the other. For if one is going to do whatever it is right to do, then it seems one will do it whether or not one has been taught. And if one is going to do whatever one has been taught to do, then it seems one will do it whether or not it is right.

In fact, however, such reasoning rests on a category mistake. These two explanations do not necessarily compete, for they are explanations of different kinds. Consider, for example, the following situation: you ask me to name the capital of Nevada, and I reply "Carson City." We can explain why I give the answer I do give in either of the following ways: First, we can point out that when I was in the fifth grade I had to memorize the capitals of the fifty states. I was taught to believe that Carson City was the capital of Nevada, and was subsequently positively reinforced for doing so. Second, we can point out that Carson City *is* the capital of Nevada, and that this was, after all, what you wanted to know. So on the one hand, I gave my answer because I was taught. And on the other, I gave my answer because it was right.

Presumably, these explanations are not unrelated. For if Carson City were not the capital of Nevada, I would not have been taught that it was. And if I hadn't been taught that Carson City was the capital of Nevada, I wouldn't have known that it was. Indeed, one might think that if the answer I gave weren't right, I *couldn't* have given it because I was taught. For no school board would have hired a teacher who got such facts wrong. And if I hadn't been taught that Carson City was the capital of Nevada, perhaps I couldn't have given this answer because it was right. For that Carson City is the capital of Nevada is not something that can be known a priori.

Similarly, we can explain why a person acts justly in either of the following ways: First, we can point out that he was taught to act justly, and was subsequently positively reinforced for doing so. Second, we can point out that it is right to act justly, and go on to say why he knows this is so. Again, these explanations are likely to be related. For if it weren't right to act justly, the person may well not have been taught that it was. And if the person hadn't been taught that he ought to act justly, the person may not have discovered this on his own. Of course, the explanations of both kinds in this case will be more complex than the explanations in the previous case. But what is relevant here is that these explanations are compatible: that one can be determined by the Good and determined by the Past.

In order for an agent to be morally free, then, he must be capable of being determined by the Good. Determination by the Good is, as it were, the goal we need freedom to pursue. We need the freedom *to* have our actions determined by the Good, and the freedom to be or to become the sorts of persons whose actions will continue to be so determined. In light of this, it should be clear that no standard incompatibilist views about the conditions of moral responsibility can be right, for, according to these views, an agent is free only if he is the sort of agent whose actions are not causally determined at all. Thus, an agent's freedom would be incompatible with the realization of the goal for which freedom is required. The agent would be, in the words, though not in the spirit, of Sartre, "condemned to be free"—he could not both be free and realize a moral ideal.

Thus, views that offer conditional analyses of the ability to do otherwise, views that, like mine, take freedom to consist in the ability *to be determined* in a particular way, are generally compatibilist views. For insofar as an agent *is* determined in the right way, the agent can be said to be acting freely. Like the compatibilists, then, I am claiming that whether an agent is morally responsible depends not on whether but on how that agent is determined. My view differs from theirs only in what I take the satisfactory kind of determination to be.

However, since on my view the satisfactory kind of determination is determination by reasons that an agent ought to have, it will follow that an agent can be both determined and responsible only insofar as he performs actions that he ought to perform. If an agent performs a morally bad action, on the other hand, then his actions can't be determined in the appropriate way. So if an agent is ever to be responsible for a bad action, it must be the case that his action is not psychologically determined at all. According to my view, then, in order for both moral praise and moral blame to be justified, the thesis of psychological determinism must be false.

Is it plausible that this thesis is false? I think so. For though it appears that some of our actions are psychologically determined, it appears that others are not. It appears that some of our actions are not determined by our interests, and some of our interests are not determined at all. That is, it seems that some of our actions are such that no set of psychological facts are sufficient to explain them. There are occasions on which a person takes one action, but there seems to be no reason why he didn't take another.

For example, we sometimes make arbitrary choices—to wear the green shirt rather than the blue, to have coffee rather than tea. We make such choices on the basis of no reason—and it seems that we might, in these cases, have made a different choice instead.

Some less trivial and more considered choices may also be arbitrary. For one may have reasons on both sides which are equally strong. Thus, one may have good reasons to go to graduate school and good reasons not to; good reasons to get married, and good reasons to stay single. Though we might want, in these cases, to choose on the basis of reasons, our reasons simply do not settle the matter for us. Other psychological events may be similarly undetermined, such as the chance occurrence of thoughts and ideas. One is just struck by an idea, but for no particular reason—one might as easily have had another idea or no idea at all. Or one simply forgets an appointment one has made, even though one was not particularly distracted by other things at the time.

On retrospect, some of the appearance of indetermination may turn out to be deceptive. We decide that unconscious motives dictated a choice that seemed at the time to be arbitrary. Or a number of ideas that seemed to occur to us at random reveal a pattern too unusual to be the coincidence we thought. But if some of the appearances of indetermination are deceptive, I see no reason to believe that all of them should be.

Let us turn, then, to instances of immoral behavior, and see what the right kind of indetermination would be. For indetermination, in this context, is indetermination among some number of fairly particular alternatives—and if one's alternatives are not of the appropriate kind, indetermination will not be sufficient to justify moral blame. It is not enough, for example, to know that a criminal who happened to rob a bank might as easily have chosen to hold up a liquor store instead. What we need to know, in particular, is that when an agent performs a wrong action, he could have performed the right action for the right reasons instead. That is, first, the agent could have had the interests that the agent ought to have had, and second, the agent could have acted on the interests on which he ought to have acted.

Corresponding to these two possibilities, we can imagine two sorts of moral failure: the first corresponds to a form of negligence, the second to a form of weakness. Moral negligence consists in a failure to recognize the existence of moral reasons that one ought to have recognized. For example, a person hears that his friend is in the hospital, but fails to attend to this when planning his evening. He doesn't stop to think about how lonely and bored his friend is likely to be—he simply reaches for the *TV Guide* or for his novel instead. If the person could have recognized his friend's sorry predicament, he is guilty of moral negligence. Moral weakness, on the other hand, consists in the failure to act on the reasons that one knows one ought, for moral reasons, to be acting on. For example, a person might go so far as to conclude that he really ought to pay his sick friend a visit, but the thought of the drive across town is enough to convince him to stay at home with his book after all. If the person could have made the visit, he is guilty of moral weakness.

There is, admittedly, some difficulty in establishing that an agent who performs a morally bad action satisfies the condition of freedom. It is hard to know whether an agent who did one thing could have done another instead. But presumably we decide such questions now on the basis of statistical evidence—and, if, in fact, these actions are not determined, this is the best method there can be. We decide, in other words, that an agent could have done otherwise if others in his situation have done otherwise, and these others are like him in all apparently relevant ways. Or we decide that an agent could have done otherwise if he himself has done otherwise in situations that are like this one in all apparently relevant ways.

It should be emphasized that the indetermination with which we are here concerned is indetermination only at the level of psychological explanation. Such indetermination is compatible with determination at other levels of explanation. In particular, a sub-psychological, or physiological, explanation of our behavior may yet be deterministic. Some feel that if this is the case, the nature of psychological explanations of our behavior cannot be relevant to the problem of free will. Though I am inclined to disagree with this view, I have neither the space nor the competence to argue this here.

Restricting the type of explanation in question appropriately, however, it is a consequence of the condition of freedom I have suggested that the explanation for why a responsible agent performs a morally bad action must be, at some level, incomplete. There must be nothing that made the agent perform the action he did, nothing that prevented him from performing a morally better one. It should be noted that there may be praiseworthy actions for which the explanations are similarly incomplete. For the idea that an agent who could have performed a morally bad action actually performs a morally good one is no less plausible than the idea that an agent who could have performed a morally good action actually performs a morally bad one.

Presumably, an agent who does the right thing for the right reasons deserves praise for his action whether it was determined or not. But whereas indetermination is compatible with the claim that an agent is deserving of praise, it is essential to the justification of the claim that an agent is deserving of blame.

Seen from a certain perspective, this dealing out of praise and blame may seem unfair. In particular, we might think that if it is truly undetermined whether a given agent in a given situation will perform a good action or a bad one, then it must be a matter of chance that the agent ends up doing what he does. If the action is truly undetermined, then it is not determined by the agent himself. One might think that in this case the agent has no more control over the moral quality of his action than does anything else.

However, the fact that it is not determined whether the agent will perform a good action or a bad one does not imply that which action he performs can properly be regarded as a matter of chance. Of course, in some situations an agent might choose to make it a matter of chance. For example, an agent struggling with the decision between fulfilling a moral obligation and doing something immoral that he very much wants to do might ultimately decide to let the toss of a coin settle the matter for him. But, in normal cases, the way in which the agent makes a decision involves no statistical process or randomizing event. It appears that the claim that there is no complete explanation of why the agent who could have performed a better action performed a worse one or why the agent who could have performed a worse action performed a better one rules out even the explanation that it was a matter of chance.

In order to have control over the moral quality of his actions, an agent must have certain requisite abilities—in particular, the abilities necessary to see and understand the reasons and interests he ought to see and understand and the abilities necessary to direct his actions in accordance with these reasons and interests. And if, furthermore, there is nothing that interferes with the agent's use of these abilities— that is, no determining cause that prevents him from using them and no statistical process that, as it were, takes out of his hands the control over whether or not he uses them—then it seems that these are all the abilities that the agent needs to have. But it is compatible with the agent's having these abilities and with there being no interferences to their use that it is not determined whether the agent will perform a good action or a bad one. The responsible agent who performs a bad action fails to exercise these abilities sufficiently, though there is no complete explanation of why he fails. The responsible agent who performs a good action does exercise these abilities—it may or may not be the case that it is determined that he exercise them.

The freedom required for moral responsibility, then, is the freedom to be good. Only this kind of freedom will be neither too much nor too little. For then the agent is not so free as to be free from moral reasons, nor so unfree as to make these reasons ineffective.

# 12

# The Incompatibility of
# Responsibility and Determinism

PETER VAN INWAGEN

Many philosophers think that determinism is incompatible with moral responsibility. Probably most of the philosophers who accept this thesis accept it on the basis of some argument very much like this one:

(i) Determinism is incompatible with free will
(ii) Moral responsibility is impossible without free will
∴. Determinism is incompatible with moral responsibility.

I am one of these philosophers.[1] I think that both (i) and (ii) are true and I believe that I am in possession of good reasons for thinking this. I am aware, however, that many philosophers think (i) is false. Many philosophers, in fact, think that anyone who accepts (i) convicts himself *ipso facto* of philosophical incompetence.[2] (I may remark that this attitude evidences very high standards of philosophical competence indeed, since among the philosophers who accept (i) are professors Anscombe, Chisholm, and Plantinga.) Because (i) is so very controversial, however, I propose in this paper to investigate the question

"The Incompatibility of Responsibility and Determinism" originally appeared in *Bowling Green Studies in Applied Philosophy*, vol. 2, ed. M. Bradie and M. Brand (Bowling Green, Ohio: Bowling Green State University, 1980), 30–37, © 1979 by Bowling Green State University, and is reprinted here with permission from the Editor.

1. See my articles "A Formal Approach to the Problem of Free Will and Determinism," *Theoria*, Vol. XL, Part 1 (1974) and "The Incompatibility of Free Will and Determinism," *Philosophical Studies* 27 (1975).
2. See, e.g., the opening paragraphs of Donald Davidson's "Freedom to Act" in Ted Honderich, ed., *Essays on Freedom of Action* (London: Routledge & Kegan Paul, 1973).

whether moral responsibility is compatible with determinism *independently* of (i). I shall argue that determinism and responsibility are incompatible, and not only shall I make no use of proposition (i) in my argument, I shall make no mention whatever of free will other than a very brief one at the end of the paper, and that in relation to a question of secondary importance. I concede that my argument will bear a certain structural resemblance to various arguments for the incompatibility of free will and determinism, but that is neither here nor there: the concept of free will will not *figure* in my argument.

## I

In the remainder of this paper, I shall often drop the word 'moral' and speak simply of responsibility. But I mean my remarks about responsibility to apply only to moral responsibility. I do not claim for example, that everything I say about "responsibility" is true of legal responsibility. I shall offer no definition or analysis of responsibility. I have no analysis to give and I doubt whether an analysis of responsibility would contribute much to my argument in any case. I *shall* argue that certain propositions involving the concept of responsibility are conceptual truths, but I am pretty sure I should simply reject any proposed analysis of responsibility that was in conflict with the conceptual claims I am going to make about responsibility. For example, I shall have occasion to claim that it is a conceptual truth that no human being can be held responsible for the way the world was before there had ever been any human beings, and if someone were to propose an analysis of responsibility that had the consequence that some human being *could* be held responsible for some preadamite state of affairs, then we should have the right to be certain, without further inquiry, that his analysis was wrong. I do not mean that I shall not defend my claims about conceptual truths involving the notion of responsibility. I shall. But my defences will be informal and will rest on no general analysis of that notion.

I *have* got an analysis of determinism. But I have given this analysis (in various more or less equivalent forms) elsewhere and I shall not repeat it here.[3] I will remark, however, that determinism is the thesis that the past and the laws of nature together determine a unique future and is *not* the thesis that every event has a cause ("universal causation"). For the thesis of universal causation might be true and determinism false.[4]

3. See the papers referred to in note 1.
4. See pp. 89 and 90 of my "Reply to Narveson," *Philosophical Studies* 32 (1977).

However the thesis of determinism (the thesis that the past and the laws of nature determine a unique future) should be spelled out in detail, it should have the following consequence. (In the sequel I shall, in order to save space, conflate use and mention to a really *shocking* extent. You have my word for it that this conflation is eliminable by dull and lengthy paraphrasis.) Let S be a sentence that, in some relevant sense, gives a complete and accurate description of the entire state of the world at some moment in the remost past. In fact, let us suppose that S gives a description of the state of the world at some moment so long ago that at that moment there were no human beings and never had been any. (It will facilitate the argument to suppose there was such a moment. This assumption could be dispensed with at the cost of uninteresting complications.) Let L be a sentence that, in some relevant sense, gives a complete and accurate statement of "the laws of nature," whatever, precisely, those may be. Let T be any truth whatever. Let '□' represent what Plantinga has called "broadly logical necessity," that is, truth in all possible worlds. Then it follows from determinism that

$$\Box(S \ \& \ L. \supset T).$$

It is this consequence of determinism that I shall show is incompatible with moral responsibility.

## II

I shall use 'N$p$' as an abbreviation for the following sentence form:

$p$ and no human being, or group of human beings, is even partly responsible for the fact that $p$.

For example, 'N Nixon received a pardon' is to be read, 'Nixon received a pardon and no human being or group of human beings is even partly responsible for the fact that Nixon received a pardon.' The qualification introduced by the words 'even partly' will play no role in the argument of this paper and I shall ignore it in the text. The curious reader may consult footnote 5. Owing to the presence of the word 'human' in this sentence-form, my arguments will be directly applicable only to questions of human moral responsibility. I have included the word 'human' in order to avoid discussing the relation between determinism and the actions of supernatural agents such as

God or angels. The argument of the sequel, however, could easily be applied to Martians, Venerians, or any other purely natural agents.

My argument will make use of two inference forms involving 'N':

(A) $\Box p \vdash N p$

and

(B) $Np, N(p \supset q) \vdash Nq$.

The validity of (A) seems to me to be beyond dispute. No one is responsible for the fact that $49 \times 18 = 882$, for the fact that arithmetic is essentially incomplete, or, if Kripke is right about necessary truth, for the fact that the atomic number of gold is 79. (According to Descartes, God is responsible for these things; but we needn't consider that vexed question.) The validity of (B) is a more difficult matter. I shall return to it later.[5]

My argument will require two premises, 'NS' and 'NL'. The former is obviously true, since no human being is morally responsible for anything that occurred before any human beings had ever been. The latter is obviously true, since, whatever may be true of God or other supernatural beings, no human being is morally responsible for the laws of nature. (For example, if it is a law of nature that nothing travels faster than light, then no human being is morally responsible for the fact that nothing travels faster than light.)

Now the argument. We begin with our consequence of determinism:

(1) $\Box (S \ \& \ L. \supset T)$.

From (1) we may deduce by elementary modal and sentential logic,

---

5. If the words 'even partly' were omitted from the sentence-form that 'N$p$' abbreviates, then (B) might be open to counterexample. Suppose, for example, that Smith kills the elder of the Jones twins and that the younger is killed by a bolt from the blue. It is at least arguable that in that case neither Smith nor anyone else is responsible for the fact that *both* the Jones twins are dead. But then the following argument has true premises and a false conclusion

N Both the Jones twins are dead
N (Both the Jones twins are dead $\supset$ the elder of the Jones twins is dead)
∴ N The elder of the Jones twins is dead

if the words 'even partly' are omitted from the reading of 'N$p$'. But it seems evident that, in the case imagined, Smith is at least *partly* responsible for the fact that both the Jones twins are dead.

(2) □ (S ⊃ (L ⊃ T)).

We now argue:

| | |
|---|---|
| (3) N(S ⊃ (L ⊃ T)) | From (2) by (A) |
| (4) NS | Premise |
| (5) N(L ⊃ T) | From (3) and (4) by (B) |
| (6) NL | Premise |
| (7) NT | From (5) and (6) by (B) |

I have called this an argument. More precisely it is an argument-form. We may derive indefinitely many arguments from it by substituting arbitrary sentences for 'T'. If we substitute for T a sentence that expresses a truth and if determinism is true, the substitution-instance of (1) so obtained will be true and the argument so obtained will be sound (assuming, of course, that it is valid). This fact about our argument-form amounts to a proof of the following proposition: substitute any *truth* you like for 'T' in the following schema

> If determinism is true, then no human being, or group of human beings, is morally responsible for the fact that T,

and you will get a truth. For example, if you substitute 'Kennedy was assassinated', 'The U.S. used atomic weapons against Japan', or 'Nixon received a pardon' for 'T', you will get a truth. This result, I think, may be properly summarized in these words: determinism is incompatible with moral responsibility.

We have proved this result provided that the reasoning employed in our argument-form is valid; that is, provided that both (A) and (B) are valid; that is—since the validity of (A) is beyond dispute—provided (B) is valid. Let us now turn to the question of the validity of (B).

### III

How could one show that (B) is valid? How, in general, does one go about showing that an argument-form is valid? There would seem to be two ways.

First, one might employ the methods of formal semantics. In the present case, since 'N' is very like a modal operator, the methods of *possible-world* semantics might seem promising. Here is a sketch of how we might apply these methods to (B). We first delimit a certain set W of worlds and say that N$p$ is true just in the case that $p$ is true in all these worlds. (This would amount to a semantical definition of 'N'.) For example, we might say that N$p$ is true if $p$ is true in both the actual world and in all worlds such that human beings can be held morally responsible for their "actuality-status" (that is, actuality or non-actuality, as applicable). Interestingly enough, the definition of W is of no *formal* significance. If we accept any definition of N$p$ of the following form: 'Np is true iff p is true in all worlds such that . . . ', where the condition that fills the blank makes no mention of $p$, then (B) will "come out" valid. (Obviously, if p is true in every member of W, and if $p \supset q$ is true in every member of $W$, then $q$ is true in every member of W.) While this formal result is not devoid of persuasive force (despite its utter triviality), it is far from decisive. It depends on the assumption that there is *some* set of worlds W such that N$p$ *can* plausibly be thought of as making the assertion that $p$ is true in every member of W. While this assumption seems right to me, I have no argument for it, and a person who was determined to reject (B) might very well reject it.

Secondly, one might attempt to show that (B) was valid by "reducing" it to certain generally accepted valid inference-forms. But it seems intuitively evident that this cannot be done. No generally accepted inference-form involves moral concepts. (The familiar principle that 'ought' implies 'can' may be an exception to this generalization. But even if this principle does count as a "generally accepted inference-form," it's hard to see how it could be of much help to the friends of (B).) And it seems wholly implausible to suppose that an inference-form essentially involving the concept of moral responsibility could be reduced to inference-forms involving only non-moral concepts.

Thus the prospect of *showing* (B) to be valid appears bleak, though perhaps no bleaker than the prospect of *showing* anything of philosophical interest. I must confess that my belief in the validity of (B) has only two sources, one incommunicable and the other inconclusive. The former source is simply what philosophers are pleased to call "intuition": when I carefully consider (B), it seems to be valid. But I can't expect *you* to be very impressed by this fact. People's intuitions, after all, have led them to accept all sorts of crazy propositions, and many sane but false propositions. (The Unrestricted Comprehension Principle in set theory and the Galilean Law of the Addition of Velocities in physics are good examples of propositions in the second category.) The latter source is the fact that I can think of no instances of (B) that have, or could possibly have, true premises and a false conclusion. That is, I can think of no instances of (B) that can be seen to have true premises and a false conclusion *independently* of the question whether moral responsibility is compatible with determinism. If moral responsibility is compatible with determinism (and if determinism is true), then the following instance of (B):

> N(S & L. ⊃ The U.S. used atomic weapons against Japan)
> N(S & L)
> ∴. N The U.S. used atomic weapons against Japan

doubtless has true premises and a false conclusion.

It may be hard to credit, but there are almost certainly philosophers who would say that this shows that my use of (B) "begs the question" against the proponents of the compatibility of determinism and moral responsibility. But if this accusation of question-begging were right, it's hard to see how any argument could avoid begging the question. If one presents an argument for a proposition Q, then, if Q is false, *some* step in the argument is wrong; and one may believe of a certain step in the argument that *if* any step is wrong, *that one* is. But it hardly follows that one is "begging the question" by taking that step. One may be begging the question (whatever, precisely, that is) but that one is begging the question is not a consequence of the mere existence of a "weakest link" in one's chain of reasoning.

But these questions about "question-begging" and where the burden of proof lies, and so on, are very tricky. Let's look at them from a different angle. Suppose a proponent of the compatibility of determinism and responsibility (let's call this doctrine R-compatibilism) replies to my argument as follows: "You employ argument-form (B). But this argument-form is invalid. I prove this as follows:

> R-compatibilism is true
> ∴. Argument-form (B) is invalid.

You yourself admit that the conclusion of this argument follows from its premise [I do]. You may not accept its premise, but that's *your* problem, for that premise is *true*. Moreover, you can hardly object to this little argument of mine on the ground that it begs the question. It's no worse in that respect than *your* argument, which is essentially this:

> Argument-form (B) is valid
> ∴. R-compatibilism is false."

What am I to say to this? I suppose I can do no more than appeal to the intuitions of my audience. Here's how it looks to me (and doesn't it look this way to you?): Argument-form (B) seems obviously right and R-compatibilism does not seem obviously right. If two principles are in conflict and one seems obviously right and the other does not seem obviously right, then (if one must choose) one should accept the one that seems obviously right.

But perhaps someone will say that he finds R-compatibilism obviously right. Presumably this attitude of his is either grounded in an immediate and intuitive relationship to R-compatibilism—he claims to *see* that it's true, just as I claim to see that (B) is valid—*or* his attitude is grounded in some argument for R-compatibilism. Let us first look at the case of the philosopher who claims to see the truth of R-compatibilism intuitively. Well, arguments, like explanations, must come to an end somewhere. Perhaps if there is such a philosopher, he and I constitute a genuine case of a conflict of rock-bottom intuitions. But I must say I should find any such claim as the one I have imagined incredible. R-compatibilism looks to me like the kind of thing one could believe only because one had an argument for it. I simply cannot see what could be going on in the mind of someone who claimed to know it intuitively. I don't know what that would *feel* like.

The philosopher who believes R-compatibilism on the basis of an *argument* is not likewise mysterious to me. But I shall want to know what the premises of his argument are. And I shall raise the following question about his (ultimate) premises: Are they *really* intuitively more plausible than (B)? I find it hard to believe that there are any propositions that entail R-compatibilism that are more plausible than (B). I'm not sure what premises might be employed in an argument for the compatibility of responsibility and determinism, but I know what the premises employed in arguments for the compatibility of *free will* and determinism are like and I expect that the premises of arguments for R-compatibilism would be of a comparable level of plausibility. The crucial premise in arguments for the compatibility of free will and determinism is usually a semantic proposition that begins in some such way as this

'S can do A' means 'S would do A if S chose to do A and . . .'

and ends in complexity.[6] When I examine premises of this sort, I find

6. See, e.g., Wilfrid Sellars, "Fatalism and Determinism," in Keith Lehrer, ed., *Freedom and Determinism* (New York: Random House, 1966); Bernard Gert and Timothy J. Duggan, "Free Will as the Ability to Will," Chapter 10 in the present volume; Keith Lehrer, "Preferences, Conditionals and Freedom," in Peter van Inwagen, ed., *Time and Cause: Essays Presented to Richard Taylor* (Dordrecht: D. Reidel, 1980).

myself without any particular convictions about their truth or falsity, owing simply to their complexity. If someone presents an argument for R-compatibilism that has a premise as complex as any of these semantical premises that figure in the free-will debate, then naturally I shall find this complex premise less plausible than (B) and will continue to accept (B) and its consequences, among which is R-incompatibilism.

No one, of course, is obliged to correct my mistaken beliefs. But if anyone thinks my belief in R-incompatibilism is false and *does* for some reason take an interest in my intellectual welfare, here is what he will have to do to get me to see the light: he will have to produce some proposition intuitively more plausible than the proposition that (B) is valid and show that this proposition entails R-compatibilism, or else he will have to devise a counterexample to (B) whose status as such can be established without assuming that determinism and moral responsibility are compatible.

# Bibliography

*Abbreviations*

| | |
|---|---|
| A | *Analysis* |
| APQ | *American Philosophical Quarterly* |
| CJP | *Canadian Journal of Philosophy* |
| JP | *Journal of Philosophy* |
| M | *Mind* |
| N | *Noûs* |
| P | *Philosophy* |
| PA | *Philosophia* |
| PAS | *Proceedings of the Aristotelian Society* |
| PPQ | *Pacific Philosophical Quarterly* |
| PQ | *Philosophical Quarterly* |
| PR | *Philosophical Review* |
| PS | *Philosophical Studies* |
| PT | *Philosophical Topics* |
| S | *Synthèse* |
| T | *Theoria* |

*References*

The list below serves as a guide to the literature on topics discussed in this book.

Adams, Marilyn. 1967. "Is the Existence of God a 'Hard' Fact?" *PR*, 74 (October), 492–503.
Adams, Robert. 1985. "Involuntary Sins." *PR*, 94 (January), 3–31.
Alston, William. 1977. "Self-Intervention and the Structure of Motivation." In Mischel (1977).
Anscombe, G. E. M. 1976. "Soft Determinism." In Ryle (1976).
Audi, Robert. 1974. "Moral Responsibility, Freedom, and Compulsion." *APQ*, 11 (January), 1–14.
———. 1978. "Avoidability and Possible Worlds." *PS*, 33 (May), 413–21.
Aune, Bruce. 1967. "Hypotheticals and 'Can': Another Look." *A*, 27 (June), 191–95.

——. 1970. "Free Will, 'Can', and Ethics: A Reply to Lehrer." *A*, 30 (January), 77–83.

Austin, J. L. 1961. "Ifs and Cans." In his *Philosophical Papers*, London: Oxford University Press; reprinted in *Philosophical Papers*, J. O. Urmson and G. J. Warnock, eds.

Bennett, Jonathan. 1980. "Accountability." In van Straaten (1980).

Berofsky, Bernard, ed. 1966. *Freewill and Determinism*. New York: Harper & Row.

——. 1971. *Determinism*. Princeton: Princeton University Press.

Blumenfeld, David. 1971. "The Principle of Alternate Possibilities." *JP* 67 (June), 339–345.

Bogdan, R. J., ed. 1981. *Keith Lehrer*. Dordrecht: D. Reidel.

Brand, M., and Walton, D., eds. 1976. *Action Theory*. Dordrecht: D. Reidel.

Brueckner, Anthony L. 1985. "Skepticism and Epistemic Closure." *PT*. 13 (Fall), 89–118.

Caplan, Lincoln. 1984a. "Annals of Law: The Insanity Defense." *New Yorker*, July 2, 1984, pp. 45–78.

——. 1984b. *The Insanity Defense and the Trial of John W. Hinckley, Jr.* Boston: David R. Godine.

Cauman, L. et al., eds. 1982. *How Many Questions? Essays in Honor of Sidney Morgenbesser*. Indianapolis: Hackett.

Chisholm, Roderick. 1958. "Responsibility and Avoidability." In Hook (1958).

——. 1964. "J. L. Austin's Philosophical Papers." *M*, 68 (January), 1–26.

——. 1966. "Freedom and Action." In Lehrer (1966).

——. 1967. "'He Could Have Done Otherwise.'" *JP*, 64 (July 6), 409–17.

Culver, Charles M., and Gert, Bernard. 1982. *Philosophy in Medicine: Conceptual and Ethical Issues in Medicine and Psychiatry*. Oxford: Oxford University Press.

Cummins, Robert. 1979. "Could Have Done Otherwise." *Personalist*, 60 (October), 411–14.

——. 1980. "Culpability and Mental Disorder." *CJP*, 10 (June), 207–32.

Davidson, Donald. 1969. "How is Weakness of the Will Possible?" In Feinberg (1969). (Reprinted in Davidson 1980.)

——. 1973. "Freedom to Act." In Honderich (1973). (Reprinted in Davidson 1980.)

——. 1980. *Essays on Actions and Events*. Oxford: Clarendon Press.

Davies, Martin. 1983. "Boethius and Others on Divine Foreknowledge." *PPQ*, 8, pp. 313–29.

Dennett, Daniel D. 1971. "Intentional Systems." *JP*, 68 (February 25), 87–106.

——. 1973. "Mechanism and Responsibility." In Honderich (1973).

——. 1976. "Conditions of Personhood." In Rorty (1976).

——. 1984a. *Elbow Room: Varieties of Free Will Worth Wanting*. Cambridge: MIT Press.

____. 1984b. "I Could Not Have Done Otherwise—So What?" *JP*, 81 (October), 553–65.

Dretske, Fred. 1970. "Epistemic Operators." *JP*, 67 (December), 1007–23.

Duggan, Timothy, and Gert, Bernard. 1967. "Voluntary Abilities." *APQ*, 4 (April), 127–35.

Dworkin, Gerald. 1970a. "Acting Freely." *N*, 4 (November), 367–83.

____, ed. 1970b. *Determinism, Free Will, and Moral Responsibility.* Englewood Cliffs: Prentice-Hall.

____. 1976. "Autonomy and Behavior Control." *Hastings Center Report*, 6 (February), 23–28.

Feinberg, Joel, ed. 1969. *Moral Concepts.* London: Oxford Press.

____. 1980a. *Doing and Deserving.* Princeton: Princeton University Press.

____. 1980b. "The Interest in Liberty on the Scales." In Feinberg (1980c).

____. 1980c. *Rights, Justice, and the Bounds of Liberty.* Princeton: Princeton University Press.

Fingarette, Herbert. 1967. *On Responsibility.* New York: Basic Books.

Fischer, John Martin. 1979. "Lehrer's New Move: 'Can' in Theory and Practice." *T*, 45, pp. 49–62.

____. 1983a. "Freedom and Foreknowledge." *PR*, 92 (January), 67–79.

____. 1983b. "Incompatibilism." *PS*, 43 (January), 127–37.

____. 1985a. "Ockhamism." *PR*, 94 (January), 80–100.

____. 1985b. "Scotism." *M*, 94 (April), 231–43.

____. 1985–1986. "Responsibility and Failure." *PAS*, 86, 251–70.

____. 1986. "Van Inwagen on Free Will." *PQ*, 36 (April), 252–60.

____. Forthcoming. "Freedom and Miracles." *N*.

Foley, Richard. 1979. "Compatibilism and Control over the Past." *A*, 39 (January), 70–74.

Frankfurt, Harry. 1973. "Coercion and Moral Responsibility." In Honderich (1973).

____. 1976. "Identification and Externality." In Rorty (1976).

____. 1978. "The Problem of Action." *APQ*, 15 (April), 157–62.

____. 1982a. "The Importance of What We Care About." *S*, 53 (November), 257–72.

____. 1982b. "What We Are Morally Responsible For." In Cauman et al. (1982).

____. Forthcoming. "Identification and Wholeheartedness." In Schoeman (forthcoming).

Gallois, Andres. 1977. "Van Inwagen on Free Will and Determinism." *PS*, 32 (July), 99–105.

Ginet, Carl. 1966. "Might We Have No Choice?" In Lehrer (1966b).

____. 1980. "The Conditional Analysis of Freedom." In van Inwagen (1980).

____. 1983. "In Defense of Incompatibilism." *PS*, 44 (November), 391–400.

Goldman, A. 1970. *A Theory of Human Action.* Englewood Cliffs: Prentice-Hall.

Greenspan, P. S. 1976. "Wiggins on Historical Inevitability and Incompatibilism." *PS*, 29 (April), 235–47.

——. Forthcoming. "Unfreedom and Responsibility." In Schoeman (forthcoming).

Hampshire, Stuart. 1975. *Freedom of the Individual.* Princeton: Princeton University Press.

Hilpinen, Risto. 1970. "Can and Modal Logic." *Ajatus,* 32, pp. 7–17.

Hintikka, Jaakko. 1964. "Aristotle and the 'Master Argument' of Diodorus." *APQ,* 2 (April), 101–14.

Hoffman, Joshua, and Rosenkrantz, Gary. 1980. "On Divine Foreknowledge and Human Freedom." *PS,* 37 (April), 289–96.

——. 1984. "Hard and Soft Facts." *PR,* 93 (July), 414–34.

Honderich, Ted, ed. 1973. *Essays on Freedom of Action.* London: Routledge & Kegan Paul.

Hook, Sidney, ed. 1958. *Determinism and Freedom in the Age of Modern Science.* New York: Collier.

Horgan, Terence. 1977. "Lehrer on 'Could'-Statements." *PS,* 32 (November), 403–11.

——. 1985. "Compatibilism and the Consequence Argument." *PS,* 47 (1985), 339–56.

Jeffrey, Richard. 1974. "Preference among Preferences." *JP,* 71 (July 18), 377–91.

Kenny, A. J. P. 1976. *Freedom, Will, and Power.* Oxford: Blackwell.

——. 1978. *Freewill and Responsibility: Four Lectures.* London: Routledge & Kegan Paul.

Lamb, James W. 1977. "On a Proof of Incompatibilism." *PR,* 86 (January), 20–35.

Lehrer, Keith. 1966a. "An Empirical Disproof of Determinism?" In Lehrer 1966b.

——, ed. 1966b. *Freedom and Determinism.* New York: Random House.

——. 1968. "Cans without Ifs." *A,* 29 (October), 29–32.

——. 1976. "'Can' in Theory and Practice: A Possible Worlds Analysis." In Brand and Walton (1976).

——. 1980. "Preferences, Conditionals, and Freedom." In van Inwagen (1980).

——. 1981. "Self Profile." In Bogdan (1981).

Levin, Michael. 1979. *Metaphysics and the Mind-Body Problem.* Oxford: Clarendon Press.

Lewis, David. 1981. "Are We Free to Break the Laws?" *T,* 47, pp. 112–21.

Locke, Don. 1973–1974. "Natural Powers and Human Abilities." *PAS,* 73, 171–87.

——. 1976. "The 'Can' of Being Able." *PA,* 6 (March), 1–20.

McCann, Edwin W. 1975. "The Conditional Analysis of 'Can': Goldman's 'Reductio' of Lehrer." *PS,* 28 (December), 437–41.

Mischel, T., ed. 1977. *The Self: Philosophical and Psychological Issues.* Oxford: Oxford University Press.

Moore, G. E. 1912. *Ethics.* Oxford: Oxford University Press.

Morgenbesser, S., Suppes, P., and White, M., eds. 1979. *Philosophy, Science, and Method: Essays in Honor of Ernest Nagel.* New York: St. Martin's Press.

Morgenbesser, S., and Walsh, J. J., eds. 1962. *Freewill.* Englewood Cliffs: Prentice-Hall.

Narveson, Jan. 1977. "Compatibilism Defended." *PS*, 32 (July), 83–87.

Neely, Wright. 1974. "Freedom and Desire." *PR*, 83 (January), 32–54.

Nozick, Robert. 1979. "Coercion." In Morgenbesser, Suppes, and White (1979).

——. 1981. *Philosophical Explanations.* Cambridge: Harvard University Press.

Pears, David. 1963. *Freedom and the Will.* New York: St. Martin's Press.

——. 1975a. "Ifs and Cans." In Pears (1975b).

——. 1975b. *Questions in the Philosophy of Mind.* London: Gerald Duckworth.

Pike, Nelson. 1965. "Divine Omniscience and Voluntary Action." *PR*, 74 (January), 27–46.

——. 1966. "Of God and Freedom: A Rejoinder." *PR*, 75 (July), 369–79.

——. 1970. *God and Timelessness.* London: Routledge & Kegan Paul.

——. 1977. "Divine Foreknowledge, Human Freedom, and Possible Worlds." *PR*, 86 (April), 209–16.

——. 1984. "Fischer on Freedom and Foreknowledge." *PR*, 93 (October), 599–614.

Prior, Arthur N. 1962. "The Formalities of Omniscience." *P*, 37 (April), 114–29.

Rorty, Amelie O., ed. 1976. *The Identities of Persons.* Berkeley: University of California Press.

Ryle, G., ed. 1976. *Contemporary Aspects of Philosophy.* Boston: Oriel.

Sankowski, Edward. 1977. "Responsibility of Persons for Their Emotions." *CJP*, 7, pp. 829–40.

——. 1980. "Some Problems about Determinism and Freedom." *APQ* 17 (October), 291–99.

Saunders, John Turk. 1968. "The Temptations of 'Powerlessness'." *APQ*, 5 (April), 100–108.

Schoeman, F. 1978. "Responsibility and the Problem of Induced Desires." *PS*, 34 (October), 293–301.

——, ed. Forthcoming. *New Directions in Responsibility.* Cambridge: Cambridge University Press.

Shatz, David. 1985. "Free Will and the Structure of Motivation." *Midwest Studies in Philosophy* 10, ed. Peter French, et al. Minneapolis: University of Minnesota Press.

Slote, Michael. 1982. "Selective Necessity and the Free-Will Problem." *JP*, 79 (January), 5–24.

Sorabji, Richard. 1983. *Necessity, Cause, and Blame: Perspectives on Aristotle's Theory.* Ithaca: Cornell University Press.

Stern, Lawrence. 1974. "Freedom, Blame, and Moral Community." *JP*, 71 (February), 72–84.

Strawson, P. F. 1962. "Freedom and Resentment." *Proceedings of the British Academy*, 48, pp. 1–25. (Reprinted in Strawson 1968.)

——. 1968. *Studies in the Philosophy of Thought and Action*. London: Oxford University Press.

Stump, Eleonore, and Kretzmann, Norman. 1981. "Eternity." *JP*, 78 (August), 429–58.

Taurek, John. 1972. "Determinism and Moral Responsibility." Ph.D. thesis. University of California, Los Angeles.

Taylor, Charles. 1976. "Responsibility for Self." In Rorty (1976).

Taylor, Richard. 1963. *Metaphysics*. Englewood Cliffs: Prentice-Hall.

Thalberg, Irving. 1978. "Hierarchical Analyses of Unfree Action." *CJP*, 8 (June), 211–26.

Thorp, John. 1980. *Free Will: A Defense against Neuro-Physiological Determinism*. London: Routledge & Kegan Paul.

Urmson, J. O., and Warnock, G. J., eds. 1979. *Philosophical Papers* [of J. L. Austin]. Oxford: Clarendon Press.

van Inwagen, Peter. 1974. "A Formal Approach to the Problem of Free Will and Determinism." *T*, pp. 9–22.

——. 1975. "The Incompatibility of Free Will and Determinism." *PS*, 27 (March), 185–99.

——. 1977a. "Reply to Gallois." *PS*, 32 (July), 107–11.

——. 1977b. "Reply to Narveson." *PS*, 32 (July), 89–98.

——, ed. 1980. *Time and Cause: Essays Presented to Richard Taylor*. Dordrecht: D. Reidel.

——. 1983. *An Essay on Free Will*. Oxford: Clarendon Press.

van Straaten, Zak, ed. 1980. *Philosophical Subjects*. Oxford: Clarendon Press.

Wallace, James. 1978. *Virtues and Vices*. Ithaca: Cornell University Press.

Walton, Douglas. 1981. "Lehrer on Action, Freedom, and Determinism." In Bogdan (1981).

Watson, Gary, ed. 1982. *Free Will*. Oxford: Oxford University Press.

——. 1977. "Skepticism about Weakness of the Will." *PR*, 86 (July), 316–39.

Wiggins, D. 1973. "Towards a Reasonable Libertarianism." In Honderich (1973).

Wolf, Susan. 1981. "The Importance of Free Will." *M*, 90 (July), 386–405.

——. 1985. "The Legal and Moral Responsibility of Organizations." In *Criminal Justice: NOMOS: XXVII*, ed. J. W. Chapman and J. R. Pennock. New York: New York University Press.

Young, Robert. 1980a. "Autonomy and the 'Inner Self.'" *APQ*, 17 (January), 35–43.

——. 1980b. "Autonomy and Socialization." *M*, 89 (October), 565–76.

Zimmerman, David. 1981. "Hierarchical Motivation and Freedom of the Will." *PPQ*, 62, pp. 354–68.

Zimmerman, Michael J. 1982. "Moral Responsibility, Freedom, and Alternate Possibilities." *PPQ*, 63, pp. 243–54.

——. 1984. *An Essay on Human Action*. New York: Peter Lang.

# Index

abilities: characterization of, 208, 239; to do otherwise, 226, 227; to will, 210, 211–13, 214, 222, 223; voluntary, 207. *See also* actions

actions, 214; kinds of, and abilities, 209; for moral good, 229; non-action, 216; psychologically determined, 225–26; consequences of, responsibility for, 157–58, 178; unfree, 214, 217; unvoluntary, 214–15, 217, 221; voluntary, 213, 219, 220, 221. *See also* free action(s)

addicts, drug, 33, 103; and freedom, 79, 125, 128, 135; happy vs. unhappy, 42–43, 45, 47, 72, 73, 79; willing vs. unwilling, 99–100, 101, 117, 177

agent: and control, 181, 239; free, man as, 96, 131, 236; morally responsible, 12, 13, 225, 227; motives of, 91–92, 106, 230–32; free, reaction to, 12, 40–41; responsible, 179, 237, 239–40; willing, 104. *See also* valuing, agent's

Anscombe, G. E. M., 187, 241

Aristotle, 217, 218–20, 221

associationist strategy, 179–80, 182

attitudes, reactive, 9, 11–13, 14, 40

Austin, John, 110, 215, 220

Berlin, Isaiah, 82, 95–96

Blumenfeld, David, 154

Campbell, C. A., 136n

causal determinism, doctrine of, 21, 32, 37, 40, 60, 185; and compulsion, 96, 189; definition, 33, 183, 232, 242–43; and free action, 109, 111–12; and free will, 80, 153, 210; and moral responsibility, 55, 56, 149, 171–73, 177–78, 189, 190, 236, 243–49; validity of argument form concerning, 245–49

Chisholm, Roderick, 77–78, 162n

*Clockwork Orange, A,* 56, 192–204

closure principle, 37–38; denial of, 39–40

coercion: examples of, 100–102, 126–28; and free action, 102, 103, 106; and moral responsibility, 115, 144–48; threat as, 104, 115, 127, 129

compatibilist analysis: of freedom, 33, 34–37, 82–83, 206; of responsibility, 43, 61

compulsion, psychological, 56, 191–92, 201, 203, 211–12; and determinism, 96, 189; and fear, 197; and free action, 102, 103, 104. *See also* addicts, drug; coercion; unfreedom

conditioning, 192, 198–99; aversive, 193, 199, 200, 204; stages, 194–96

control: according to Frankfurt, 47, 174, 175; of behavior, 192–204;

control (*cont.*)
  and moral responsibility, 179–87;
  from outside, 11; over the past,
  23; positive, 203. *See also* coercion; compulsion, psychological;
  manipulation, direct

Davidson, Donald, 158–60, 179–80
Descartes, René, 244
desires: Frankfurt's hierarchal theory, 43–46, 48–49, 67–73, 75, 77,
  94–95, 100–101, 115–16, 119–
  20, 218; and valuing, 85–89, 90,
  92; Watson's view, 48, 83, 85,
  218n
determinism. *See* causal determinism, doctrine of
Devil/neurologist, concept of, 105,
  106, 119–21; alternate model,
  186–87
Donagan, Alan, 223
Duggan, Timothy J., 55–56, 57, 58
Dworkin, Gerald: example of willing action, 99, 102, 105

essentialist principle, 179, 180
events, 158–61; as particulars vs.
  universals, 186

facts, hard/soft, 24, 29, 30; control
  over, 31; and time, 25
fatalism: arguments from, 26, 28,
  30
Fischer, John: argument of, 54–55
fixity-of-the-past premise, 27–31,
  33
foreknowledge, 22, 23–25; divine,
  29–30, 31; human, 29–30
Frankfurt, Harry G.: account of
  acting freely, 46–47, 103, 104–5,
  124–28, 174, 187; arguments
  against, 47–51, 54, 55, 137, 177–
  85, 188–90; cases, 54–55, 57–60,
  175; on control, 47, 174, 175;
  theory of wanton, 44, 48, 71–73,
  93, 115. *See also* desires; free will;

person; principle of alternate
  possibilities
free action(s): and ability to do otherwise, 107, 108–12, 123, 148–
  52; and agent's wants, 110; and
  choice, 16, 18, 237, 239; defini-
  tions of, 98, 104, 107, 109, 214,
  217; different meanings of, 10–
  11, 14, 40–41, 55–60, 75, 81–82,
  83, 112; as freedom to do otherwise, 107, 108–12, 138; and free
  will, 44, 45, 58, 74; Hobbesian
  concept, 102–7; and idea of unwillingness, 113–18; Locke on,
  98, 103, 115–16; Moore's concept, 107–9; and moral responsibility, 116–18, 121–23, 225; as
  willing actions, 98–102, 105, 106.
  *See also* Frankfurt, Harry G.
free will, 44, 74–80, 82; account of
  Moore, 209, 210; accounts of
  Frankfurt, Neely, and Watson,
  93, 124–28, 130–32, 134–35,
  138–39; description of, 205–6,
  210–13, 214, 221–22; and freedom of action, 44, 45, 58, 74;
  and moral responsibility, 78–80,
  153, 213; as philosophical problem, 97, 138, 153, 206, 228, 234.
  *See also* will
freedom: agent with, reaction to,
  12, 40–41; conditional analysis,
  evaluation of, 15–21, 33, 34; different kinds of, 41–46; enjoyment of, 77; importance of topic,
  11; metaphysical conditions of,
  228–29, 232, 233; and moral responsibility, 13, 14, 46, 234, 240;
  philosophical tradition concerning, 74, 81, 95, 136; reasons for,
  lack of, 21; threats to, 23. *See also*
  free action(s); free will
freedom to do otherwise: as requirement of free action, 107,
  108–12, 138; explanations of, 15,
  19n; and God's existence 21–23,

freedom to do otherwise (*cont.*)
24, 26, 30, 31, 228; incompatibilist arguments about, 22–24, 26, 30–37, 111–12; and moral responsibility, 22, 40, 51, 55, 109
Freud, Sigmund, 90

Gert, Bernard, 55–56, 57–58
Ginet, Carl, 188
God, 244; existence of, 27, 40; as free agent, 96; and freedom to do otherwise, 21–23, 24, 26, 30, 31, 228; as omniscient, 22, 23, 24, 29. *See also* foreknowledge
Goldman, Alvin, 179
Greenspan, P. S., arguments of, 55–57

Hart, H. L. A., 220–21
Hobbes, Thomas, 82, 97, 220, 221; concept of free action, 102–3
Hume, David, 83–84

identification, notion of, 49, 50, 51, 94, 95, 120, 183
incompatibilist arguments, 40, 174, 175, 185, 198, 227, 228, 241–42; causal determinism vs. freedom to do otherwise, 32–33, 34, 111–12, 153; different versions of conclusion, 171–73; about God's existence and freedom to do otherwise, 22–24, 26, 30, 31, 228; about moral responsibility, 43, 60, 151–52, 182; responses to, 34–37
indetermination, 237–39
insanity defense, 13, 57

Locke, Don: criticism of Frankfurt, 177–78; on free action, 98, 103, 115–16; notion of willingness, 115–23; strategy of, 49, 50

McNaughten Rule, 13
manipulation, direct, 56, 149, 203; examples of, 9–11, 14, 19–20, 105, 119–21; as unfreedom, 201, 202
Milton, John, 97
Moore, G. E.: concept of free action, 107–9; discussion of free will, 209, 210
moral responsibility: "actual-sequence" model of, 42, 51, 55, 183, 184, 187–89; asymmetrical approach, 58–60; and consequences of actions, 157–58, 178; description of, 12, 13, 14, 52, 59; threats to, 60–61; traditional approach to, 14–15, 58, 59, 183, 187–88. *See also* causal determinism, doctrine of; coercion; control; free action(s); free will; freedom; freedom to do otherwise; principle of alternate possibilities; unfreedom

Neely, Wright, 95n; theory of freedom, 124, 125–28. *See also* free will
Nietzsche, Friedrich, 96

Ockham, William of, theory of, 24–32

PAP. *See* principle of alternate possibilities
PPA. *See* principle of possible action
PPP. *See* principles of possible prevention
Paradigm Case Argument, 136
Pears, David, 110–11
person: concept of, 65–66; Frankfurt's theory, 44, 46–51, 66–67, 73n, 74–78, 92–93; and freedom of the will, 68–70, 74; Strawson's definition, 65
Plantinga, Alvin, 241, 243
Plato, 83–85, 88n, 93
power necessity, 18–19, 28
principle of alternate possibilities (PAP), 51–55, 128; counterexam-

principle of alternate possibilities (*cont.*)
ples to, 53, 54, 148, 154–55, 170;
definition of, 53, 144, 153–54;
evaluation of, 151–52, 153;
Frankfurt-type cases, 54–55, 57–
60; illustrations of, 144–48, re-
placement principle for, 152; re-
visions of, 175–85
principle of possible action (PPA),
155–57, 171–73
principles of possible prevention
(PPP), 157–73

Reason: vs. Appetite, 83, 89; according to Hume, 83–84; according to Plato, 83–85; and the
Stoics, 132n
resonance, notion of, 49

Sartre, Jean-Paul, 236
Sellars, Wilfrid, 221, 223–24
Skinner, B. F., 192, 201; behaviorist
science of, 194
Slote, Michael, strategy of, 49–50
Smart, J. J. C., 82
Socrates, 85n, 96n
Sorabji, Richard, 187
Spinoza, Benedict de: on emotional
detachment, 133–34; rationality
theory of freedom, 124, 130, 132
Stoics: concept of freedom, 132–34,
212
Strawson, Peter, 11–12, 65

Taylor, Richard: *Metaphysics*, 105
transfer of blamelessness, principle
of, 40, 60–61
transfer of knowledge, principle of.
*See* closure principle

transfer of powerlessness, principle
of, 19–21, 22, 30–34, 38, 40, 60–
61

unfreedom, 45; and action, 82, 214,
217; and behavior control, 192–
204; and hypnotism, 10, 20, 202;
kinds of, 56–57, 201, 202; and
lack of knowledge, 56; and moral
responsibility, 55–58, 119. *See also*
addicts, drug; control
universals, examples of, 161–63,
168, 170–71

valuing, agent's: definition of, 91;
and desires, 85–89; and motivation, 89–91, 91–92
van Inwagen, Peter, 179–80, 181;
argument of, 51–54; criticism of
Frankfurt, 179–80, 181, 184

wanton, in Frankfurt's theory, 48,
115; definition of, 44, 71–73, 93
Watson, Gary: argument against
Frankfurt, 48; on desires, 48, 83,
85, 218n; theory of freedom,
124–25, 128, 187. *See also* free
will
will: ability to, 210, 211–13, 214,
222, 223; as action, 43; agent's,
68–70; disability of, 2, 8, 57, 58,
221, 223
willingness, Locke's notion of, 115–
23
Wisdom, John: *Problems of Mind and
Matter*, 105
Wolf, Susan, asymmetrical approach of, 58–60

Library of Congress Cataloging-in-Publication Data

Moral responsibility.

Bibliography: p.
Includes index.
1. Free will and determinism. 2. Responsibility.
I. Fischer, John Martin, 1952 –
BJ1461.M59 1986     170     86-6282
ISBN 0-8014-1828-3
ISBN 0-8014-9341-2 (pbk.)